The Era of Chinese Multinationals

The Era of Chinese Multinationals

Competing for Global Dominance

Lourdes Casanova
Anne Miroux

ACADEMIC PRESS

An imprint of Elsevier

ELSEVIER

Academic Press is an imprint of Elsevier
125 London Wall, London EC2Y 5AS, United Kingdom
525 B Street, Suite 1650, San Diego, CA 92101, United States
50 Hampshire Street, 5th Floor, Cambridge, MA 02139, United States
The Boulevard, Langford Lane, Kidlington, Oxford OX5 1GB, United Kingdom

Notices
Knowledge and best practice in this field are constantly changing. As new research and experience
broaden our understanding, changes in research methods, professional practices, or medical treatment
may become necessary.

Practitioners and researchers must always rely on their own experience and knowledge in evaluating
and using any information, methods, compounds, or experiments described herein. In using such
information or methods they should be mindful of their own safety and the safety of others, including
parties for whom they have a professional responsibility.

To the fullest extent of the law, neither the Publisher nor the authors, contributors, or editors, assume
any liability for any injury and/or damage to persons or property as a matter of products liability,
negligence or otherwise, or from any use or operation of any methods, products, instructions, or ideas
contained in the material herein.

Library of Congress Cataloging-in-Publication Data
A catalog record for this book is available from the Library of Congress

British Library Cataloguing-in-Publication Data
A catalogue record for this book is available from the British Library

ISBN 978-0-12-816857-8

For information on all Academic Press publications
visit our website at https://www.elsevier.com/books-and-journals

Publisher: Candice Janco
Acquisition Editor: Candice Janco
Editorial Project Manager: Ruby Smith
Production Project Manager: Kamesh Ramajogi
Cover Designer: Christian J. Bilbow

Typeset by SPi Global, India

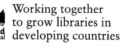

Working together
to grow libraries in
developing countries

www.elsevier.com • www.bookaid.org

Dedication

Special thanks go to my dear husband Soumitra, my daughter Sara, and my beloved mother Paquita, who left us while writing the book. Her values, love and dedication live in her eight children, grandchildren, and extended family.

Lourdes Casanova

Special thanks go to my parents for the example they set; to my husband Bruno for his love and unwavering support, to my children Hadrien, Thomas, Victoria, and Eve-Anne, the joy of my life, for giving me strength and faith in the future. And to little Oscar, who will live in the world we all are shaping today.

Anne Miroux

Endorsement

The rise of emerging-market multinationals has become mostly a story about the rise of Chinese multinationals. Casanova and Miroux provide a rich overview of how and why Chinese firms rose to prominence globally and the challenges they will face in the future. The book draws on firm-level data painstakingly compiled from multiple sources, and is enriched by a handful of case studies. If you're interested in the global economy and China's vital role in it, you must read this book.

Ravi Ramamurti, University Distinguished Professor and Director, Center for Emerging Markets, Northeastern University, Boston, U.S.

China's extraordinary economic growth over the past few decades is, first and foremost, a story of its companies. This story is aptly told by Casanova and Miroux, who are uniquely qualified to dispel the still widespread myth of China's role as the world's workbench. Instead, as the authors show, a growing number of Chinese companies compete at the global technology frontier. This book is an invaluable resource for business leaders, investors, and policy makers alike.

Peter Cornelius, AlpInvest Partners, Carlyle, New York City, U.S.

This book is more than a book on China and Chinese multinationals. It is a well-researched and very interesting explanation of why China has rocketed the world since the 2008 global crisis and the trajectory of Chinese firms overseas. Casanova and Miroux provide an insightful account of the rise of Chinese firms in different industries, with very exciting cases of the successful and not so successful ones.

Maria Teresa Fleury, Director and Professor FGV/EAESP, São Paulo, Brazil

This is an excellent and compelling book that charts the rise of Chinese multinationals and explores how they have become a force to reckon with in the world economy. The book is well written, rich in detail, and broad in its analytical scope. It is a must-read for anyone who wants to understand the spectacular rise and dynamism of Chinese corporations.

Eswar Prasad, Tolani Senior Professor of Trade Policy at Cornell University and a senior fellow at the Brookings Institution

I would like to congratulate Prof. Casanova and Dr. Miroux for their new publication on Chinese MNCs. I started to know Prof. Casanova almost 10 years ago, when she was teaching at INSEAD. We have studied Chinese MNCs and tried to compare them with Latin American MNCs. We were together for WEFs, and EMFs, and I do enjoy working with her. She is, as far as I know, one of the few Latin academies who, early on, started working on emerging multinationals from both China and Latin America. Combining her rich experience with that of Dr. Miroux, an expert with a deep knowledge of FDI and emerging economies and a long experience in this area at UNCTAD, this book enables us to know more about this new breed of firms.

Dr. Taotao Chen
Director of Latin America Center, Tsinghua University
Professor of International Business, School of Economics & Management, Tsinghua University

This book is a great tool for anyone trying to grasp the changing dynamics in emerging markets as they deal with the trade war and economic uncertainties. Casanova and Miroux's book is essential reading at a time when new trends are diffusing the dividing line between economic and political risks with political leaders acting in unexpected ways.

Saibal Dasgupta, journalist Voice of America, Beijing Office and author of the upcoming book, "Running with the dragon: How India should do business with China"

Chinese multinationals have become key actors in the global business landscape. This book is a thoughtful and well-researched contribution to a better understanding of this major change in the global economy, identifying the forces behind it and offering insights on possible consequences for well-established multinationals. Based on insightful analysis of major Chinese companies, and on vividly presented case studies of firms—some of them not well known to the public at large—it highlights how Chinese enterprises have become formidable competitors worldwide, while also pointing out to some challenges ahead.

James Zhan, Director of Investment and Enterprise at the United Nations Conference on Trade and Development

Contents

Author's biographies

Lourdes Casanova is the senior lecturer and director of the Emerging Markets Institute in the S.C. Johnson School of Management, at Cornell University. Formerly at INSEAD, she specializes in international business. In 2014 and 2015, Esglobal named her one of the 50 most influential Iberoamerican intellectuals, and in 2017 Esglobal named her as one of the 30 most influential Iberoamerican women intellectuals. She was a Fulbright Scholar, earned her Master's degree from the University of Southern California and her PhD from the University of Barcelona.

She has been a visiting professor at the Haas School of Business, University of California at Berkeley; Judge Business School, Cambridge University, and Latin American Center, Oxford University. She was a consultant for the Inter-American Development Bank and she taught and directed executive programs at INSEAD for large multinationals. Lourdes Casanova's publications include: Entrepreneurship and the Finance of Innovation in Emerging Markets (2017) coauthored with P. Cornelius and S. Dutta; the 2018, 2017, and 2016 Emerging Market Multinationals Reports, coauthored with A. Miroux; The Political Economy of an Emerging Global Power: In Search of the Brazil Dream (2014) coauthored with J. Kassum; and Global Latinas: Latin America's emerging multinationals (2009). She has also coauthored "Innovalatino, Fostering Innovation in Latin America" (2011) and has contributed articles in numerous economic journals.

She was a member of Latin America Global Agenda Council and the Competitiveness in Latin America taskforce of the World Economic Forum, the B20 Task Force on ICT and Innovation in G20 summit, Los Cabos (2012), and responsible for the Goldman Sachs 10,000 women initiative at INSEAD. She is a member of the board of Boyce Thompson Institute. She is a founding board member of the Emerging Multinationals Research Network and cofounder of the Ithaca Hub of Global Shapers. She is a regular contributor of CNN en español and writes an op-ed at Latin Trade.

Anne Miroux is a faculty fellow at the Emerging Markets Institute, S.C. Johnson School of Management at Cornell University. She has over 30 years of experience in international trade and finance. She began her career in the United Nations Center on Transnational Corporations in New York, and later joined the United Nations Conference on Trade and Development (UNCTAD) where she specialized in developing country debt, foreign direct investment and transnational corporations, and technology and innovation policies. For several years she headed the Investment Analysis Branch in UNCTAD and directed the World Investment Reports (WIR), the United Nations flagship report on FDI and transnational corporations and served as the editor of the UN Transnational Corporations Journal. She has published numerous papers and articles and led research projects on debt, transnational corporations, FDI (foreign direct investment), and technology and innovation policies. She has also led many technical assistance activities on these topics in developing countries.

Till 2015, Anne Miroux was the director of the Division on Technology and Logistics in UNCTAD, and head of the Secretariat of the UN Commission on Science and Technology for Development (CSTD). She is a member of the Advisory Board of the Technology and Management Center of the Department of International Development at Oxford University. Anne Miroux has an MBA from HEC (Paris) and a diploma from IEP (Institut d'Etudes Politiques—Paris). She holds a PhD in economics from University of Paris I—Sorbonne.

EMERGING MARKETS INSTITUTE

Founded in 2010, Cornell's Emerging Markets Institute at the Samuel Curtis Johnson Graduate School of Management provides thought leadership on the role of emerging markets—and emerging market multinationals—in the global economy. The Institute brings together preeminent practitioners and academics from around the world to develop the next generation of global business leaders and create the premier research center on the role of emerging markets in the global economy.

Preface

Jessica Tan
Deputy CEO Ping An

I first started working in China in 2003. As a young McKinsey consultant who had just relocated to Asia from the United States, my first project was to help Ping An set up one of the largest nationwide integrated operations center, centralizing more than 30,000 people across the country. Back then, Ping An and other Chinese companies were still looking toward best practices globally. The China I saw in the early 2000s conformed to conventional narratives. Its economy was export focused, particularly in manufacturing. Its companies were good at execution but relied on the West for design and intellectual capital. Its society was rapidly modernizing and becoming affluent, but consumer tastes and spending patterns were expected to play catch up to global trends for at least another generation.

But since 2010, many of these old narratives are no longer true. China is now leading many technology innovations. Consumption has emerged as the main driver of economic growth, accounting for more than 75% of the gross domestic product growth in 2018. The sharp rise in Chinese consumer spending has in turn driven pioneering innovations in many consumer sectors, such as the rapid growth and now dominance of mobile payments, and the broad adoption of online retail, already accounting for a quarter of total Chinese retail spending. The 2018 sales of plug-in electric cars in China have also nearly equaled the United States and Europe combined. Chinese consumers now lead and set technology adoption trends; any futurist studying consumer use of technology can no longer confine himself to the Silicon Valley, but must equally study Beijing, Shenzhen, and Shanghai.

Spurred by consumer demand, Chinese companies are also becoming innovators in their own right. Taking artificial intelligence (AI) as an example, according to a study by Tsinghua University, two-thirds of global investments in AI industry went to China, and China's AI industry has grown 67% in just 1 year since 2017, making China's AI market exceed US$ 4.3 billion. A study by the Boston Consulting Group further found that 85% of Chinese companies were piloting or deploying AI in their businesses, compared to just about 50% in the United States and Europe.

Various Chinese companies are now leading in many Fintech, HealthTech, and Smart City technology innovations. For example, at Ping An, we apply AI to empower our core financial services, providing end-to-end coverage from sales, operations to service optimization, and use new technologies to create new businesses in domains such as health care and smart cities. We service over 11 million auto claims a year, of which 98.7% are paid within the day and 60% are self-service through a mobile app where an AI engine automatically adjudicate claims recognizing 60,000 different car models and 24 million spare parts. In health care, Ping An provides online health-care consultations and services to over 290 million users, with more than 660,000 consultations per day, of which 75% are answered by AI powered doctor assistants. In building smart cities, Ping An supports over 100 Chinese cities across 21 service lines on city management, economy development, and citizen services, such as using AI to reduce traffic accident handling time from 40 to 5 min, reduce traffic congestion, and to improve speed by 15%–20% during peak periods; providing end-to-end AI agricultural solution that allows better disaster prediction and management by 30%; and providing over 3000 citizen governmental services in a seamless mobile app. You can use the app to take public transport, apply for various licenses, and manage electronic health records.

Another two examples are Tencent and Alibaba. Tencent's WeChat, with over a billion users worldwide, has been rapidly evolving to meet consumer needs, taking care of every aspect of people's daily life, following one of the company's slogans being "AI in all." WeChat Pay allows people to pay quickly with a simple QR code scan, providing over 1 billion transactions per day. Home to two China's top online marketplaces, Alibaba built its mobile payment platform Alipay and has accumulated over half a billion users so far.

In 2018, through Alipay and its competitor, Tencent's WeChat Pay around 83% of all payments in China were made via mobile. Consequently, mobile payments are almost indispensable in China, and Alibaba intensively uses AI to manage all the transactions. Based on all the data these firms have accumulated, Alibaba online lender MYbank and WeBank are able to provide microloans for its sellers online to support their business.

Besides being innovators, these companies are also expanding their blueprints into wider domains and broader markets: Alibaba's AliExpress has opened up to businesses in multiple European countries, showing the company's attempt outside the domestic market; Tencent's WeChat gradually prevails in foreign countries, and the firm starts to invest in American Fintech companies.

Lourdes Casanova and Anne Miroux's book on *"The Era of Chinese Multinationals"* is thus a timely examination of the massive changes taking place in the nature and impact of Chinese multinational companies. From being just the factories for the world, Chinese companies are fast becoming global innovators, with leading ideas and technologies. In time, they will seek to work with partners overseas to bring their innovations globally to consumers everywhere.

Acknowledgments

Writing a book is always a demanding journey, tougher than expected, full of rewards, and reflections. In such circumstances, it is important to be surrounded by reliable colleagues, trusted friends, and enthusiastic students. The Emerging Markets Institute (EMI) at Cornell University provided us with this environment and we thank the institute and the Cornell SC Johnson College of Business for it; we also want to thank all those whom we met along the way (academics, entrepreneurs, company executives, and experts from international organizations in particular) with whom we shared opinions and discussed our respective understandings. Special thanks go to the executives and high-level officials of companies interviewed who shared their insights on the future of their respective industries, their own firms, and the opportunities and threats looming on the horizon. It did not always fit the conventional wisdom, or the official view. The rise of Chinese firms, and the global economic future overall, leaves few people indifferent. Our debates were all the livelier and enriching for it.

Our research has always tried to rely as much as possible on verifiable facts and quantitative information. In this, student interns from Universidad de los Andes in Colombia have provided invaluable research assistance support: Mariana Rodríguez Díaz, Jorge Andrés Forero Fajardo, Carlos Alonso Delgado López, and last year Angélica Soraya Camacho, Nicolás Clavijo, and Thomas Merizalde, and Advisory Council member Rob Cañizares, who funded the program. Our thanks also go to Astrit Sulstarova for sharing his knowledge of and experience in the field of Foreign Direct Investment statistics.

We are indebted to our dedicated students at EMI for their research assistance: Vineetha Pachava, Rawling scholars Michael Pocress (for the Belt and Road Initiative) and John Ninia. Special thanks to César Bustillo Dias and Daryl Aung Lwin for the ICBC (Industrial and Commercial Bank of China) case study, to Cornell Tech student Siqi Shi and Angelica Soraya Camacho for the chapter on State Grid Corporation of China, to Cornell Tech student Wen Gao for the chapter on Chinese innovation, and to Cornell Alum Devesh Verma for the case study on Tencent. MBA students Abdellah Bouhamidi and Fayrouz Hares were great data analysts and excellent in translating our words into graphs.

Our special thanks, too, go to Jennifer Wholey for her copyediting, substantive and developmental editing, work she performed diligently and very constructively. We are also very grateful to the PhD student Eudes Lopes who not only contributed to editing but also provided comments and suggestions that were always very pertinent and enhanced the analysis. Our discussions with both were inspiring and the book would not have been possible without them.

The report also benefited from the dynamic discussions at Cornell University, especially with Andrew Karolyi, Deputy Dean of the college, Shanjun Li, Eswar Prasad, Ravi Kanbur, Kaushik Basu, Christopher Marquis, Arnab Basu, Sharon Poczter, Chris Barrett, Iwan Aya Azis and also members of the advisory council at EMI specially Rob Cañizares, Rustom Desai, Henry Renard, Georges Ugeux, and Timothy Heyman to name a few. The work of Ravi Ramamurti from Northeastern University, Mike Peng from the University of Texas in Dallas, and Professor Taotao Chen from Tsinghua University were all inspiring. Conversations with the members of the Emerging Markets Research Network Moacir Miranda de Oliveira and Fernanda Cahen from FEA, University of São Paulo, Veneta Andonova and Juana García from Universidad de los Andes in Colombia, Anabella Dávila from Tec de Monterrey in México, Diego Finchelstein from Universidad de San Andres/CONICET in Argentina, and Hugh Dang from the Transnational Corporations Council of Studies in Canada were also very helpful.

We would also like to mention colleagues from the OECD Development Center, a close partner of EMI at Cornell, and in particular Mario Pezzini, Bathylle Missika, and Lorenzo Pavone, with whom we have a fruitful and stimulating working relationship.

Lastly, both authors benefited from the opinions of Soumitra Dutta and Bruno Lanvin, the authors' husbands, who provided insights on innovation, and much more. We would like to thank them for their tremendous support.

EMERGING MARKETS INSTITUTE

Introduction

Acronyms

AIIB	**Asian Infrastructure Development Bank**
BRI	**Belt and Road Initiative**
EMR	**emerging markets report**
ICBC	**Industrial and Commercial Bank of China**
GFC	**Global Financial Crisis**
MOFCOM	**China Ministry of Commerce**
NDB	**National Development Bank**
OFDI	**Outward Foreign Direct Investment**
R&D	**Research and Development**
SGCC	**State Grid Corporation of China**
S&T	**Science and Technology**
UNCTAD	**United Nations Conference on Trade and Development**
VASs	**Valued-added services**
M&As	**mergers and acquisitions**
VC	**venture capital**

There is no hyperbole in stating that China has rocketed to the forefront of the world economy since the 2008 Global Financial Crisis (GFC). As many countries treaded carefully and turned inward to find surer financial footing, Chinese firms experienced a renaissance that flew largely under the radar. A little more than a decade since the crisis, Chinese companies stand as major global players—if not the victors—in many sectors such as construction, engineering, technology, white goods, mobile payments, and banking.

Seizing upon unprecedented growth in their domestic market to unleash scale, Chinese firms made aggressive forays as investors into markets overseas, particularly those bearing opportunities triggered by the GFC. The Chinese government supported and encouraged the démarche. Firms in most countries around the world must now contend with these new competitors, an uncommon phenomenon a decade ago. Moreover, China has catapulted itself into an innovation powerhouse, not just an efficient price leader. The country outranks the United States with the highest number of technological researchers, patents, and publications in the world, a feat increasingly made visible in the products and services Chinese firms champion, most notably in 5G technology, the cornerstone of the digital revolution.

China's leadership is not, however, limited to telecom. Firms such as Alibaba and Tencent dominate the burgeoning ecommerce and social media markets, among others. Nor is the far-reaching significance of the innovation emanating from Chinese firms limited to the IT sector per se. State Grid Corporation of China (SGCC), for instance, the second-largest company in the world by revenue, envisions its ultrahigh voltage IP (transmission line loss reducer) as the centerpiece of a paradigmatic gambit toward international, and even intercontinental, electricity grids, the implications of which elude measurement.

This book embarks on a longitudinal examination of Chinese firms as they mature. The authors contend that fully comprehending the factors that led to the expansion of Chinese companies are also key markers for understanding the forces behind China's economic rise and increased geopolitical influence. This connection serves as the book's crux.

The raw materials that make up the empirical core of the text derive from databases including the Fortune Global 500 ranking, Standard & Poor's Capital IQ, Financial Times fDi Markets, the Statistical Bulletin of China's Outward Foreign Direct Investment published by China Statistics Press (MOFCOM), UNCTAD, and World Bank statistics. We sourced analyses from work undertaken at the Emerging Markets Institute of the Cornell SC Johnson College of Business at Cornell University, and the series of Reports on Emerging Market Multinationals published since 2016 under its auspices. Finally, the project is informed by direct interviews with executives from Chinese multinational corporations and experts in multilateral institutions, as well as think tanks.

The book is divided into two parts. The first part describes the backdrop behind the rise of Chinese multinationals parallel to the country's economic growth and takes stock of the great global strides these companies have made. We examine Chinese corporate characteristics: how they compare with Western multinationals in terms of revenues and profits, and also the role that external environments played into their success. The second part outlines Chinese firms' strategic advantages (innovation, efficiency, and global reach) as they move beyond cost leadership and position themselves as global brands, as well as unique challenges they face. We intersperse four case studies of Chinese firms (the Industrial and Commercial Bank of China (ICBC), SGCC, Tencent, and Hainan Airlines (HNA) Group), each of which we identify as leaders emblematic of structural shifts to the country's key economic sectors.

The core conceit throughout the book is that examination of China and its corporate champions provides a vantage point from which to make sense of the world economy's transformation. We also explore the need for Western multinationals to collaborate and compete with emerging Chinese leaders.

Part I: Speed—Chinese multinationals conquering the world

Chapter 1 (*Chinese Firms Take the Helm*) sets the contours of the phenomenon, illustrating the rise of Chinese firms in global business. The expansion of China's domestic economy provided the foundation on which Chinese companies could build their development plans. With the GFC as a springboard, these firms rode the wave of remarkable growth in the decade that followed. By 2018, the Fortune Global 500 listed 111 Chinese firms (nearly at par with the United States), a spike from only 16 in 2005. Yet, Chinese firms show gaps in profitability, market capitalization, and international presence compared to more established Western multinationals. Nonetheless, the chapter reveals that Chinese companies are on track to narrow lingering disparities.

Even with the Chinese economy slowing down to 6.6% in 2018 as compared to past decades, the country's firms prove resilient, in large part thanks to their domestic market. Given their relative youth, the expansion plans of these companies portend more pronounced movement into global markets, a trend well underway in mobile phones, computers, railways equipment, and chemicals, to name a few. This disruptive shock will likely be felt across sectors and geographies, as demonstrated by trade conflicts that have openly erupted since 2018.

Chapter 2 (*Chinese Firms Venturing Abroad*) recounts the journey of Chinese multinationals as they have expanded abroad. In 2000, Chinese firms were hardly visible as outward investors. Over the next 16 years, China became one of the largest investors in the world, ranking second only to the United States in 2016. The GFC marks a turning point in this respect. After the crisis, financially distressed firms became affordable targets at an opportune moment for Chinese firms looking for technology and knowledge-driven ventures in advanced economies.

In their outward ventures, Chinese firms have employed both greenfield expansion and mergers and acquisitions (M&As). Several high-profile Chinese acquisitions of Western companies, however, have drawn more public attention. Chinese multinationals are no longer confined to their natural markets in Asia, nor even to other emerging economies, but have made moves to advanced markets, too. In addition, Chinese firms branched out beyond traditional domains such as natural resources or heavy industries. In fact, service-based and consumer-related industries have become more attractive for Chinese investors, while heavy or more traditional industries such as Energy (Oil, Coal, and Gas) or Materials (such as Metals) either stagnated or declined in importance. This indicates that Chinese multinationals' investment strategies increasingly prioritize consumer markets around the world. It points to the ambitions of Chinese multinationals in light of the new capabilities they have built over the years.

Meanwhile, China has consistently ranked among the top three countries for outward foreign direct investment (OFDI). Following buying sprees in 2016 and 2017, Chinese M&A activity slowed, reflecting a double policy blow of increased government scrutiny and controls both at home and abroad. It is unknown whether this slowdown will hold in the medium term, though the underlying motivations for OFDI expansion remain. For enterprises, access to natural resources, brands, and knowledge are key motivations; for the government, the overall strategy of advancing high value-added sectors and innovation continues to guide policy-making in support of OFDI in specific sectors. The country's "Made in China 2025" plan as well and other development initiatives indicate that OFDI support is likely to endure.

Chapter 3 (*A Heavyweight on the Global Scene*) turns to the Chinese economy's dramatic transformation that instigated the rise of Chinese multinationals in global business. From a poor, mostly rural nation in the 1970s, China has become the second largest economy in the world 40 years after the launch of its "Reform and Opening" policy.

China gradually accelerated its economic performance, integrated into international markets, and expanded its technology and innovation capabilities. Over time, it gained a number of trophy titles: leading exporter, second largest importer, number one FDI recipient, and top global investor, to name of few.

Backed by increased economic might, the country has also grown in global political influence and soft power. Through a number of initiatives—the establishment of new multilateral banks like the Asian Infrastructure Development Bank (AIIB) and the New Development Bank (NDB), and the launch of the Belt and Road Initiative (BRI), among the most visible—China has bolstered its international profile. The BRI, one of the largest infrastructure development programs in history, lies at the heart of President Xi Jinping's grand strategy to render China into a global power. As with all projects of such size and scope, it has generated concerns and criticisms. Yet, the BRI's ambitious infrastructure projects and wide geographical reach is reshaping longstanding global alliances and steering nations toward a rapprochement with China.

However, some of the conditions that contributed to China's rapid growth have waned as of 2019. As open trade and technological tensions increase, the geopolitical climate is pulling away from a world in which China and emerging economies could rely on favorable international relations as a source for growth and a basis for global expansion. The rule-based global trade system in particular is being upended. While it is too early to assess the implications, it is clear that the rules of the game are being reshuffled for all.

The emergence of China's multinationals on the global scene does not only reflect China's economic trajectory and its transformation into a major economic powerhouse. In Chapter 4 (*Forty Years of Opening Up: Policy Support and Chinese OFDI Expansion*), we explore the role of China's government policies in Chinese firms' growth and outward expansion. In less than two decades, the Chinese government charted a course from restriction to facilitation, and finally to support and promotion of outward FDI. These changes took place within a broader context of significant economic and institutional reforms in China that boosted the development of the business sector.

Chinese firms, however, have also faced policy headwinds as they have expanded further afield. In view of the massive FDI outflows in 2015–16, the Chinese government became concerned about speculation motivating investment and the potential impacts on the Chinese economy. In 2016, the government began to introduce regulations to rein in capital outflows, and followed up with a series of measures to monitor Chinese OFDI. Overseas, serious policy challenges have been brewing. Several governments, especially in developed countries, have stepped up their scrutiny and control of acquisitions by foreign investors on national security grounds since 2018. Here again, the increasingly dramatic technology rivalry between the United States and China looms large.

In Chapter 5 (*ICBC—The Global Bank*), we examine the success story of ICBC, emblematic of a Chinese bank growing domestically and then strategically expanding abroad. In 2019, ICBC was the largest bank by assets and the second one by market capitalization in the world; it operated about 17,000 Chinese domestic institutions and 400 institutions overseas. Founded in 1984, ICBC's main operating segments are corporate banking, personal banking, and treasury. Like many Chinese counterparts,

ICBC benefited from the sizeable domestic market, leveraging government policies to support growth into foreign markets. First China's "Going Out" strategy (launched in 2000) and then the country's entry into the WTO (World Trade Center) boosted Chinese firms' overseas expansion. ICBC entered foreign markets for the first time in the mid-2000s as a prime example of a "follow the customer strategy." The presence of its branches in other countries soon facilitated other Chinese firms to expand abroad.

ICBC has pioneered Internet banking in the Chinese market. The bank faces strong competition from mobile payment leaders such as Tencent's WeChat and Alibaba's Alipay, but the huge potential of the digital banking market in Asia offers ample growth opportunities. Given the size of the Chinese market, foreign operations still represent 10% of ICBC's total assets. ICBC views international expansion as an important area of growth, including in BRI countries.

Part II: Strategic advantages and challenges for Chinese firms

SGCC, a state-owned company examined in Chapter 6 (*State Grid, Powering China and the World*), was the second largest multinational company in the world by revenues in 2018; yet it has largely flown under the radar. Founded in 2002, it builds and operates power grids in China, but has rapidly expanded into Australia, Brazil (where it is the largest power distributor), Greece, Italy, the Philippines, and Portugal, among others. Despite this impressive movement into global markets, the company looks to expand even further.

Technological development and innovation are key factors in SGCC's international expansion, reflected in its Global Energy Interconnection project that envisions a global smart gird network by 2050, based on ultrahigh voltage (UHV) technology. To that end, the company has innovated technology that reduces energy line loss, which facilitates rapid energy transmission over long distances. However, political challenges abound, particularly in the Western countries as growing mistrust of investment is exacerbated by the fact that SGCC is a state-owned company. Energy transition concerns also linger. For instance, electricity production in China is still heavily reliant on coal.

Chapter 7 (*China, an Innovation Hub*) details how science and technology (S&T) policy reform and innovation supported China's remarkable progress in higher education and research and development (R&D). China has launched and adjusted a wide range of S&T policies that have nurtured an innovation ecosystem and significantly increased the size of the educated workforce, laying a solid foundation for future development. This chapter also highlights some technological frontiers in which Chinese firms have established strong leadership claims: artificial intelligence, mobile payments, and high-speed trains.

Chinese firms wrested significant leading positions in several sectors globally. Long considered to be low-cost competitors relative to their G-7 counterparts, Chinese companies built upon their growing domestic market and leveraged their lower input costs to compete on price in foreign markets, focusing on efficiency, productivity, and quality. However, as shown in Chapter 8 (*Chinese Multinational Companies Move Beyond Price Competition*), this strategy of cost leadership is evolving, with important implications for established leaders and competitors from developed economies. Chinese companies are still cost leaders in many sectors, but the price differential is shrinking. As they build brand equity and move up the technology ladder, Chinese firms have hiked price points in some sectors to earn higher profit margins and invest in future innovation. Chinese companies such as Huawei and Lenovo have moved beyond cost leadership altogether as their top priority, focusing on innovation and technology to consolidate brand leadership and solidify their market standings. Even as they prove serious contenders, Chinese firms still lag in efficiency relative to their Western counterparts in some key metrics such as revenues per employee. However, our analyses of the world's most valuable brands indicate that Chinese firms, while not yet on equal footing, have made significant gains in global brand recognition.

While still relatively unknown outside China, Tencent Holdings Limited, examined in Chapter 9 (*Tencent: An Innovative Tech Giant*), is ranked among the five most valuable Internet companies globally. It is one of the most innovative multinationals in the world. Headquartered in Shenzhen, China, Tencent provides Internet value-added services (VASs) and applications across various web-based and mobile platforms, as well as online advertising services to mainland China, Hong Kong, North America, Europe, and other Asian countries. Tencent is a world leader in video games, messaging services, and patent submissions. Its dominance in large part is thanks to its messaging app WeChat, which offers free text, voice, video messaging, social media, ride sharing, and most importantly, mobile payments and gaming. Ultimately, WeChat Wallet (along with Alipay) is responsible for China's global leadership in mobile payments and other mobile transactions.

Tencent stands out in that it comprises an entire universe of interlinked businesses, reflecting its "one stop shop" philosophy. Its gaming business contributes most to the company's revenue and is at the center of the company's universe. Its instant messaging platforms (such as WeChat) revolve around it. Other services (such as online search, software and apps, e-commerce platforms, web portal, mobile payments, entertainment, and social media platforms) only further cement user loyalty. Altogether, this ecosystem of interconnected products provides a platform for brands to engage with customers through multiple access points. Tencent's venture capital (VC) arm has also been critical to the company's ability to broaden its ecosystems fueled by a network of associated companies in which it is invested. Its strategic VC investments enable Tencent to provide a more complete range of services across its different platforms.

Tencent has sought to expand its products and services to a more global audience. While it is present in several countries (such as India, Korea, Russia, and the United States), it is still heavily dependent on the Chinese market.

Chapter 10 (*The Growth of HNA—Navigating an Uncertain World*) turns to the case of Hainan Airlines, one of the fastest growing and most acquisitive Chinese firms. HNA rose from a provincial airline to global prominence with a forceful campaign of international expansion. Founded in 1993 in Haikou, China, the company entered the

Fortune Global 500 in 2015, a remarkable achievement in view of its humble origins. HNA was emblematic of the new Chinese global acquirers that emerged in the late 2000s. One of the key factors behind its expansion was its global pursuit of vertical diversification into a wide array of upstream and downstream industries, a growth strategy heavily reliant on M&As (often highly leveraged).

As with other Chinese firms, the GFC also triggered HNA's internationalization. Responding to growing demand from Chinese consumers for overseas travel, it bought stakes in airlines overseas, major hotel chains, and high-end properties, in addition to acquiring firms in aircraft maintenance, cargo handling, and airline catering, as well as container and trailer leasing. The company also expanded into some horizontal diversification, investing into IT as well as banking and asset management. By 2017, HNA Group was a diversified international conglomerate with 45 foreign companies in 18 countries and territories.

By late 2017, HNA suffered a reversal of fortunes. Its glut of acquisitions had made it financially vulnerable: the firm found itself loaded with significant debt at a time of slowing global growth. Meanwhile, the attitude of Chinese authorities quickly shifted on M&As, further precipitating HNA's financial difficulties as the government clamped down on them and other prolific buyers. The company took a number of actions to redress the situation, triggering an intense selling-off period. In less than 2 years, the conglomerate sold a large part of its assets. As of mid-2019, the future of HNA is still uncertain. Its experience is suggestive of the challenges facing fast-growing Chinese multinationals, in particular those guided by an aggressive M&A-based outward expansion strategy. China's expanding domestic market and favorable OFDI policy environment at home may have provided HNA with a false sense of security, enabling it to grow at a breakneck pace. As some of those parameters changed, the company found itself hard-pressed to weather the storm.

In the chapters that follow, we will guide you through the different elements of the Chinese ecosystem that together have allowed Chinese firms to grow and to thrive at home, regionally, and all over the world. In their own unique ways, Chinese companies have become drivers of growth, power, and innovation for China as a whole.

Part I

Speed—Chinese multinationals conquering the world

Chinese firms take the helm

1

In every crisis, there is opportunity.

Chinese proverb

Acronyms

eMNCs	emerging market multinational companies
G-7	Group of 7: Canada, France, Germany, Italy, Japan, United States, and United Kingdom
GDP	gross domestic product
GFC	global financial crisis
GPM	gross profit margins
E20	Emerging markets 20: Argentina, Brazil, Chile, China, Colombia, Egypt, India, Indonesia, Iran, Malaysia, Mexico, Nigeria, the Philippines, Poland, Republic of Korea, Russia, Saudi Arabia, South Africa, Thailand, and Turkey
M&As	mergers and acquisitions
ROA	return on investments
SGCC	state grid corporation of China
SOE	state-owned enterprises

In both scale and reach, Chinese companies have grown at an accelerated pace, particularly since the 2008 Global Financial Crisis (GFC). While China's extraordinary rise on the global stage has garnered international publicity, the success of China's companies has made significantly fewer headlines. Even as analysts recognize significant changes in the world economies in the decade since the crisis, Chinese firms have been comparatively less studied. On closer inspection, they are major players in banking, construction, and other sectors, as well as shapers of global industry (Backaler, 2014; Fishman, 2006; Guo & Gallo, 2017; Healy, 2018; Li-Hua, 2014).

In parallel with China's overall economic growth, Chinese firms leveraged the opportunities triggered by the GFC to acquire global assets (see Chapter 2; Nie, Dowell, & Lu, 2012). The Chinese government also supported and encouraged the global expansion of Chinese multinationals (see Chapter 4). Drawing on databases including the Fortune Global 500 ranking, Standard & Poor's Capital IQ, Financial Times fDi Markets, UNCTAD Statistics, the World Bank, and the Statistical Bulletin of China's Outward Foreign Direct Investment published by China Statistics Press (MOFCOM— Ministry of Commerce of the People's Republic of China), this book studies the ascent of Chinese firms to become some of the world's largest companies (Casanova & Miroux, 2016, 2017, 2018).

While many Chinese firms gained scale in the large Chinese domestic market, they also pushed forward aggressively into many global markets (Pearce, 2011;

The Era of Chinese Multinationals. https://doi.org/10.1016/B978-0-12-816857-8.00001-X

Wang & Miao, 2016). According to MOFCOM (2017), 25,000 Chinese domestic enterprises had established more than 39,000 overseas enterprises in 189 countries with total assets of $6 trillion. Chinese firms that once competed on the basis of lower prices (see Chapter 8) are now positioning themselves as innovators rather than cost leaders and disrupting the competitive landscape (Tse, 2014). According to the Global Innovation Index (2018), China in 2018 ranked 17th in the world in innovation at par with countries such as Japan (ranked 13th), France (16th), and Canada (17th). In 2018, China also had the highest number of researchers, patents, and publications in the world, besting the United States.

Chinese firms quickly evolved to compete with visibly improved products and services, such as Huawei's lead on 5G technology, thereby raising the bar for global competition. China's embrace of technological innovation as a means of growth has increased global recognition for some Chinese firms such as Alibaba and Tencent (see Chapter 9). However, many other success stories have emerged below the radar of public and private sector leaders. One such example is State Grid Corporation of China (SGCC), the second-largest company in the world by revenue with a significant presence in more than 15 global markets. From producing innovative technology (ultrahigh voltage technology capable of reducing losses in transmission line) to the development of an international (and even intercontinental) grid, SGCC's strategy for growth has potentially far reaching disruption (see case study in Chapter 6).

1.1 Chinese companies at the top of the Fortune Global 500 ranking

The Fortune Global 500, a long-established and broadly accepted ranking of global companies based on revenues, comprises companies from 36 countries, Hong Kong, and Taiwan. As of 2018, nearly half of the listed firms were from the United States and China, far more than from any other country. In the years since the GFC, China has increased its share of firms listed on the Fortune Global 500 from 16 in 2005 to 111 in 2018, second only to the United States with 126 firms. No other emerging economy has yet been able to mirror the rise of Chinese firms (see Fig. 1.1). The ascent of Chinese firms in the ranking is even more impressive if one adds the nine firms from Hong Kong to those from mainland China—bringing the 2018 total to 120 firms—just six firms fewer than the United States.

Spurred by aggressive international acquisitions (see Chapter 2; Nolan, 2014), China increased the number of companies in the Fortune Global 500 year after year. Fig. 1.2 depicts the share of all 36 countries included in the ranking. While G-7 economies have retained their lead with 55% of the firms on the Fortune Global 500, nearly a third (155 firms) of the list comes from the top 20 emerging markets (by nominal gross domestic product (GDP) and demographics), a group known as the E20 (see Chapter 3, Box 3.1 for more on the E20). Chinese companies make up an astonishing 74% of these E20 firms.

A ranking based on market capitalization tells a somewhat different story. Market capitalization is defined as the total market value of a company's outstanding shares

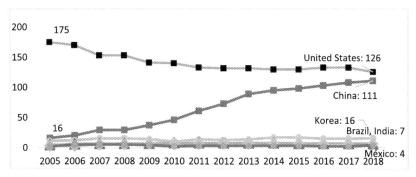

Fig. 1.1 Growth in China's representation in Fortune Global 500, 2005–18.
Source: Authors' based on Fortune Global 500 data 2005–18, (Accessed August 2018).

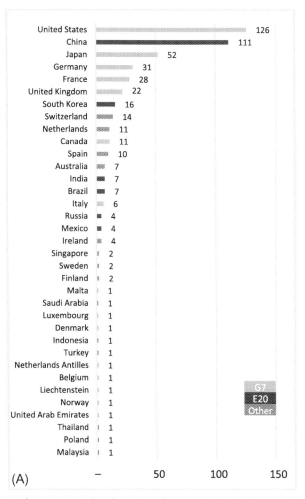

(A)

Fig. 1.2 (A) Countries represented and number of companies in the Fortune Global 500, 2018.
(A) *Source:* Authors' based on Fortune Global 500 data 2018, (Accessed August 2018);

(Continued)

Fig. 1.2 (B) Countries represented and number of companies in the Fortune Global 500, 2018 by market capitalization. Excluding private or state-owned companies. *Note of (B):* The data on market capitalization for China include the market capitalization of firms from Hong Kong. (B) *Source:* Authors' based on Fortune Global 500 data 2018, (Accessed February 2019).

of stock. The United States, Japan, and China have the highest number of firms in the Fortune Global 500 by market capitalization (excluding state-owned companies or those not publicly traded). The United States has 111 companies (28.6%), China has 54 companies (13.9%), and Japan has 49 companies (12.6%), and the three together hold approximately 55.2% of the companies in the list by market capitalization. The G-7 countries have 252 companies (64.95%). The E20 countries and other countries account for 85 (21.91%) and 51 companies (13.14%), respectively (Fig. 1.2B).

While it is common for the G-7 and other developed economies (such as Spain and Netherlands) to have a high number of Fortune-ranked companies, China and South Korea are the only E20 economies with a disproportionately high share of Fortune Global 500 firms. Fig. 1.3 depicts the relationship between a country's nominal GDP and the number of companies from the country in the Fortune Global 500 rankings. Other emerging market nations such as India, Brazil, Russia, and Mexico have failed to replicate China's distinct success.

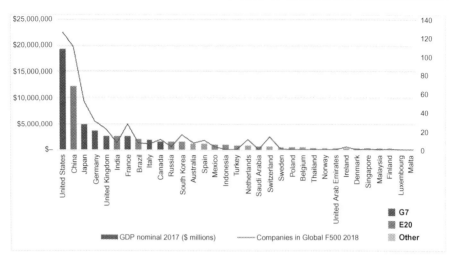

Fig. 1.3 Country's GDP nominal and number of companies ranked in Fortune Global 500.
Source: Fortune Global 500 Ranking 2018, (Accessed August 2018).

One-fifth of the top 100 companies in the world are Chinese as of the 2018 Fortune Global 500 rankings (see the Table 1.A1). A closer look at the top 15 Chinese firms in the Fortune Global 500 reveals that Chinese energy firms are particularly prominent, occupying the second (SGCC), third (Sinopec Group), and fourth (China National Petroleum) ranks in the world by revenue. Chinese firms in 10 sectors make up the 21 Chinese companies in the top 100: petroleum refining/crude oil production, engineering and construction, network and other communications, telecommunications, banks—commercial and savings, trading, insurance—life/health, motor vehicles and parts, pharmaceuticals, and utilities. This strength across sectors contrasts with the examples of many other emerging markets, in which one or two sectors have tended to dominate and expand abroad. For example, the seven firms from Brazil in the Fortune 500 come from only two sectors: finance (4) and commodities (3).

Chinese firms are also showing depth in addition to breadth, proving their dominance in a number of key industry sectors. Fig. 1.4 lists the top five companies in eight major industries across a decade and a half. Once again, Chinese firms showed impressive growth within a short period of time. In 2004, no Chinese firm appeared in any industry sector, but by 2018 the top five engineering and construction firms were all Chinese, and four of the top five banks are also Chinese. With the exception of the United States, no other country can match the dominance of large Chinese firms across such a range of sectors.

The Chinese companies being relatively young make their breakneck growth even more remarkable. As shown in Fig. 1.5, the average founding year for Chinese firms in the Fortune Global 500 rankings is 1981, compared to 1926 for American firms. While firms from other emerging market economies are younger than most of their G-7 counterparts (with average founding years of 1945 for Indian firms and 1964 for South Korean firms), China's global firms are the youngest, at less than 40 years old (Fig. 1.5).

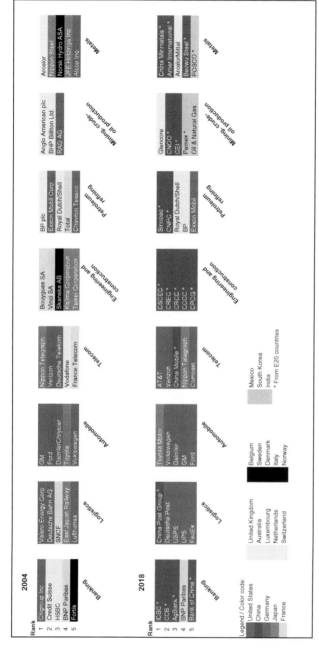

Fig. 1.4 China dominates top five companies and country of origin across different industries in the Fortune Global 500 in 2018 compared to 2004 and 2015.

Source: Authors based on Fortune Global 500 data 2004–18, (Accessed August 2018).

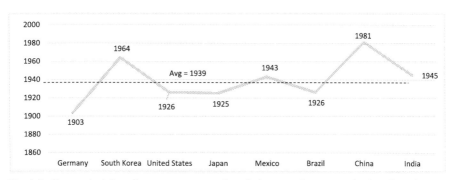

Fig. 1.5 Companies' founding years: average foundation year for companies in selected countries, from Fortune Global 500, 2018.
(*Source:* Authors based on Fortune Global 500 data 2018, (Accessed August 2018)).

1.2   An expanding international footprint

China's large domestic market is partly responsible for the successful international expansion of numerous Chinese firms. The size of China's market—which increased by a factor of six between 2004 (GDP of $1.95 trillion) and 2018 ($13.4 trillion)—allowed Chinese companies to gain scale at home before venturing abroad (see Chapter 3). In this way, the local market became a safe testing ground on which Chinese firms could innovate to create the foundations for foreign expansion.

However, many Chinese firms have a smaller international presence than firms from both developed economies and some emerging markets, as shown by their number of announced greenfield foreign direct investment (FDI) projects (Lee, 2018; Yeung, 2011; Yip & McKern, 2016). Based on fDi Markets data, Fig. 1.6 compares the average number of countries in which E20, United States, and Japanese companies had announced projects in 2017 and 2018. Firms from South Korea, Japan, and the United States lead in the number of international subsidiaries, while China lags behind. This discrepancy is likely due to the fact that, many global Chinese firms being relatively young, the attractive growth potential of the domestic market may encourage them to stay within the boundaries of their local economy.

Data from Standard & Poor's (S&P) Capital IQ, which include mergers and acquisitions (M&As) in addition to greenfield developments, mirror this trajectory (see Chapter 2). Likewise, the number of stock exchanges a company is listed on can indicate the extent of the company's internationalization. US firms lead with an average of 5.4 stock market listings, followed by other E20 countries and Japan (see Table 1.1). On average, Chinese initial public offerings (IPOs) occurred in two stock markets, usually on the Shanghai and Hong Kong exchanges. While "other E20" firms suffered a reduction in international presence from 2017 to 2018 (see Fig. 1.6), China and Korea made gains in their geographical footprint as indicated by greenfield projects.

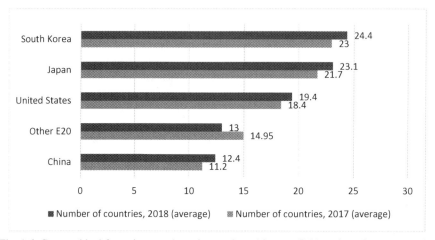

Fig. 1.6 Geographical footprint: number of countries with greenfield projects from companies in selected countries, 2017 and 2018.
Source: Authors based on data from fDI Markets, (Accessed August 2018).

1.3   Return metrics reveal room for growth

Despite Chinese gains, US firms still outperform their Chinese counterparts in several return indicators. Even though leading Chinese firms listed on the Fortune Global 500 hold more assets and have more employees than American firms, the former generate less revenue (and around half the profits) compared to the latter. Fig. 1.7 gives a snapshot of the profit margins of Chinese firms in the Fortune Global 500.

Table 1.1   Firms' international presence by average number of stock markets in which firms are listed and countries where firms are present, greenfield or M&A, 2016–18.

Group or country	Average number of stock markets in which firms are listed (2018)	Average number of countries in which firms are present (Capital IQ, 2016 EMR report)	Average number of countries in which firms are present (fDi Markets, 2017 EMR report)	Average number of countries in which firms are present (fDi Markets) 2018
Other E20	3.6	19	15	13
China	2	10	11	12.4
Japan	3.2	26	22	21.7
South Korea	2.3	17	23	24.4
United States	5.4	28	18	19.4

Source: Authors based on data from fDI markets and Capital IQ, (Accessed August 2018).

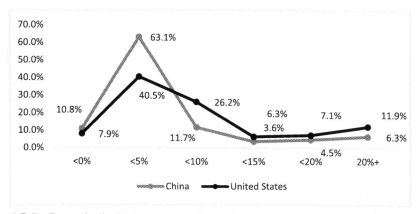

Fig. 1.7 Profit margin distribution between United States and Chinese companies in Fortune Global 500.
Source: Authors based on Fortune Global 500 data 2018, (Accessed August 2018).

As shown in Fig. 1.7, nearly 74% of Chinese firms have profit margins below 5%, lower than those of US firms. Likewise, Chinese companies demonstrated a lower return on assets (ROA) and return on employment. There are varied reasons for this. First, tight competition in much of the Chinese domestic market keeps pressure on price points. Second, many Chinese firms have not yet developed a global brand and must enter foreign markets with lower prices to compete. Finally, many Chinese firms are state-owned or have a strong government influence. As a result, firms may seek to keep employment high, which reduces operational efficiency as Chinese labor costs continue to rise.

If we look at the profit margins of Chinese companies in the top 100 of the Fortune Global 500 (Table 1.A1), banks (with profit margins over 20%) are outliers by far. Ping An Insurance has a profit margin of 9%, Huawei has ~8%, and China Mobile Communications has almost ~10%. There seems to be no simple connection between profit margins and ownership. For example, China National Petroleum, a publicly traded state-owned enterprise (SOE) ranked fourth in the Fortune Global 500 list, has a negative profit margin of −0.21%.

Fig. 1.8 shows a similar gap between Chinese and US profit to asset ratios (1% for China vs 2.1% for the United States) and return on employment (1.7% for China vs 1.9% for the United States). The disparity across a number of return metrics suggests that China has yet to do some legwork in order to catch up to the United States on efficiency.

1.4   Profitability still low for Chinese firms

American firms also have higher profit margins than their Chinese counterparts based on gross profit margins (GPM). As Fig. 1.9 shows, the gap is particularly prominent between the two countries' profit margins in the technology industry. The lone exception to this is in the financial sector: the high profitability of the Chinese banking sector is driven by the country's favorable financial policies and high savings rates. As a result of the policy enforced by the Chinese central bank, Chinese banks benefited from large spreads between lending and deposit rates.

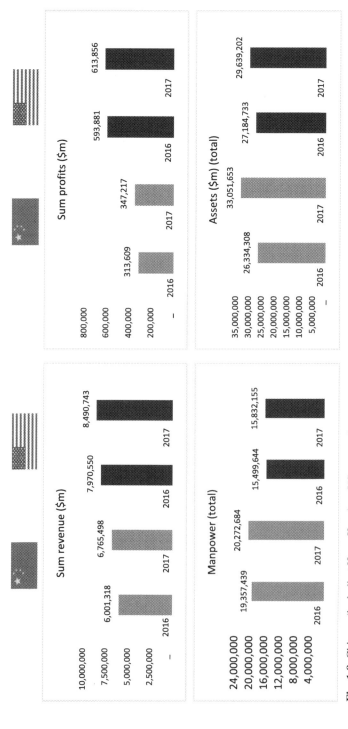

Fig. 1.8 Chinese (including Hong Kong) vs US companies: aggregated revenues, profits, labor, and assets, 2017 and 2018 Fortune Global 500. *Source:* Authors based on Fortune Global 500 data 2018. (Accessed August 2018).

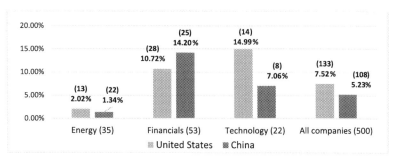

Fig. 1.9 Gross profit margins (GPM) of Chinese vs US companies in selected industries, Fortune Global 500, 2017. Industries selection criteria: More than 25 companies per industry and more than 10 companies by industry for each group (either G-7 or E20). Number of companies in parentheses.
Source: Authors' analysis based on data from S&P Capital IQ—Fortune Global 500 Financials.

Fig. 1.10 Return on Assets (ROA) of companies from China and United States in selected industries, Fortune Global 500, 2017. Industries selection criteria: More than 25 companies per industry and more than 10 companies by industry in each group (either G-7 or E20). Number of companies in parentheses.
Source: Authors' analysis based in data from S&P Capital IQ—Fortune Global 500 Financials.

Although the divide is smaller, the US firms on the Fortune Global 500 list also beat out Chinese firms on ROA. The average Chinese firm's ROA amounted to only about half of that of a US firm (1.19% vs 2.24%, see Fig. 1.10). The only lead for Chinese companies is in the financial sector, and even that is only slightly.

1.5 Gaining ground in market capitalization

In 2018, the market capitalization of 47 publicly listed Chinese companies was $14.6 trillion, about 21% of the value of 111 US-based publicly listed companies. As shown in Fig. 1.11, only 21% of Chinese companies in the 2018 Fortune Global 500 were public, vs 79% of US companies in the ranking. Meanwhile, 47% of Chinese companies were state-owned compared to only 1% of US companies, and 67% of Chinese companies were at least partially state-owned. The government's role is much larger in the capital structure of Chinese companies vs US firms, and this state influence places further emphasis on revenues over profits.

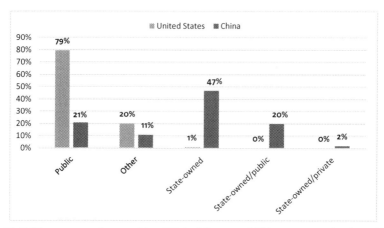

Fig. 1.11 Different types of ownership of United States and Chinese companies from 2018 Fortune Global 500.
Source: Author's analysis based on data from Capital IQ and companies' websites, (Accessed October 2018).

Fig. 1.12 displays the average total market capitalization of public companies in the Fortune Global 500.

While the gap with the United States remains large, Chinese companies have made great strides in market capitalization. The average market capitalization for the publicly traded Chinese companies in the Fortune Global 500 is around $65.6 billion, higher than the average of any non-US country. As of the first quarter of 2019, two

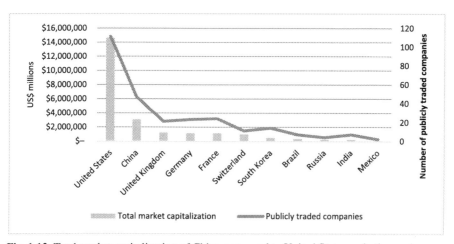

Fig. 1.12 Total market capitalization of China compared to United States and other major countries and number of publicly traded companies listed on the Fortune Global 500 compared to other major countries.
Source: Author's analysis based on data from S&P Capital IQ—Fortune Global 500 Financials, (Accessed August 2018).

Chinese companies were among the 10 largest by market capitalization: e-commerce retailer Alibaba was seventh, with a value of $485 billion, and Internet company Tencent came in eighth place with a value of $461 billion. Although the United States dominates the ranking, China now has 12 companies within the top 100 ranked by market capitalization, and 3 in the top 15.

Meanwhile, three stock exchanges in China and Hong Kong now rank among the 10 largest in the world—the Shanghai Stock Exchange, Shenzhen Stock Exchange, and Hong Kong Exchange. Their increasing sphere of influence amid primarily developed market stock exchanges may spark Chinese companies to shift their financing structures to rely more heavily on exchanges (Fig. 1.13).

While Chinese companies, like those in other countries in the E20, have traditionally relied on debt compared to equity, the US debt-to-equity ratio is also particularly high due to low interest rates, lower perception of risk, and the wider availability of financing options (see Fig. 1.14). The United States experienced a significant increase in its debt-to-equity ratio, while its debt-to-capital ratio was somewhat consistent.

China is a notable exception to the rule that emerging economies typically face higher interest rates (see Fig. 1.15). The country's low interest rates have supported its high debt-to-equity ratios. Interest rates have substantially decreased since 2017; as a result, China's prime lending interest rates matched those of the United States for the first time.

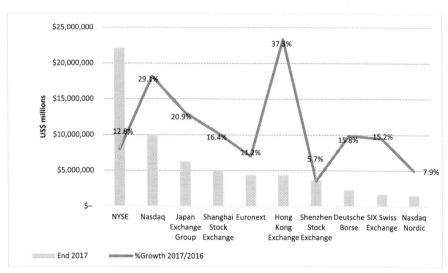

Fig. 1.13 Total value of top 10 stock exchange markets for 2018. *Note:* Excludes London Stock Exchange because it is not part of the World Federation of Exchanges.
Source: Author's analysis based on data from World Federation of Exchanges, 2018. WFE Annual Statistics Guide 2017. Available at: https://www.world-exchanges.org/home/index. php/statistics/annual-statistics.

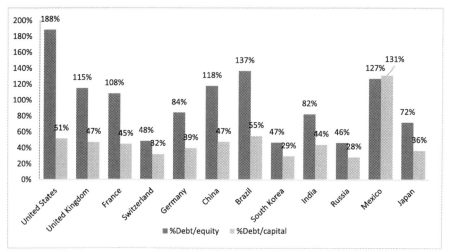

Fig. 1.14 Capital structure analysis by country for nonfinancial companies in the 2018 Fortune Global 500. *Note:* Excludes financial services companies.
Source: Author's analysis based on data from S&P Capital IQ—Fortune Global 500 Financials 2017, (Accessed August 2018).

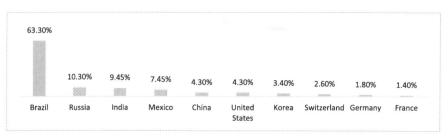

Fig. 1.15 Commercial bank prime lending interest rate (%) from selected economies, estimated data 2017. *Note:* The lending rate is the bank rate that usually meets the short- and medium-term financing needs of the private sector. This rate typically differentiates according to the borrower's creditworthiness and financing objectives. The terms and conditions attached to these rates differ by country, however, limiting their comparability.
Source: Author's analysis based on data from CIA World Factbook's estimates for December 2017. Available at: https://www.cia.gov/library/publications/the-world-factbook/fields/2208. html, (Accessed August 2018).

1.6 Moving forward

Chinese firms were able to use the GFC as a springboard, launching themselves on trajectory of stellar growth in just a single decade. As a result, three of the top five companies on the 2018 Fortune Global 500 rankings were Chinese. Seizing opportunities presented by the GFC, a growing Chinese economy provided Chinese firms with a strong foundation on which to build their plans for globalization. While the Chinese economy has slowed since, it has maintained a growth rate upwards of 6%.

This platform provides room for Chinese firms to grow further on the basis of their domestic market alone. This favorable environment may continue to increase the number of Chinese firms in the Fortune Global 500 rankings.

Not content with growth in the Chinese domestic market, successful Chinese firms ventured abroad. Overseas investments by Chinese firms increased significantly since the GFC, buoyed by the presence of cheap acquisition targets in many economies and the support and encouragement of the Chinese government to globalize (Chapters 2 and 3). Chinese firms still generally lag behind their peers in developed economies and other emerging markets in terms of their global presence, but they have made significant investments in their capabilities to innovate in order to compete on an international scale. In particular, an emphasis on technological innovation has produced several global leaders like Huawei, Alibaba, and Tencent. These Chinese tech companies have even been able to out-innovate their best competitors from developed markets (Chapters 7 and 8).

Given that Chinese firms are relatively young (with average founding year of 1981 for the firms in the Fortune Global 500 list, as mentioned above), their expansion plans may further mature in the future. Combined with the strength of their large domestic markets, Chinese companies are expected to become formidable competitors in global markets. This disruptive shock will be felt across geographies and in multiple sectors. Chinese firms will be able to combine the benefits of the immense scale of their domestic market, access to significant financial resources, a talented human resource pool, and competence in technological innovation to challenge established incumbents from developed markets. Firms from other countries will have to learn how to partner and compete with Chinese firms as they do their part to shape the coming "Asian century."

Appendix

Table 1.A1 Chinese companies among the 100 biggest in the 2018 Fortune Global 500.

Rank	Company	Industry	Revenues ($M)	Profit margin (%)	HQ[a]	Short business description	Year[b]	Ownership
2	State Grid Corporation of China	Utilities	$348,903	2.73	China	State Grid China Co., Ltd. constructs and operates power grids in China	2002	State-owned
3	Sinopec Group	Petroleum refining	$326,953	0.47	China	China Petrochemical Corporation is a petroleum and petrochemical company operating in China and abroad	1998	Public
4	China National Petroleum	Petroleum refining	$326,008	−0.21	China	China National Petroleum Corporation produces and supplies oil and gas	1955	State-owned
23	China State Construction Engineering	Engineering and construction	$156,071	1.71	China	China State Construction Engineering Corporation Ltd. operates as an integrated construction and real estate company in China	1982	State-owned/ public

26	Industrial & Commercial Bank of China	Banks: Commercial and savings	$153,021	27.66	China	Industrial and Commercial Bank of China Ltd. provides various banking products and services primarily in China and internationally	1984	State-owned/public
29	Ping An Insurance	Insurance: Life, Health (stock)	$144,197	9.14	China	Ping An Insurance (Group) Company of China, Ltd. provides various financial products and services focusing on Insurance, Banking, Asset Management, and Fintech and HealthTech businesses in China	1988	State-owned/public
31	China Construction Bank	Banks: Commercial and savings	$138,594	25.86	China	China Construction Bank Corporation provides various banking and related financial services in China	1954	State-owned/public
36	SAIC Motor	Motor vehicles and Parts	$128,819	3.95	China	SAIC Motor Corporation Ltd. researches, produces, and sells passenger and commercial vehicles in China	1955	State-owned/public

Continued

Table 1.A1 Continued

Rank	Company	Industry	Revenues ($M)	Profit margin (%)	HQ[a]	Short business description	Year[b]	Ownership
40	Agricultural Bank of China	Banks: Commercial and savings	$122.366	23.33	China	Agricultural Bank of China Ltd. provides corporate and retail banking products and services in China and internationally	1951	State-owned/public
42	China Life Insurance	Insurance: Life, health (stock)	$120,224	0.22	China	China Life Insurance Company Limited, together with its subsidiaries, operates as a life insurance company in China	1949	State-owned/public
46	Bank of China	Banks: Commercial and savings	$115,423	22.10	China	Bank of China Ltd., together with its subsidiaries, provides a range of banking and related financial services in China and abroad	1912	State-owned/public

53	China Mobile Communications	Telecommunications	$110,159	9.92	China	China Mobile Communications Group Co., Ltd., through its subsidiaries, operates in LTE/fourth generation digital mobile telecommunication and fixed-line telecommunications businesses	1997	State-owned
56	China Railway Engineering Group	Engineering and construction	$102,767	1.14	China	China Railway Group Ltd., together with its subsidiaries, operates as an integrated construction company in China	1950	State-owned
58	China Railway Construction	Engineering and construction	$100,855	1.30	China	China Railway Construction Corporation Ltd., together with its subsidiaries, engages in the construction of infrastructure projects in China and internationally	2007	State-owned/ public
65	Dongfeng Motor	Motor vehicles and parts	$93,294	1.50	China	Dongfeng Motor is a large-scale automobile enterprise which researches, manufactures, and sells commercial, passenger, and military vehicles in China	1969	State-owned/ public

Continued

Table 1.A1 Continued

Rank	Company	Industry	Revenues ($M)	Profit margin (%)	HQ[a]	Short business description	Year[b]	Ownership
72	Huawei Investment & Holdings	Network and other communications equipment	$89,311	7.86	China	Huawei Investment & Holdings provides information and communications technology (ICT) infrastructure and smart devices in China and internationally	1987	Private
86	China Resources National	Pharmaceuticals	$82,184	3.84	China/ Hong Kong	China Resources operates in the health, large consumption, real estate, cement, gas, and finance sectors in China	1938	State-owned
87	China National Offshore Oil	Mining, crude-oil production	$81,482	3.70	China	China National Offshore Oil is the largest offshore oil and gas producer in China, and provides oil and gas to China and internationally	1982	State-owned

91	China Communications Construction	Engineering and construction	$79,417	1.95	China	China Communications Construction Co. and its subsidiaries provide integrated infrastructure services in China and internationally	2005	Public
96	Pacific Construction Group	Engineering and construction	$77,205	4.07	China	Pacific Construction Group operates as an infrastructure investment, construction, and management company in China and internationally	1995	Private
98	Sinochem Group	Trading	$76,765	0.98	China	Sinochem Group operates in the energy, chemical, agricultural, real estate, and finance sectors, providing products and services in China and internationally	1950	State-owned

[a] HQ: Country Headquarters.
[b] Foundation year.
Source: Authors' analysis based on Fortune Global 500 data 2018. (Accessed August 2018).

References

Backaler, J. (2014). *China goes west: Everything you need to know about Chinese companies going global.* Basingstoke: Palgrave Macmillan.

Casanova, L.; Miroux, A. (2016). Emerging market multinationals report: The China surge. Emerging Markets Institute in collaboration with the OECD development Center. S.C. Johnson School of Management. Cornell University. https://www.johnson.cornell.edu/wp-content/uploads/sites/3/2019/04/2016-EMR-Updated-EMR-Consolidated.v3.pdf.

Casanova, L.; Miroux, A. (2017). Emerging market multinationals report: Emerging multinationals in a changing world. Emerging Markets Institute in collaboration with the OECD development Center. S.C. Johnson School of Management. Cornell University. https://www.johnson.cornell.edu/wp-content/uploads/sites/3/2019/04/EMR-2017-FINAL-FINAL-4dec2017.pdf.

Casanova, L., & Miroux, A. (2018). Emerging market multinationals report 2018. In *Emerging markets reshaping globalization.* https://www.johnson.cornell.edu/wp-content/uploads/sites/3/2019/04/EMR2018_V3_FIN-11Jan.pdf (Accessed June 2019).

Fishman, T. (2006). *China, Inc: How the rise of the next superpower challenges America and the world.* London: Pocket Books.

Global Innovation Index. (2018). https://www.globalinnovationindex.org/gii-2018-report.

Guo, X., & Gallo, F. (2017). *Multinational companies in China: Navigating the eight common management pitfalls.* Bingley: Emerald Publishing.

Healy, J. (2018). *Chinese firms going global: Can they succeed?* Singapore: World Scientific Publishing Pte.

Lee, K. (2018). *AI Superpowers: China, silicon valley, and the new world order.* New York: Houghton Mifflin Harcourt.

Li-Hua, R. (2014). *Competitiveness of Chinese firms: West meets east.* Basingstoke: Palgrave Macmillan.

Ministry of Commerce of the People's Republic of China (MOFCOM), National Bureau of Statistics, State Administration of Foreign Exchange. (2017). *2017 statistical bulletin of China's outward foreign direct investment.* China Statistics Press.

Nie, W., Dowell, W., & Lu, A. (2012). *In the shadow of the dragon: The global expansion of Chinese.* New York, NY: Amacom.

Nolan, P. (2014). *Is China buying the world?* Cambridge: Polity Press.

Pearce, R. (2011). *China and the multinationals: International business and the entry of China into the global economy.* Cheltenham: Edward Elgar Publishing.

Tse, E. (2014). *China's disruptors.* New York, NY: Penguin Publishing Group.

Wang, H., & Miao, L. (2016). *China goes global.* London: Palgrave Macmillan.

Yeung, A. (2011). *The globalization of Chinese companies strategies for conquering international markets.* John Wiley & Sons (Asia): Singapore.

Yip, G., & McKern, B. (2016). *China's next strategic advantage: From imitation to innovation.* Cambridge: MIT Press.

Further reading

Chattopadhyay, A., Batra, R., & Ozsomer, A. (2012). *The new emerging market multinationals: Four strategies for disrupting markets and building brands.* New York, NY: McGraw-Hill.

FDiMarkets. 2017/2018. Accessed through Johnson Library. Cornell University.

Fortune (n.d.), Fortune Global 500 directory 2018. <http://fortune.com/fortune500/> (Accessed August 2018).

Guillén, M., & García-Canal, E. (2013). *Emerging markets rule: Growth strategies of the new global giants*. New York, NY: McGraw-Hill Education.

Haour, G., & Zedtwitz, M. (2016). *Created in China: How China is becoming a global innovator*. London: Bloomsbury.

Larçon, J., & Barré, G. (2009). Technology-based competition and Chinese multinationals. In J. Larçon & L. Chuanzhi (Eds.), *Chinese multinationals* (pp. 127–149). Singapore: World Scientific Publishing Co.

Liu, H. (2009). *Chinese business: Landscapes and strategies*. Abingdon: Routledge.

Liu, C. (2012). *Multinationals, globalisation and indigenous firms in China (Routledge studies on the Chinese economy)*. Routledge.

Standard & Poor's. Capital IQ. Database. Accessed through Johnson Library. Cornell University.

UNCTAD. (2006). *World Investment Report. FDI from developing and transition economies: Implications for development*. Geneva: United Nations Conference on Trade and Development.

UNCTAD. (2016). FDI recovery is unexpectedly strong, but lacks productive impact. In *Global Investment Trends Monitor No. 22, United Nations Conference on Trade and Development, January 20, 2016*. http://unctad.org/en/PublicationsLibrary/webdiaeia2016d1_en.pdf (Accessed June 2019).

Chinese firms venturing abroad

Pearls don't lie on the seashore. If you want one, you must dive for it.
Chinese proverb

Acronyms

BRI	Belt and Road Initiative
CCCC	China Communications Construction Company
CNOOC	China National Offshore Oil Corporation
CPNC	China National Petroleum Corporation
CSCEC	China State Construction Engineering Corporation
CTG	China Three Gorges
FDI	foreign direct investment
GFC	Global Financial Crisis
HKND	HK Nicaragua Canal Development Investment Co., Ltd.
M&As	mergers and acquisitions
MOFCOM	Ministry of Commerce of the People's Republic of China
OBOR	One Belt One Road Initiative
TEV	total enterprise value
UNCTAD	United Nations Conference on Trade and Development

Chinese companies have evolved into major cross-border investors as they grew in both size and strength. This chapter examines the ways that Chinese firms have chosen to invest abroad: through mergers and acquisitions (M&As), greenfield, or joint venture. While M&As and greenfield have been the most popular options for Chinese firms, their strategies have evolved over time.

Using available data on announced greenfield foreign direct investment (FDI) projects from Financial Times fDi Markets (starting in 2003), and Standard & Poor's Capital IQ for M&As, this chapter analyzes these two popular modes of investment. In a greenfield investment scenario, the parent company sets up a firm abroad and builds its operation from scratch, while in M&As, one firm takes control of another. In both cases, the data relate to investment projects or mergers that have been announced, and not necessarily completed projects.

China first outperformed all emerging markets in both FDI inflows and outflows in 2000 (Casanova & Miroux, 2016). By 2009, China's FDI inflows surpassed that of all economies except the United States. Nine years later, China ranked second in global yearly outflows, and third in outward foreign direct investments (OFDI) stock (UNCTAD, 2019). In the same year, China invested $134 billion overseas, edged out only by Japan ($143 billion). All in all, the country touted a massive 13% of the world's OFDI flows, which is only expected to grow.

As per MOFCOM data (2018), China's OFDI activity is concentrated in "South-South" investments, which account for almost 86% of Chinese OFDI, as compared

The Era of Chinese Multinationals, https://doi.org/10.1016/B978-0-12-816857-8.00002-1

to 12.7% among advanced markets. In 2017, China directed the majority (63%) of its outward investments to Asia, its "natural market" followed by Latin America (21%), Europe (6.1%), North America (almost 5%), and Africa and Oceania (2.5%) (MOFCOM, 2018). Among the developed economies, China's OFDI stock and flow are both higher in the European Union than in the United States, paralleling its M&A activity.

China's investments are diversified into six main industries that represent 86% of the total OFDI stock. Leasing and business services (34%), IT and technical services (13%), wholesale and retail trade (12.5%), financial services (11%), mining (8.7%), and manufacturing (7%). China is also a net exporter of capital: in 2017, the country invested $50 billion more abroad than it received. A total of 39,000 Chinese companies contributed to an investment spree in 189 countries, with total assets of $6 trillion and an accumulated OFDI (stock) of $1.8 trillion (MOFCOM, 2018).

State-owned enterprises (SOEs) have historically dominated China's outward investment, accounting for about 70% of its OFDI stock in 2007 (MOFCOM, 2018). However, this share has been steadily declining. In 2017, SOEs were the source of about 50% of total investments abroad, a 5% decrease from the previous year.

2.1 Going solo: China's greenfield investments

Since 2008, China has significantly increased the number of its greenfield FDI projects the world over. According to fDiMarkets 2019 data, Chinese greenfield projects quadrupled in Asia (to $281 billion), Europe (to $94 billion) and Africa (to $88 billion) and ballooned 5- and 12-fold in Latin America (to $86 billion) and North America (to $57 billion), respectively. China's greenfield OFDI remains concentrated in emerging and developing economies (80% of projects), especially in Asia, its natural market, defined by Casanova (2009) as markets that share history, cultural similarities, language, and/or geographical proximity. Beyond Asia, Chinese greenfield investments have increasingly targeted advanced markets and Latin America (Fig. 2.1).

Across the industries of interest for Chinese investors, greenfield investments in real estate, coal, oil and gas, renewable energy, and metals accounted for 52.5% of the greenfield outward investments from 2009 to 2018. Comparing China's outward greenfield projects pre- and post-2008 Global Financial Crisis (GFC), we can observe that coal, oil and natural gas, and metals industries, while significant in absolute amounts, decreased in relative importance: coal and oil and natural gas industry saw its share reduced by almost 60%, and the share of metals was halved (Fig. 2.1). By contrast, less traditional sectors such as real estate and renewable energy became much more attractive to international investors. Renewable energy, a relatively new industry, quadrupled its share in China's OFDI portfolio. Business services also gained prominence over the period, though this change mostly reflects a 2013 peak that was not maintained (Fig. 2.2). Similarly, 5 of the 10 most important greenfield investments (Fig. 2.5) were in real estate (one of them in warehousing), four in energy/natural resources or related and the most important in business services.

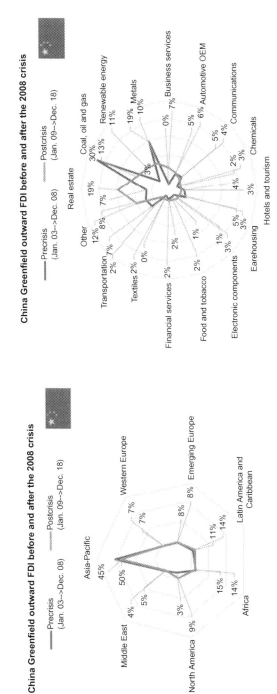

Fig. 2.1 China's outward announced greenfield FDI pre-(2003–08) and post-2008 GFC (2009–18). *Note:* Periods compared are 2003–08 and 2009–18. Data include greenfield FDI projects from China and Hong Kong. FDI data starts at 2003. *Source:* Authors based on data from fDi Markets. (Accessed January 2019).

Industry	2009	2010	2011	2012	2013	2014	2015	2016	2017	2018	Grand total
Real estate	1.5%	1.7%	0.0%	15.3%	15.2%	31.4%	9.6%	44.5%	12.1%	14.3%	19.5%
Coal, oil and gas	30.7%	9.6%	21.4%	1.5%	3.2%	10.5%	24.4%	10.6%	8.2%	12.8%	12.5%
Renewable energy	7.9%	9.7%	8.1%	22.3%	2.2%	8.4%	15.3%	5.3%	4.8%	26.3%	10.7%
Metals	11.9%	16.9%	28.1%	6.7%	7.5%	9.2%	14.0%	3.0%	11.8%	6.9%	9.8%
Business services	0.8%	0.8%	0.5%	0.7%	45.5%	0.3%	0.5%	1.3%	0.4%	0.3%	6.9%
Automotive OEM	13.9%	15.5%	7.4%	11.4%	3.0%	8.4%	3.3%	2.7%	7.7%	2.5%	5.6%
Communications	3.3%	7.9%	7.6%	2.3%	2.6%	6.0%	3.5%	3.3%	4.2%	3.1%	4.0%
Chemicals	0.5%	3.6%	0.8%	2.9%	1.8%	3.1%	0.4%	0.5%	13.7%	3.5%	2.9%
Hotels and tourism	5.8%	2.3%	1.0%	11.6%	3.7%	1.3%	5.2%	0.9%	0.1%	3.3%	2.9%
Warehousing	3.3%	0.0%	0.0%	1.1%	6.8%	1.5%	1.0%	5.1%	0.0%	1.1%	2.6%
Electronic components	1.0%	9.4%	1.2%	5.9%	0.4%	0.9%	2.9%	3.9%	2.5%	2.2%	2.5%
Food and tobacco	0.4%	0.7%	4.2%	4.8%	1.4%	1.7%	1.4%	2.5%	4.2%	1.2%	2.1%
Financial services	5.9%	4.9%	2.6%	4.0%	1.2%	1.8%	1.6%	1.6%	2.5%	0.9%	2.0%
Textiles	0.5%	1.5%	0.1%	0.6%	1.0%	3.3%	0.9%	0.7%	5.1%	3.7%	1.9%
Transportation	0.5%	0.8%	1.0%	0.5%	0.4%	0.8%	2.4%	5.4%	0.6%	0.7%	1.7%
Industrial equipment	4.8%	3.3%	2.0%	1.8%	0.7%	4.7%	0.7%	0.6%	0.8%	0.3%	1.6%
Building materials	2.1%	0.6%	4.1%	0.6%	0.2%	1.0%	3.5%	1.3%	2.7%	0.4%	1.5%
Paper, printing and packaging	0.5%	0.0%	1.1%	0.0%	0.2%	2.5%	2.0%	0.8%	2.6%	2.2%	1.4%
Leisure and entertainment	0.0%	0.0%	0.0%	0.0%	0.0%	0.0%	0.0%	0.4%	1.0%	6.4%	1.1%
Automotive components	1.1%	0.8%	1.2%	1.8%	0.4%	0.5%	1.5%	0.7%	2.3%	0.7%	1.0%
Other	3.6%	10.0%	7.6%	4.4%	2.6%	2.6%	5.8%	4.8%	12.9%	7.2%	5.7%
Total	100.0%	100.0%	100.0%	100.0%	100.0%	100.0%	100.0%	100.0%	100.0%	100.0%	100.0%

Fig. 2.2 Industry distribution of China's announced greenfield OFDI investments (in %), from 2009 to 2018. *Source*: Authors based on data from fDiMarkets. (Accessed January 2019).

China's greenfield investments cast a moderately wide geographical footprint relative to the country's smaller range of M&A activity. The 20 target countries with the largest number of greenfield projects represent 70% of total Chinese investments, with a relatively balanced distribution: virtually all of the countries have a share between 1.5% and 7% (see Fig. 2.3). Most of these target countries are emerging and developing economies; half of them are from Asia. The most notable outlier to this pattern is the United States, which ranks second as a destination for Chinese greenfield investments post-GFC. The same pattern repeats among the 10 largest greenfield investment deals (Fig. 2.5): all are "South-South" investments, that is, in emerging markets, in all regions but one (the Shanghai Greenland Group in the United States).

China's greenfield cross-border OFDI is quite diversified across companies. The five largest Chinese greenfield investors account for an estimated 19.5% of total investments (Fig. 2.4)—unlike in other emerging markets like Latin America, in which only two or three companies in Mexico and Brazil account for about 50% of each country's OFDI (Casanova, 2018). The most significant Chinese greenfield investor until 2018 was HK Nicaragua Canal Development Investment Co., Ltd. also known as HKND, founded in 2012 to develop the Nicaragua Canal (Fig. 2.5). Despite an announced 2014 IPO, HKND shuttered in 2018 as it succumbed to financial difficulties. Some of the largest investors in greenfield projects are resource companies—oil companies like China National Petroleum Corporation (CPNC), Sinopec, and China

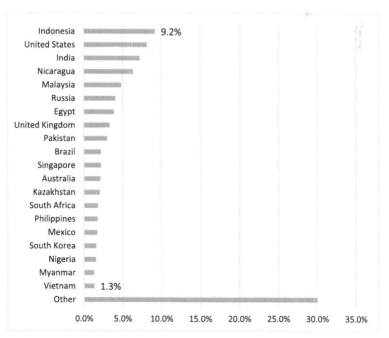

Fig. 2.3 Distribution of announced Chinese outward greenfield investments, from 2009 to 2018 by targeted country.
Source: Authors based on data from fDiMarkets, (Accessed January 2019).

Top investing company	2009	2010	2011	2012	2013	2014	2015	2016	2017	2018	Grand total
Hong Kong Nicaragua Canal Development Investment (HKND Group)	0.0%	0.0%	0.0%	0.0%	45.0%	0.0%	0.0%	0.0%	0.0%	0.0%	6.3%
China Fortune Land Development (CFLD)	0.0%	0.0%	0.0%	0.0%	0.0%	0.0%	0.0%	0.0%	0.0%	19.1%	4.2%
Power Construction Corporation of China (PowerChina)	0.0%	0.0%	0.0%	0.0%	0.1%	0.0%	2.8%	0.0%	3.4%	0.0%	3.5%
China National Petroleum (CNPC)	28.8%	5.7%	3.7%	0.1%	0.5%	0.8%	0.0%	6.1%	0.1%	0.1%	2.8%
Shanghai Greenland Group	0.0%	0.0%	0.0%	0.0%	8.2%	11.3%	0.0%	0.9%	0.0%	0.0%	2.7%
Dalian Wanda Group	0.0%	0.0%	0.0%	2.0%	2.4%	4.8%	1.4%	2.8%	0.0%	0.0%	1.7%
Huawei Technologies	1.2%	5.2%	1.8%	1.0%	1.0%	2.6%	0.7%	1.2%	1.7%	0.7%	1.4%
Shanghai Electric	0.0%	0.0%	0.0%	1.5%	0.1%	3.3%	2.5%	3.4%	0.0%	0.0%	1.4%
Sany	0.3%	2.1%	0.2%	0.3%	0.0%	0.3%	4.2%	1.5%	3.1%	0.0%	1.2%
China Communications Construction Company	0.0%	0.0%	0.0%	0.0%	2.1%	0.0%	0.2%	3.9%	0.6%	0.1%	1.1%
Zendai Group	0.0%	0.0%	0.0%	0.0%	0.0%	8.0%	0.0%	0.0%	0.0%	0.0%	1.0%
Hutchison Whampoa	0.9%	0.3%	0.0%	0.9%	5.0%	1.0%	0.4%	0.0%	0.0%	0.2%	1.0%
China State Construction Engineering Corporation (CSCEC)	0.0%	0.0%	0.0%	0.1%	0.0%	0.0%	0.3%	3.3%	1.6%	0.6%	0.9%
China Petroleum and Chemical (Sinopec)	0.8%	0.0%	6.3%	0.4%	0.1%	1.7%	1.3%	0.0%	0.0%	0.0%	0.9%
China National Offshore Oil Corporation (CNOOC)	0.4%	0.0%	0.0%	0.0%	0.0%	2.1%	0.0%	0.0%	0.0%	3.6%	0.8%
China Huaneng	4.9%	0.0%	0.0%	1.1%	0.3%	0.0%	4.2%	0.0%	0.0%	0.0%	0.8%
Jiangsu Delong Nickel Industry	0.0%	0.0%	0.0%	0.0%	0.0%	0.0%	6.9%	0.0%	0.0%	0.0%	0.8%
Zhejiang Geely Holding Group (Geely Holding Group)	0.6%	1.4%	1.2%	1.1%	0.1%	1.0%	2.1%	0.4%	0.5%	0.4%	0.8%
China Gezhouba (CGGC)	0.0%	0.0%	2.3%	0.0%	0.0%	4.4%	0.1%	0.1%	0.0%	0.0%	0.7%
Zhejiang Hengyi Group	0.0%	0.0%	10.0%	0.0%	0.0%	0.0%	0.0%	0.0%	0.0%	0.0%	0.7%
Other	70.2%	85.3%	74.4%	91.4%	34.9%	58.9%	72.8%	53.8%	88.9%	75.2%	65.3%
Total	100.0%	100.0%	100.0%	100.0%	100.0%	100.0%	100.0%	100.0%	100.0%	100.0%	100.0%

Fig. 2.4 Company contribution to total greenfield OFDI investments from China, 2009–18. *Source*: fDiMarkets, (Accessed January 2019).

Project date	Investment ($USmm)	Investing company	Parent company (investor)	Destination country	Industry sector
Jun 2013	$40,000	Hong Kong Nicaragua Canal Development Investment (HKND Group)	Hong Kong Nicaragua Canal Development Investment (HKND Group)	Nicaragua	Business services
Oct 2016	$20,000	China Fortune Land Development (CFLD)	China Fortune Land Development (CFLD)	Egypt	Real estate
Apr 2018	$17,800	Sinohydro	Power Construction Corporation of China (PowerChina)	Indonesia	Renewable energy
Apr 2014	$6,400	Shanghai Zendai Property	Zendai Group	South Africa	Real estate
Jan 2015	$5,000	Jiangsu Delong Nickel Industry	Jiangsu Delong Nickel Industry	Indonesia	Metals
Oct 2013	$4,900	Shanghai Greenland Group	Shanghai Greenland Group	United States	Real estate
Jan 2016	$4,900	China Fortune Land Development (CFLD)	China Fortune Land Development (CFLD)	India	Real estate
Jul 2011	$4,300	Zhejiang Hengyi Group	Zhejiang Hengyi Group	Brunei	Coal, oil and gas
Oct 2013	$4,098	Hutchison Port Holdings (HPH)	Hutchison Whampoa	Mexico	Warehousing
Mar 2016	$4,000	China Petroleum Pipeline Bureau (CPP)	China National Petroleum (CNPC)	Mozambique	Transportation

Fig. 2.5 Top 10 OFDI greenfield investment deals from China 2009–18.
Source: Authors based on data from fDiMarkets. (Accessed January 2019).

National Offshore Oil Corporation (CNOOC), infrastructure and construction companies such as China Communications Construction Company (CCCC) and China State Construction Engineering Corporation (CSCEC)—they also include the world's largest telecommunications electronic equipment company, Huawei, in seventh position. One of the most internationalized Chinese firms, Huawei earns almost 50% of its $100 billion revenue from abroad. At the time of the publication of this book, Huawei was facing difficulties in the European market as the US-China trade war continues to escalate. (The United States is making efforts to block the company, citing security concerns that Huawei denies.)

2.2   China's new status as a global acquirer

In the late 1990s-early 2000s, China barely contributed to OFDI. Cross-border M&As began to pick up in the early 2000s, and since 2009 China has been an important actor on the global M&A market (Fig. 2.6).

China became one of the most active global acquirers after the GFC, ranked second among the top 10 in 2016, its peak year. Chinese M&As accounted for about 20% of the total value of announced M&As by the top 10 global acquirers that year. Over the decade leading up to 2016, the value of Chinese M&A deals continuously increased, as shown in Fig. 2.7. The most significant cross-border deal by a Chinese acquirer was the state-owned chemical company ChemChina's announced acquisition of Swiss firm Syngenta for $43 billion.

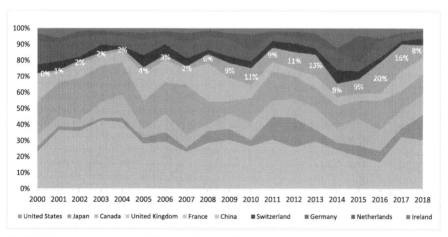

Fig. 2.6 Outbound announced M&A deals from China as percentage of the value of total outbound M&A deals by top 10 investing countries by OFDI stock. Countries selected on the basis of highest OFDI stock as of 2018 (UNCTAD data). China includes transactions by China and Hong Kong. The percentages reflect (%) share for the top 10 countries.
Source: Authors' analysis based on data on M&A transactions from Standard & Poor's Capital IQ, (Accessed February 2019).

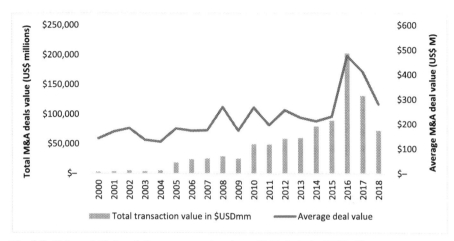

Fig. 2.7 Chinese M&A activity: announced outbound M&A deals, 2000–18.
Source: Authors' analysis based on data on M&A transactions from Standard & Poor's
Capital IQ.

Comparing data from the United States to China, Korea, Brazil and India, we
can observe that the US dominates both greenfield (since 2003, the earliest year
with available data) and M&As (since 2000) for cross-border investments (see
Table 2.1). Since the GFC, the total value of China's activity has been roughly half
of the United States while also showing impressive growth from precrisis levels in
both greenfield and M&As at 354% and 391%, respectively. Although starting from
a much lower level, Korea also had impressive growth in M&A activity (424%)
and greenfield (118%). Brazil and India both have increased greenfield projects but
reduced M&As. Given its high volumes, the United States has also grown, but at
more moderate pace.

China not only became a more frequent acquirer, but was also involved in progressively larger M&A deals, including 10 of the top 100 global transactions in 2017,
a feat only topped by the United States (26), Canada (16), and the United Kingdom
(15). In 2018, China nearly repeated the achievement, accounting for 7 of the top
100 transactions (Fig. 2.A1). That year, the $35 billion acquisition of EDP (Energias
de Portugal) announced by China Three Gorges (CTG) was the fourth-largest cross-
border deal in the world, and China's largest deal. At the time this book was going to
press, however, the announced purchase was not realized, and EDP was considering
other options involving a joint venture with CTG.

Since 2017, Chinese M&A activity has faced some headwinds from local and
global policy changes (see Chapters 3 and 4). Chinese authorities made efforts to
curtail capital outflows following a rapid flurry of Chinese M&A activity in 2016.
M&A activity declined as a result of targeted government regulations, but China still
proved a leading global acquirer. By mid-2017, Chinese activity accounted for 16%
of worldwide M&A deals in the first semester of 2017, a result only surpassed by the

Table 2.1   Changes in announced outbound M&A deals and greenfield investments by country: comparing pre-GFC (2000–08 for M&As and 2003–08 for Greenfield) and post-GFC (2009–18).

Investor	Greenfield OFDI (total amount in million)	Outbound M&A (total amount in million)
China (with Hong Kong)	Precrisis period: $184,674 Postcrisis period: $578,751 Growth: +181% Rank precrisis period: No 7 Rank postcrisis: No 2	Precrisis period: $166,325 Postcrisis period: $798,013 Growth: +380% Rank precrisis: Rank postcrisis: No 4 (No 2 in 2016)
Korea	Precrisis period: $126,601 Postcrisis: $276,368 Growth: +118%	Precrisis period: $26,324 Postcrisis period: $138,059 Growth: 424%
India	Precrisis period: $86,476 Postcrisis period: $158,925 Growth: +84%	Precrisis period: $63,250 Postcrisis period: $61,792 Growth: −2%
Brazil	Precrisis period: $29,408 Postcrisis period: $45,773 Growth: +55%	Precrisis period: $60,767 Postcrisis period: $47,463 Growth: −22%
China	Precrisis: $141,448 Postcrisis: $642,950 Growth: +354%	Precrisis: $166,325 Postcrisis: $817,533 Growth: +391%
United States	Precrisis period: $977,553 Postcrisis period: $1,288,383 Growth: +32%	Precrisis period: $1,518,855 Postcrisis period: $1,814,891 Growth: +19%

Source: Authors' analysis based on data on announced M&A transactions originating from China and Hong Kong, excluding canceled transactions (value in million US$) from Standard & Poor's Capital IQ. Consortium investments where Korean companies were minority stakeholders were removed manually for Korean M&A figures.

United States (Fig. 2.6). The US and European policy shifts since early 2018 have further stagnated Chinese overseas acquisitions (Chapter 4), and subsequently China's share of global M&A activity decreased to 8%, dropping in global acquirer rankings to sixth place between France and Switzerland (see Fig. 2.8). It is unclear if the growth volumes of 2016 and 2017 were outliers and 2018 represents a return to normality, or the beginning of a downturn. Time will tell if Chinese firms want to focus on regaining ground in outward M&A deals (see Fig. 2.9) or prefers to concentrate on their domestic market.

2.3   Increase in the size of M&A deals from China

Along with the increase in the total value of M&A deals, the average deal size of Chinese acquisitions has surged from $186.6 million in 2000–08 to $289.7 million in 2009–18

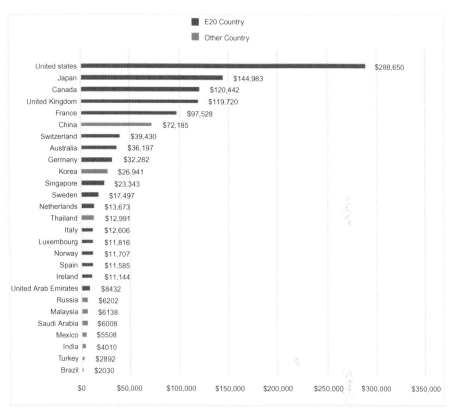

Fig. 2.8 Top 15 economies and other selected E20 by announced outbound M&A deals (in million US$) in 2018.
Source: Authors' analysis based on data on M&A transactions from Standard & Poor's Capital IQ. Excludes financial centers in the Caribbean.

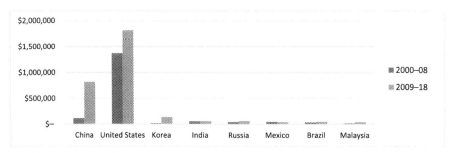

Fig. 2.9 Total value of announced M&A deals by China, other emerging markets 2003–16, pre-GFC (2000–08), and post-GFCs (2009–18) in million US$.
Source: Authors' analysis based on data on M&A transactions from Standard & Poor's Capital IQ. Cross-border M&A transactions, involving local companies of their respective countries and excluding cancelled transactions, (Accessed February 2019).

(Fig. 2.10). As deal size increased, Chinese companies were willing to pay higher prices for the targeted assets, according to valuation metrics commonly used in M&A transactions such as total enterprise value (TEV)/revenues[1] and price/earnings ratios (average premium), which measure a firm's total value. The average TEV/revenue ballooned from 2.3 multiples in 2000–08 to 8.3 multiples in 2009–18 (Fig. 2.10). For publicly traded M&A targets, the average acquisition premium grew from 18.8% to 28.7%.

Comparing Chinese outbound M&A deals with those of the United States, we observe notable differences (Fig. 2.11). While China's recent M&A deals have grown

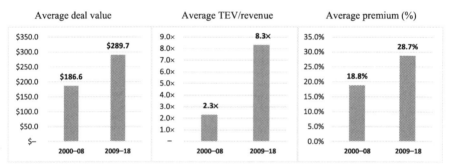

Fig 2.10 Price and valuation of Chinese outbound M&A deals (2000–18) in million US$. *Note:* Average % premium based on "Target Stock Premium, 1 Week Prior" (Capital IQ) Target Stock Premium calculation: [(Purchase price/Historical price) − 1] × 100. TEV: Total enterprise value, a measure of a company's total value, is calculated as the market capitalization plus debt, minority interest, and preferred shares, minus total cash and cash equivalents. Data points available: TEV/revenue (231), premium (401). *Source*: Authors' analysis based on Standard & Poor's Capital IQ data on M&A transactions.

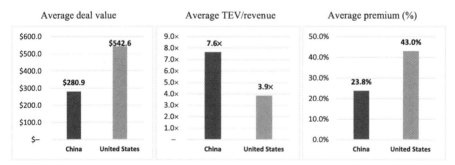

Fig 2.11 Price and valuation of China and United States outbound M&A deals (2018). *Note:* Average premium based on "Target Stock Premium—1 Week Prior (%)" (Capital IQ) Data points available: China TEV/Revenue (231), US TEV/Revenue (1011), China Premium (401), US Premium (1364). *Source*: Authors' analysis based on Standard & Poor's Capital IQ data on M&A transactions.

---

[1] TEV is total market capitalization, preferred stock value, and total debt less cash and cash equivalents.

in size, up to $280.9 million, they remain substantially smaller than the average US outbound deal, valued at $542.6 million. Higher premium paid by the US companies compared to the Chinese companies (43.0% and 23.8%, respectively) explains some of this gap. This effect is offset, however, by the lower average TEV/revenue that American companies offered than what Chinese firms paid (3.9 multiples and 7.6 multiples, respectively). However, in part due to increased government scrutiny (Chapters 3 and 4), some analysts predict that China will avoid large acquisitions and the average Chinese deal value will continue to be smaller than that of the United States (in spite a brief role reversal in 2016). Lower premiums may signal that China is a more recognized player in the M&A space and does not need, as before, to offer higher premiums for acquired shareholders to accept their bid. Alternatively, Chinese firms may have become more adept at avoiding bidding wars. Additional analysis of longitudinal data is necessary to reach more definitive conclusions regarding both average TEV/revenue and premiums.

2.3.1   China's increased focus on services

Like greenfield investments, the industry distribution of Chinese outbound M&A activity has changed since the GFC.[2] According to Capital IQ data, prior to the GFC, the majority of Chinese investments abroad were focused on the energy and materials sectors, which accounted for a combined 45% of total transaction value of announced Chinese M&As between 2000 and 2008. At the other end of the spectrum, real estate (3%), consumer staples (2%), and health-care (1%) transactions were insignificant (Fig. 2.12). Since 2009, however, deal activity has spread more evenly across the sectors. The share of energy and materials declined in the Chinese M&A portfolio (by about half) while less traditional sectors have increased in importance. Real estate

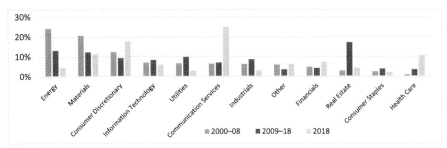

Fig. 2.12 Industry distribution of all Chinese outbound M&A deals (%) pre-(2000–08) and post-GFC (2009–18) and in 2018.
Source: Authors' analysis based on data on M&A transactions from Standard & Poor's Capital IQ, (Accessed February 2019).

---

[2] Industry distribution based on Standard & Poor's Capital IQ's primary industry sector classification, including industrials, consumer, financials, information technology, health care, utilities, materials, and energy sectors. Materials includes primarily natural resources, but also chemicals and container and packaging companies.

took the number one spot (17% of the value of the deals over 2009–18), while other sectors such as industrials and utilities grew as a percentage of total deals (Fig. 2.12). Furthermore, in 2018, over 50% of Chinese outbound deals were in the communication services, consumer discretionary, and materials sectors.

All in all, real estate, consumer discretionary, information technology, and materials amount to more than half of acquisition value from 2014 to 2018 (S&P Capital IQ, 2019). As a sign of a more mature economy, the second largest in the world, this sectoral focus closely tracks US outbound acquisitions and foreshadows the sectors that the "Made in China 2025" strategy prioritizes (see Fig. 2.13). The implications of China's widespread acquisitions across multiple sectors have caused concern in several advanced markets, breeding distrust. On the local level, the Chinese government placed new restrictions on real estate (see Chapters 3 and 4), as transactions increasingly took a speculative tone.

2.3.2   Europe becomes a top destination for Chinese M&As

In parallel with target sector diversification, the geographical footprint of Chinese announced M&As also changed. In the pre-GFC period, a significant amount of Chinese cross-border M&As already targeted developed markets. This trend only reinforced in the crisis' aftermath: while Asia was the main target of Chinese M&As from 2000 to 2008 (Fig. 2.15), advanced markets received 57% of China's M&As from 2009 to 2018. The United States was China's most important target market, but Europe amassed the most transactions (39%) postcrisis (Figs. 2.14–2.16). Within Europe the most prominent target countries (in decreasing order of importance) were the United Kingdom, Switzerland, Italy, Germany, Netherlands, Finland, and France. Chinese financial investors made a number of substantial acquisitions during this time. For instance, one of the largest acquisitions occurred in 2016 when a consortium of Chinese investors consisting of Beijing Jianguang Asset Management Co., Ltd ("JAC Capital") and Wise Road Capital LTD ("Wise Road Capital") announced the purchase of Standard Products business from the Netherlands-based semiconductor company, NXP Semiconductors N.V. for $2.75 billion.

The dual desire to both acquire advanced technologies and capture market share explains Chinese firms' focus on developed economies. An early prominent example was Lenovo's acquisition of IBM's PC business (Thinkpad unit) in 2005. Thinkpad's success encouraged other Chinese firms to make bold acquisitions in advanced markets. For example, Haier acquired General Electric's appliances division in 2016.

Asia, China's main OFDI recipient, accounts for the second highest (24.6%) volume of M&A activity from Chinese firms. Most of China's M&A deals in Asia are focused on logistics and transportation. In July 2017, a consortium of five Chinese companies, including Bank of China's investment unit, won a bid to acquire Singapore-based warehousing company GLP, formerly Global Logistic Properties. The deal, worth 16 billion Singapore dollars ($11.6 billion), was one of the largest

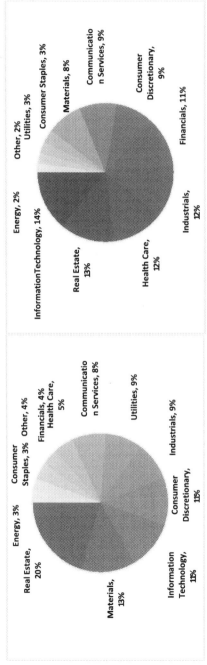

Fig. 2.13 Sector distribution of Chinese (left) and United States (right) announced M&A deals (2014–18). *Source*: Authors' analysis, based on data from Standard & Poor's Capital IQ, accessed January 2019.

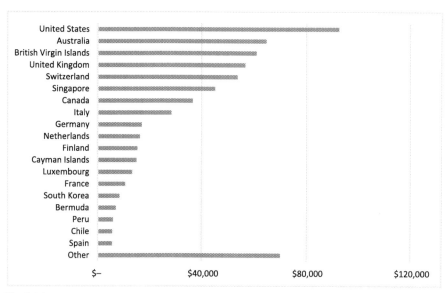

Fig. 2.14 Distribution of Chinese outward M&A from 2009 to 2018 by country. *Note:* Other countries include the following from largest to smallest total transactions of Chinese M&A activity: Portugal, Israel, Russia, Brazil, Norway, Sweden, Japan, Pakistan, New Zealand, Barbados, Belgium, Jersey, South Africa, Malaysia, Macau, Hungary, Slovakia, Turkey, India, Democratic Republic of the Congo, Thailand, Kazakhstan, Isle of Man, Slovenia, Taiwan, Cyprus, Jordan, Greece, Vietnam, Mongolia, Indonesia, Austria, Czech Republic, Nigeria, Samoa, Benin, Namibia, Malta, Denmark, Sierra Leone, Liechtenstein, Panama, Argentina, Poland, United Arab Emirates, Bangladesh, Seychelles, Gibraltar, Georgia, Mauritius, Kyrgyzstan, Sri Lanka, Philippines, Eritrea, Ecuador, Serbia, Estonia, Cambodia, Ireland, Croatia, Myanmar, Belarus, Guyana, Laos, Bahamas, Saint Kitts and Nevis, Suriname, Trinidad and Tobago, Vanuatu, Papua New Guinea, Bolivia, Botswana, Ukraine, Tonga, Brunei, Gabon, Anguilla, Monaco, Nicaragua, Romania, Fiji, Macedonia, Egypt, Lithuania, Antigua & Barbuda, Marshall Islands, and Latvia. *Source*: Authors' analysis based on data on M&A transactions from Standard & Poor's Capital IQ, (Accessed February 2019).

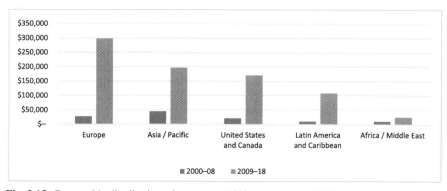

Fig. 2.15 Geographic distribution of announced Chinese outbound M&A deals pre-(2000–08) and post-GFC (2009–18).
Source: Authors' analysis based on data on M&A transactions from Standard & Poor's Capital IQ, (Accessed February 2019).

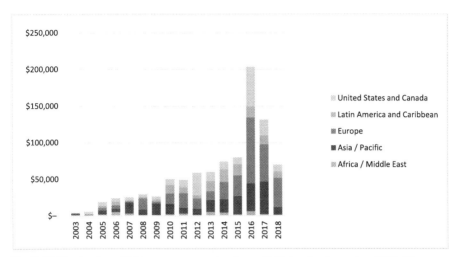

Fig. 2.16 Destination of Chinese announced outbound M&A value by region 2003–18, million US$.
Source: Authors' analysis based on data on M&A transactions originating from China and Hong Kong (value in million US$) from Standard & Poor's Capital IQ.

Chinese acquisitions in 2017. Chinese conglomerate HNA Group also bought more than 90% of Singaporean logistics operator CWT that same year.

Latin America's share in total outbound M&A deals from China increased slightly from <10% pre-GFC to just under 13% post-GFC. Cheap currencies, new opportunities from postcrisis financial hardships, and Chinese firms' desire to seek both new markets and sources for natural resources supported a pivot toward Latin America. For example, State Grid acquired the Brazilian energy company CPFL for $3.4 billion. Africa and the Middle East, however, have yet to capture the attention of much of China's M&As.

Fig. 2.A1 provides a list of top M&A deals in 2017 and 2018 and shows that the United States topped the list with 23 deals, which was almost double the total value of the next contender, Canada. China ranked third, with 12 deals.

2.4 Strategies for going global

There is a vast body of literature on the motivations for companies to go global (Ciprian, Peng, & Bruton, 2014; Cuervo-Cazurra, 2012; Cuervo-Cazurra & Ramamurti, 2014; Dunning, 1993, 2005). One or more of the following may be motives for international expansion:

– Efficiency: Firms are able to benefit from lower labor costs and lower production costs by establishing units in foreign markets, typically in less developed economies. Examples include setting up garment manufacturing units in Bangladesh (as of 2016 the country has become the second largest garment manufacturer in the world after China).

- Growth in new markets: Companies also seek to grow beyond their domestic market and acquire new customers in foreign markets. This is especially true for countries and regions that have large populations with an appetite for new products and services, such as Africa and Asia.
- Natural resources: Firms also require natural resources to sustain their economic development and seek to acquire them from resource-rich nations or regions. Many firms have sought to protect their access to key natural resources such as oil and gas by expanding in foreign markets.
- Knowledge: Companies also seek to acquire new technologies and market-specific knowledge by establishing units in particular countries or regions. It is not uncommon to see many technology firms seeking to acquire or set up subsidiaries in key tech hubs such as Silicon Valley and Boston.

Different companies' specific motives will differ, between for instance European and US firms and Chinese or Latin American firms (see Fig. 2.17). China, for example, has traditionally benefited from lower labor and production costs at home, integrated value chains, and scale, which make production quite efficient. Many firms from the United States and Europe opened their units in China to benefit from the lower production costs and efficient and well-integrated value chains and logistics. Hence, efficiency has not been a driving factor for China's OFDI strategy, though this could change if labor costs were to rise or to avoid trade restrictions (Chapter 3). The other three reasons listed above have typically motivated Chinese firms' foreign investments, as in the case of Lenovo's acquisition of IBM's PC division.

As China lacks natural resources in many categories, Chinese firms have also targeted access to resources in their globalization drive. For example, Ming Metals, China's biggest metal trading firm purchased a majority stake in Sherwin, the second largest US aluminum company in 2008, and purchased Oz Minerals, an Australian mining firm in 2009. Although they represent a reduced share of total

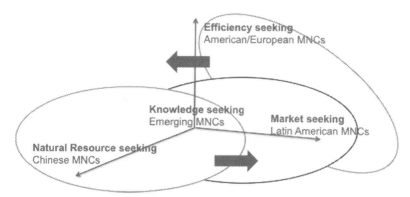

Fig. 2.17 Motivations for internationalization by companies from different countries of origin. *Note: Arrows* indicate that Chinese companies are seeking new markets and Western companies are also learning from emerging markets.
Source: Authors based on analyzed data and company interviews.

OFDI compared to pre-GFC, Figs. 2.1 and 2.2 demonstrate the continued appetite of Chinese overseas investments for natural resources.

Access to natural resources and intangibles such as brand recognition and technology remain the main drivers of overseas investments in 2019. Markets seeking is also a motive, but of much less importance, as illustrated in Fig. 2.17.

Chinese firms have typically followed a five-staged process to rapidly expand internationally, as outlined in Fig. 2.18. The first stage has always been growth in the domestic market, similar to most US firms. Chinese firms have leveraged the rapid growth of the Chinese domestic market to gain scale while also competing against and learning from foreign companies operating in China.

In the second stage, Chinese companies have typically expanded into their natural markets in Asia as a first step toward going global. These markets are particularly effective for testing new products or services since they share information flows and access to talent. The US companies similarly moved into their natural markets in Europe and North America in early stages of globalization.

Chinese firms have prioritized other emerging markets in Latin America and Africa in the third stage. Emerging markets share similar population strata, and Chinese firms have recognized that their products and services are well positioned to serve the bottom of the pyramid (Prahalad, 2005). As Chinese firms continue to pursue growth in new markets and access to natural resources, they have expanded into other emerging markets around the world. For instance, Chinese smartphone manufacturers like Oppo, Xiaomi, and Huawei have opened Internet access for African and Latin American consumers who cannot afford more expensive options like Apple's iPhones. American firms have also focused on selected emerging markets in their third stage of globalization, mainly in Latin America.

After developing global skills in their natural markets and in other emerging markets, Chinese firms have typically pursued acquisitions in the more developed markets in Europe and the United States in the fourth stage. Through these acquisitions,

Internationalization phases	Chinese companies	United States companies
1	Domestic	Domestic
2	**Natural market: Asia and neighboring countries**	**Europe (United Kingdom as springboard) and neighboring countries: Canada and Mexico**
3	Latin America, Africa	Latin America, Australia
4	Western countries: United States/European Union	Global
5	Increasing investments in OBOR countries	"Coming back home?"

Fig. 2.18 Comparing internationalization in China vs the United States.
Source: Authors.

Chinese firms hope to gain access to (developed) markets, and desirable brand and technology assets in advanced economies. Rather than trying to learn about new markets, the Chinese firms hope to learn about new technologies and innovation. By contrast, when American firms enter this mature stage of globalization, they typically bring new technologies from home and continue to focus on access to new markets or resources.

In response to the US policies' effect on global trade, China is focusing more on the new Silk Road, or One Belt One Road (OBOR) initiative, also known as the Belt and Road Initiative (BRI), launched in 2013 to support the country's global expansion. At the same time, American firms are contemplating "coming back home" to return global operating units (especially in manufacturing) to support domestic policy agendas and job creation initiatives.

2.5   Conclusion

Chinese firms have had indisputable success in globalization. China became one of the world's largest investors, ranking second in 2016 for instance. In their outward ventures, Chinese firms have employed both greenfield expansion and M&As to great success.

China's surge in M&A activity has run the gamut from technology and knowledge-driven ventures in advanced markets to natural resource-focused acquisitions in Africa and Latin America, to market diversification activities. Cross-border M&As have enabled Chinese firms to establish new marketing and distribution channels at an opportune moment, due to a favorable exchange rate with many developed markets. Especially in the United States after 2008 and Europe since 2011, valuations of foreign targets became more affordable, boosting Chinese outbound M&A activity from less than $40 billion in 2007 to over $200 billion in 2016.

Our analysis has highlighted five critical facts:

- M&As have gained importance as a mode of international expansion for Chinese firms since the GFC.
- The United States and other major developed countries have not matched China's pace of growth overseas.
- China's greenfield investments remain predominantly of a South-South nature, mainly in Asia, though the share of Chinese investment into advanced markets has increased noticeably postcrisis.
- Chinese M&A activity is still focused on Europe and North America. Europe has taken the lead over North America as the primary target for M&As by Chinese multinationals.
- In both greenfield FDI projects and M&As, service-based and consumer-related industries have grown in attractiveness for Chinese companies, while heavy or more traditional industries such as energy (oil, coal, and gas) and materials (such as metals) have either stagnated or declined in importance. This change suggests that emerging market multinationals will increasingly prioritize consumer markets around the world. The alternative and renewable

industry has become a significant part of the Chinese greenfield project portfolio, further illustrating a shift in the investment strategies of emerging market multinationals. Together, these trends demonstrate that Chinese multinationals are pursuing new markets and industries, as well as to the capabilities these firms have built—and will most likely continue to build—over the years.

China's companies have become major global investors, a radical change compared to their activity even as recently as the early 2000s. To achieve this growth, they have had to take greater risks, sometimes paying high prices for overseas acquisitions (although since the 2016–17 buying spree, Chinese M&A activity has slowed). This retrenchment in activity reflects a double blow: at home, the Chinese government has increased scrutiny of outflows, while abroad, especially in developed countries, host governments have tightened the control and supervision of foreign acquisitions, often citing national security concerns.

The long-term overall trend in Chinese M&As—and broadly speaking OFDI—points to continued fast expansion of Chinese overseas activities. Chinese firms still look for new and innovative ways to expand into global markets, and despite the increasing scrutiny, the Chinese government will continue to encourage outbound investment in line with its overall strategy for the transformation of the Chinese economy, whether in emerging markets around the Belt and Road Initiative or beyond. Together, these factors are powerful drivers for robust Chinese overseas investments into the future, albeit possibly at a more sustainable level.

Appendix

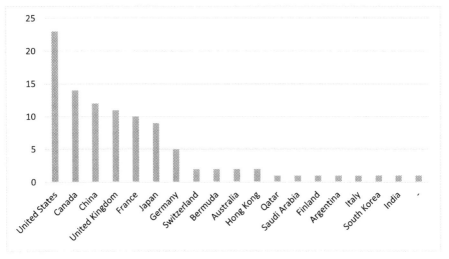

Fig. 2.A1 Top 100 outbound announced M&A transactions in 2018 by country of origin. *Source*: Authors based on available data from Capital IQ, (Accessed March 2019).

Table 2.A1 Top 100 outbound announced M&A transactions in 2018.

Announced date	Transaction value in $USDmm	Target/issuer	Geography (target)	Primary sector (target)	Buyers/investors	HQ—Ultimate parent (buyers)
04/19/2018	80,853	Shire plc	Jersey	Health care	Takeda Pharmaceutical Company Limited (TSE:4502)	Japan
04/29/2018	69,248	Sprint Corporation (NYSE:S)	United States	Communication services	T-Mobile US, Inc. (NasdaqGS:TMUS)	Germany
02/27/2018	49,687	Sky Limited	United Kingdom	Communication services	Comcast Corporation (NasdaqGS:CMCS.A)	United States
05/11/2018	35,299	EDP—Energias de Portugal, S.A. (ENXTLS:EDP)	Portugal	Utilities	China Three Gorges (Europe) S.A.	China
02/15/2018	26,226	RELX NV	Netherlands	Industrials	RELX PLC (LSE:REL)	United Kingdom
05/09/2018	21,819	Unitymedia GmbH and UPC Ceská republika, s.r.o. and UPC Magyarország Kft. and UPC Romania S.R.L.	–	Communication services	Vodafone Czech Republic a.s.; Vodafone Investments Luxembourg S.a.r.l.; Vodafone Magyarország Mobil Távközlési Zartkoruen Mukodo Részvénytársaság; Vodafone Europe B.V.; Vodafone Romania S.A.	Vodafone Czech Republic a.s. (United Kingdom); Vodafone Europe B.V. (United Kingdom); Vodafone Investments Luxembourg S.a.r.l. (United Kingdom); Vodafone Magyarország Mobil Távközlési Zartkoruen Mukodo Részvénytársaság (United Kingdom); Vodafone Romania S.A. (United Kingdom)

Date	Value	Target company	Target country	Sector	Acquirer	Acquirer country
07/03/2018	17,109	Wind Tre S.p.A.	Italy	Communication services	CK Hutchison Holdings Limited (SEHK:1)	Hong Kong
05/09/2018	16,000	Flipkart Private Limited	Singapore	Consumer discretionary	Walmart Inc. (NYSE:WMT)	United States
03/05/2018	15,443	XL Group Ltd	Bermuda	Financials	AXA SA (ENXTPA:CS)	France
05/17/2018	15,263	Enbridge Energy Partners, L.P.	United States	Energy	Enbridge (US) Inc.	Canada
11/13/2018	13,244	Power Solutions business of Johnson Controls	—	Utilities	Caisse de dépôt et placement du Québec: Brookfield Business Partners L.P. (NYSE:BBU)	Brookfield Business Partners L.P. (NYSE:BBU) (Canada); Caisse de dépôt et placement du Québec (Canada)
03/27/2018	12,525	Nouryon	—	Materials	The Carlyle Group L.P. (NasdaqGS:CG); GIC Pte. Ltd.	GIC Pte. Ltd. (Singapore): The Carlyle Group L.P. (NasdaqGS:CG) (United States)
01/22/2018	11,474	Bioverativ Inc.	United States	Health care	Sanofi (ENXTPA:SAN)	France
07/31/2018	10,590	Forest City Realty Trust, Inc.	United States	Real estate	Brookfield Asset Management Inc. (TSX:BAM.A)	Canada
07/26/2018	10,500	Petrohawk Energy Corporation	United States	Energy	BP American Production Company	United Kingdom
12/17/2018	9410	Power Grids Business of ABB Ltd	—	Industrials	Hitachi, Ltd. (TSE:6501)	Japan
04/09/2018	8696	AveXis, Inc.	United States	Health care	Novartis AG (SWX:NOVN)	Switzerland

Continued

Table 2.A1 Continued

Announced date	Transaction value in $USDmm	Target/issuer	Geography (target)	Primary sector (target)	Buyers/investors	HQ—Ultimate parent (buyers)
10/01/2018	8447	Luxottica Group S.p.A.	Italy	Consumer discretionary	EssilorLuxottica Société anonyme (ENXTPA:EL)	France
11/01/2018	8059	Newfield Exploration Company	United States	Energy	Encana Oil & Gas (USA) Inc.	Canada
11/11/2018	8000	Qualtrics International Inc.	United States	Information technology	SAP America, Inc.	Germany
03/31/2018	7745	Joy City Property Limited (SEHK:207)	Bermuda	Real estate	Grandjoy Holdings Group Co., Ltd. (SZSE:000031)	China
09/10/2018	7582	Integrated Device Technology, Inc. (NasdaqGS:IDTI)	United States	Information technology	Renesas Electronics Corporation (TSE:6723)	Japan
05/07/2018	7241	Frutarom Industries Ltd.	Israel	Materials	International Flavors & Fragrances Inc. (NYSE:IFF)	United States
05/07/2018	7150	Marketing and Distribution Rights of Various Brands of Starbucks Corporation	–	Consumer staples	Nestlé S.A. (SWX:NESN)	Switzerland
10/22/2018	7109	Magneti Marelli S.p.A.	Italy	Consumer discretionary	Ck Holdings Co. Ltd.	Japan

12/27/2018	7084	Gatwick Airport Limited	United Kingdom	Industrials	California Public Employees' Retirement System; Abu Dhabi Investment Authority; Global Infrastructure Partners; Australian Government Future Fund; National Pension Service; VINCI Airports SAS	Abu Dhabi Investment Authority (United Arab Emirates); Australian Government Future Fund (Australia); California Public Employees' Retirement System (United States); Global Infrastructure Partners (United States); National Pension Service (South Korea); VINCI Airports SAS (France)
10/23/2018	7080	Hanergy Thin Film Power Group Limited	Bermuda	Information technology	Hanergy Mobile Energy Holding Co., Ltd.	China
08/06/2018	6829	Bemis Company, Inc. (NYSE:BMS)	United States	Materials	Amcor Limited (ASX:AMC)	Australia
08/30/2018	6730	Sydney Motorway Corporation Pty Limited	Australia	Industrials	Transurban Group (ASX:TCL); Canada Pension Plan Investment Board; AustralianSuper Pty Ltd; Tawreed Investments Ltd.	AustralianSuper Pty Ltd (Australia); Canada Pension Plan Investment Board (Canada); Tawreed Investments Ltd. (United Arab Emirates); Transurban Group (ASX:TCL) (Australia)

Continued

Table 2.A1 Continued

Announced date	Transaction value in $USDmm	Target/issuer	Geography (target)	Primary sector (target)	Buyers/investors	HQ—Ultimate parent (buyers)
09/12/2018	6700	Sedgwick Claims Management Services, Inc.	United States	Information technology	Stone Point Capital LLC: The Carlyle Group L.P. (NasdaqGS:CG); Caisse de dépôt et placement du Québec	Caisse de dépôt et placement du Québec (Canada); Stone Point Capital LLC (United States); The Carlyle Group L.P. (NasdaqGS:CG) (United States)
03/26/2018	6610	USG Corporation (NYSE:USG)	United States	Industrials	Gebr. Knauf KG.	Germany
09/24/2018	6516	Randgold Resources Limited	Jersey	Materials	Barrick Gold Corporation (TSX:ABX)	Canada
06/28/2018	6490	Real estate Business of CaixaBank, S.A.	–	Real estate	Lone Star Funds	United States
09/11/2018	6469	Amer Sports Corporation (HLSE:AMEAS)	Finland	Consumer discretionary	Tencent Holdings Limited (SEHK:700); ANTA Sports Products Limited (SEHK:2020); FountainVest Partners	ANTA Sports Products Limited (SEHK:2020) (British Virgin Islands); FountainVest Partners (Hong Kong); Tencent Holdings Limited (SEHK:700) (China)
01/17/2018	6164	UBM plc	Jersey	Communication services	Informa plc (LSE:INF)	United Kingdom

Date	Number	Company	Country	Sector	Acquirer	Acquirer country
10/26/2018	5795	Essar Steel India Limited	India	Materials	Nippon Steel & Sumitomo Metal Corporation (TSE:5401); Arcelormittal India Private Limited	Arcelormittal India Private Limited (Luxembourg); Nippon Steel & Sumitomo Metal Corporation (TSE:5401) (Japan)
07/05/2018	5748	Praxair Deutschland Holding GmbH & Co. KG/Praxair España, S.L.U/ Praxair Italia S.r.l.	–	Materials	Taiyo Nippon Sanso Corporation (TSE:4091)	Japan
09/18/2018	5615	Jardine Lloyd Thompson Group plc (LSE:JLT)	United Kingdom	Financials	Marsh & McLennan Companies, Inc. (NYSE:MMC)	United States
01/22/2018	5564	Validus Holdings, Ltd.	Bermuda	Financials	American International Group, Inc. (NYSE:AIG)	United States
03/01/2018	5478	Snowy Hydro Limited	Australia	Utilities	–	–
12/03/2018	5468	Tesaro, Inc.	United States	Health care	GlaxoSmithKline plc (LSE:GSK)	United Kingdom
03/15/2018	5394	NEX Group Limited	United Kingdom	Financials	CME Group Inc. (NasdaqGS:CME)	United States
05/18/2018	5391	Irish Residential Mortgage Portfolio of LLcyds Banking Group plc	–	Financials	Barclays Bank PLC	United Kingdom

Continued

Table 2.A1   Continued

Announced date	Transaction value in $USDmm	Target/issuer	Geography (target)	Primary sector (target)	Buyers/investors	HQ—Ultimate parent (buyers)
02/27/2018	5363	AccorInvest Group SA	Luxembourg	—	GIC Pte. Ltd.; Public Investment Fund; Colony Capital, Inc. (NYSE:CLNY); Crédit Agricole Assurances S.A.; Amundi (ENXTPA:AMUN)	Amundi (ENXTPA:AMUN) (France); Colony Capital, Inc. (NYSE:CLNY) (United States); Crédit Agricole Assurances S.A. (France); GIC Pte. Ltd. (Singapore); Public Investment Fund (Saudi Arabia)
05/25/2018	5362	Techem GmbH	Germany	Industrials	Caisse de dépôt et placement du Québec; Ontario Teachers' Pension Plan Board	Caisse de dépôt et placement du Québec (Canada); Ontario Teachers' Pension Plan Board (Canada)
08/31/2018	5062	Costa Limited	United Kingdom	Consumer discretionary	The Coca-Cola Company (NYSE:KO)	United States
11/21/2018	5000	Grifols Diagnostic Solutions Inc.	United States	Health care	Shanghai RAAS Blood Products Co., Ltd. (SZSE:002252)	China
01/23/2018	4950	Maersk Oil Exploration International	—	Energy	TOTAL S.A. (ENXTPA:FP)	France
06/29/2018	4850	Clean Fuel Project	—	Energy	Thai Oil Public Company Limited (SET:TOP)	Thailand

Date	No.	Target company	Target country	Sector	Acquirer	Acquirer country
01/29/2018	4769	Ablynx NV	Belgium	Health care	Sanofi (ENXTPA:SAN)	France
02/22/2018	4702	Naturgy Energy Group, S.A. (BME:NTGY)	Spain	Utilities	CVC Capital Partners Limited; Corporación Financiera Alba, S.A. (BME:ALB)	Corporación Financiera Alba, S.A. (BME:ALB) (Spain); CVC Capital Partners Limited (United Kingdom)
04/21/2018	4700	Sky Betting and Gaming	–	Consumer discretionary	The Stars Group Inc. (TSX:TSGI)	Canada
02/15/2018	4653	Canadian Real Estate Investment Trust	Canada	Real estate	Choice Properties Real Estate Investment Trust (TSX:CHP.UN)	United Kingdom
01/04/2018	4600	Westinghouse Electric Company LLC	United States	Industrials	Brookfield Business Partners L.P. (NYSE:BBU)	Canada
01/17/2018	4358	Equital Ltd. (TASE:EQTL)	Israel	Energy	Y.H.K. Investment Limited Partnership	United States
12/10/2018	4350	Travelport Worldwide Limited (NYSE:TVPT)	Bermuda	Information technology	Elliott Management Corporation; Siris Capital Group. LLC; Evergreen Coast Capital Corp.	Elliott Management Corporation (United States); Evergreen Coast Capital Corp. (United States); Siris Capital Group, LLC (United States)
11/06/2018	4223	Public Joint Stock Company Rosneft Oil Company (LSE:ROSN)	Russia	Energy	Qatar Investment Authority	Qatar
11/20/2018	4221	BTG plc (LSE:BTG)	United Kingdom	Health care	Boston Scientific Corporation (NYSE:BSX)	United States

Continued

Table 2.A1 Continued

Announced date	Transaction value in $USDmm	Target/issuer	Geography (target)	Primary sector (target)	Buyers/investors	HQ—Ultimate parent (buyers)
10/11/2018	4209	BMW Brilliance Automotive Ltd.	China	Consumer discretionary	BMW Holding B.V.	Germany
07/20/2018	4200	Arysta LifeScience Corporation	Japan	Materials	UPL Corporation Limited	India
10/08/2018	4166	Rowan Companies plc (NYSE:RDC)	United Kingdom	Energy	Ensco plc (NYSE:ESV)	United Kingdom
05/14/2018	4104	Healthscope Limited (ASX:HSO)	Australia	Health care	Brookfield Capital Partners Ltd.; Brookfield Business Partners L.P. (NYSE:BBU)	Brookfield Business Partners L.P. (NYSE:BBU) (Canada); Brookfield Capital Partners Ltd. (Canada)
05/17/2018	4066	Sociedad Química y Minera de Chile S.A. (NYSE:SQM)	Chile	Materials	Tianqi Lithium Corporation (SZSE:002466)	China
08/20/2018	3916	China Biologic Products Holdings, Inc. (NasdaqGS:CBPO)	Cayman Islands	Health care	CDH Investments; Bank Of China Group Investment Limited; GL Capital Group	Bank Of China Group Investment Limited (China); CDH Investments (China); GL Capital Group (China)
06/20/2018	3809	China Merchants Port Holdings Company Limited (SEHK:144)	Hong Kong	Industrials	China Merchants Port Group Co., Ltd. (SZSE:201872)	China
01/22/2018	3692	YOOX Net-A-Porter Group S.p.A.	Italy	Consumer discretionary	Richemont Italia Holding S.p.A.	Switzerland

Date		Company	Country	Industry	Acquirer	Acquirer Country
12/14/2018	3671	Antelliq	France	Information technology	Merck Animal Health	United States
07/22/2018	3670	Atos Syntel	United States	Information technology	Atos SE (ENXTPA:ATO)	France
05/21/2018	3628	EMI Music Publishing Limited	United Kingdom	Communication services	Sony Corporation of America	Japan
06/29/2018	3535	Fimei—Finanziaria Industriale Mobiliare ed Immobiliare S.P.A.	Italy	—	CVC Capital Partners Limited; Public Sector Pension Investment Board; StepStone Group LP	CVC Capital Partners Limited (United Kingdom); Public Sector Pension Investment Board (Canada); StepStone Group LP (United States)
03/19/2018	3517	Orbotech Ltd.	Israel	Information technology	KLA-Tencor Corporation (NasdaqGS:KLAC)	United States
11/30/2018	3500	IDI Logistics, LLC	United States	Real estate	Oxford Properties Group, Inc.; Ivanhoé Cambridge, Inc.	Ivanhoé Cambridge, Inc. (Canada); Oxford Properties Group, Inc. (Canada)
03/21/2018	3433	Telenor Bulgaria/Telenor Hungary/Telenor Real Estate/Telenor Common Operation/Other Companies	—	Communication services	PPF Group N.V.	Netherlands

Continued

Table 2.A1 Continued

Announced date	Transaction value in $USDmm	Target/issuer	Geography (target)	Primary sector (target)	Buyers/investors	HQ—Ultimate parent (buyers)
10/23/2018	3418	Healthscope Limited (ASX:HSO)	Australia	Health care	Canada Pension Plan Investment Board; Ontario Teachers' Pension Plan Board; AustralianSuper Pty Ltd; BGH Capital; Carob Investment Private Limited	AustralianSuper Pty Ltd (Australia); BGH Capital (Australia); Canada Pension Plan Investment Board (Canada); Carob Investment Private Limited (Singapore); Ontario Teachers' Pension Plan Board (Canada)
05/11/2018	3403	ZPG Limited	United Kingdom	Communication services	Silver Lake; GIC Special Investments Pte. Ltd.; Psp Investments Holding Europe Ltd	GIC Special Investments Pte. Ltd. (Singapore); Psp Investments Holding Europe Ltd (United Kingdom); Silver Lake (United States)
08/20/2018	3393	SodaStream International Ltd.	Israel	Consumer discretionary	PepsiCo, Inc. (NasdaqGS:PEP)	United States
12/14/2018	3341	Belmond Ltd. (NYSE:BEL)	Bermuda	Consumer discretionary	LVMH Moët Hennessy Louis Vuitton S.E. (ENXTPA:MC)	France
09/04/2018	3324	Ocean Rig UDW Inc.	Cayman Islands	Energy	Transocean Ltd. (NYSE:RIG)	Switzerland

Continued

Date	Value	Target	Target country	Sector	Acquirer	Acquirer country
07/16/2018	3300	Assets in the Americas of Linde Aktiengesellschaft	—	Materials	CVC Capital Partners Limited; Messer Group GmbH	CVC Capital Partners Limited (United Kingdom); Messer Group GmbH (Germany)
02/05/2018	3290	Nuovo Trasporto Viaggiatori S.p.A.	Italy	Industrials	Global Infrastructure Partners	United States
05/17/2018	3289	Spectra Energy Partners, LP	United States	Energy	Enbridge Inc. (TSX:ENB)	Canada
07/04/2018	3278	NorthRiver Midstream Inc.	—	Energy	Brookfield Infrastructure Partners L.P. (NYSE:BIP)	Bermuda
06/25/2018	3250	INNIO	—	Industrials	Advent International Corporation	United States
08/01/2018	3244	EnerCare Inc.	Canada	Consumer discretionary	Brookfield Infrastructure Partners L.P. (NYSE:BIP)	Bermuda
02/07/2018	3222	Saeta Yield, S.A.	Spain	Utilities	TerraForm Power, Inc. (NasdaqGS:TERP)	United States
12/10/2018	3200	Linde Aktiengesellschaft (DB:LNA)	Germany	Materials	Linde plc (XTRA:LIN)	United Kingdom
05/22/2018	3143	Denizbank Anonim Sirketi (IBSE:DENIZ)	Turkey	Financials	Emirates NBD Bank PJSC (DFM:EMIRATESNBD)	United Arab Emirates
04/17/2018	2983	Eletropaulo Metropolitana Eletricidade de São Paulo S.A. (BOVESPA:ELPL3)	Brazil	Utilities	Enel Brasil Investimentos Sudeste, S.A.	Chile

Table 2.A1 Continued

Announced date	Transaction value in $USDmm	Target/issuer	Geography (target)	Primary sector (target)	Buyers/investors	HQ—Ultimate parent (buyers)
09/04/2018	2953	Oxford Investa Property Partners	Australia	Real estate	Oxford Properties Group, Inc.	Canada
12/11/2018	2948	Ahlsell AB (publ)	Sweden	Industrials	CVC Capital Partners Limited	United Kingdom
10/31/2018	2925	Colonial First State Global Asset Management	–	Industrials	Mitsubishi UFJ Trust and Banking Corporation	Japan
09/13/2018	2866	MPM Holdings Inc. (OTCPK:MPMQ)	United States	Materials	KCC Corporation (KOSE:A002380); Wonik QnC Corporation (KOSDAQ:A074600); SJL Partners	KCC Corporation (KOSE:A002380) (South Korea); SJL Partners (South Korea); Wonik QnC Corporation (KOSDAQ:A074600) (South Korea)
05/15/2018	2865	SIX Payment Services Ltd	Switzerland	Information technology	Worldline S.A. (ENXTPA:WLN)	France
06/21/2018	2800	SKY Aviation Leasing International Limited	Cayman Islands	Industrials	Goshawk Aviation Limited	Ireland
04/05/2018	2776	Hispania Activos Inmobiliarios SOCIMI, S.A. (BME:HIS)	Spain	Real estate	The Blackstone Group International Partners LLP	United States
12/27/2018	2746	FT Life Insurance Company Limited	Bermuda	Financials	Earning Star Limited	Hong Kong

07/16/2018	2736	VTG Aktiengesellschaft (DB:VT9)	Germany	Industrials	Morgan Stanley Infrastructure Inc.	United States
10/25/2018	2719	Ceva Logistics AG (SWX:CEVA)	Switzerland	Industrials	CMA CGM S.A.	Lebanon
10/25/2018	2655	Nexperia B.V.	Netherlands	Information technology	Wingtech Technology Co., Ltd (SHSE:600745)	China
11/08/2018	2622	Quadgas Midco Limited	United Kingdom	Financials	Allianz Capital Partners GmbH; Hermes Investment Management Limited; Qatar Investment Authority; International Public Partnerships Limited (LSE:INPP); Macquarie Infrastructure and Real Assets (Europe) Limited; Amber Fund Management Ltd.; Dalmore Capital Limited; CIC Capital Corporation	Allianz Capital Partners GmbH (Germany); Amber Fund Management Ltd. (United States); CIC Capital Corporation (China); Dalmore Capital Limited (United Kingdom); Hermes Investment Management Limited (United States); International Public Partnerships Limited (LSE:INPP) (United States); Macquarie Infrastructure and Real Assets (Europe) Limited (Australia); Qatar Investment Authority (Qatar)

Source: Authors based on available data from Capital IQ. (Accessed March 2019).

Table 2.A2 Data points available from Capital IQ (2000–18) based on which the graphs/ tables are derived in this chapter.

Country	Data points available (deal value)	Total number of deals referenced
China	3395	5394
United States	11.675	27,630
India	822	1607
Japan	1.920	3766
Brazil	226	416
South Korea	825	1173
United Kingdom	6584	12,611
Germany	2373	7374
Netherlands	1392	3841
Switzerland	1420	4243
Ireland	1171	2431
Canada	5792	10,190
France	2158	7132

Source: Standard & Poor's Capital IQ.

References

Casanova, L. (2018). La internacionalización de las empresas latinoamericanas. In A. Blanco-Estévez (Ed.), *Global Latam. Series Inversión extranjera*: ICEX. Secretaría General Iberoamericana. Ministerio de Industria y Comercio. http://www.investinspain.org/invest/es/canal-de-informacion/documentacion/informacion-sobre-inversion-extranjera-directa-ied/DOC2018804475.html?orderBy=xfwm_cnt_Fecha1&orderType=desc (Accessed June 2019).

Casanova, L., & Miroux, A. (2016). *Emerging market multinationals report: The China surge*. Emerging Markets Institute in collaboration with the OECD development Center. S.C. Johnson School of Management. Cornell University. https://www.johnson.cornell.edu/wp-content/uploads/sites/3/2019/04/2016-EMR-Updated-EMR-Consolidated.v3.pdf (Accessed June 2019).

Casanova, L. (2009). *Global Latinas: Latin America's emerging multinationals*. Palgrave Macmillan.

Ciprian, S., Peng, M. W., & Bruton, G. D. (2014). Slack and the performance of state-owned enterprises. *Asia Pacific Journal of Management, 31*, 473–495.

Cuervo-Cazurra, A. (2012). Extending theory by analyzing developing country multinational companies: Solving the Goldilocks debate. *Global Strategy Journal, 2*, 153–167. Strategic Management Society, Chicago.

Cuervo-Cazurra, A., & Ramamurti, R. (Eds.), (2014). *Understanding multinationals from emerging markets*. Cambridge: Cambridge University Press.

Dunning, J. H. (1993). *Multinationals Enterprises and the Global Economy*. Reading, MA: Addison-Wesley.

Dunning, J. H. (2005). The evolving world scenario. In S. Passow & M. Runnbeck (Eds.), *What's next? Strategic views on foreign direct investment* (pp. 12–17). Stockholm: Invest in Sweden Agency.

Ministry of Commerce of the People's Republic of China (MOFCOM), National Bureau of Statistics, State Administration of Foreign Exchange. (2018). 2017 Statistical Bulletin of China's Outward Foreign Direct Investment. China Statistics Press.

Prahalad, C. K. (2005). *The Fortune at the bottom of the pyramid: Eradicating poverty through profits*. Upper Saddle River, NY: Wharton School Publishing.

S&P Capital IQ. (2019). *M&A data retrieved from S&P Capital IQ database*. https://www.capitaliq.com/ (Accessed March 2019).

UNCTAD. (2019). *World Investment Report: Special Economic Zones*. New York and Geneva: United Nations.

Further reading

Casanova, L., & Miroux, A. (2017). *Emerging market multinationals report: Emerging multinationals in a changing world*. Emerging Markets Institute in collaboration with the OECD development Center. S.C. Johnson School of Management. Cornell University. https://www.johnson.cornell.edu/wp-content/uploads/sites/3/2019/04/EMR-2017-FINAL-FINAL-4dec2017.pdf (Accessed June 2019).

Casanova, L., & Miroux, A. (2018). *Emerging market multinationals report 2018. Emerging markets reshaping globalization*. https://www.johnson.cornell.edu/wp-content/uploads/sites/3/2019/04/EMR2018_V3_FIN-11Jan.pdf (Accessed June 2019).

ECLAC. (2013). *Foreign Direct Investment in Latin America and the Caribbean 2012*. Santiago de Chile: United Nations Economic Commission for Latin America and the Caribbean.

Fleury, A., & Fleury, M. T. L. (2012). *Brazilian multinationals: Competences for internationalization*. Cambridge: Cambridge University Press.

Fortune. *Fortune Global 500 directory*. (n.d.). http://fortune.com/fortune500/ (Accessed May 2019).

Garcia, A., & Xu, J. (2018). *China's overseas mergers and acquisitions may not have slowed down in 2017 and will probably boom in 2018*. http://unctad.org/en/Pages/DIAE/World%20Investment%20Report/Annex-Tables.aspx (Accessed July 2018).

Guillén, M. F., & García-Canal, E. (2009). The American model of the multinational firm and the 'new' multinationals from emerging economies. *Academy of Management Perspectives, 23*(2), 23–35. Briarcliff Manor, NY http://www-management.wharton.upenn.edu/guillen/PDF-Documents/New_MNEs_Acad_Mgmt_Perspectives-2009.pdf (Accessed June 2019).

Lall, S. (1984). *New multinationals: Spread of third world enterprises*. Wiley/IRM series on multinationals. New York: John Wiley & Sons Ltd.

Nie, W., Dowell, W., & Lu, A. (2012). *In the shadow of the dragon: The global expansion of Chinese companies—How it will change business forever*. New York: AMACOM.

Porter, M. E. (1980). *Competitive Strategy*. New York: Free Press.

Sauvant, K. P., Mendoza, K., & Ince, I. (2008). *The rise of transnational corporations from emerging markets: Threat or opportunity?* Cheltenham: Edward Elgar.

Sauvant, K. P., McAllister, G., & Maschek, W. A. (2010). *Foreign direct investments from emerging markets: The challenges ahead*. New York: Palgrave Macmillan.

UNCTAD. (2018). *World investment report: Investment and new industrial policies*. New York and Geneva: United Nations.

UNCTAD. (n.d.) Statistical data for FDI and OFDI. United Nations: New York and Geneva. https://unctadstat.unctad.org/EN/.

A heavyweight on the global scene

We should increase China's soft power, with a good Chinese narrative, and better communicate China's messages to the world.

**Chinese President Xi Jinping, policy address to top leaders of the
Communist Party, November 2014**

Acronyms

ADB	Asian Development Bank
AfDB	African Development bank
AIIB	Asian Infrastructure Investment Bank
BCIMEC	Bangladesh-China-Indian-Myanmar Economic Corridor
BRICS	Brazil, Russia, India, China, and South Africa
CCWAEC	China-Central and West Asia Economic Corridor
CELAC	Community of Latin America and the Caribbean
CICPEC	China-Indochina Peninsula Economic Corridor
CMREC	China-Mongolia-Russia Economic Corridor
CPEC	China-Pakistan Economic Corridor
GDP	gross domestic product
GFC	Global Financial Crisis
IADB	Inter-American Development Bank
IBRD	International Bank for Reconstruction and Development
IsDB	Islamic Development Bank
PPP	purchasing power parity
MFN	most-favored nation principle
NDB	New Development Bank
NELB	New Eurasian Land Bridge
OBOR	One Belt One Road Initiative
TANAP	Trans-Anatolian Natural Gas Pipeline
UNCTAD	United Nations Conference on Trade and Development

China solidified its stance as one of the top global powers when it became the second largest economy in the world by nominal gross domestic product (GDP) in 2010, with increased soft power at its disposal and growing geopolitical influence. By 2018, China's $13.4 GDP trillion contributed 15% to global nominal GDP (three times its weight in the global economy a decade earlier). China boasts a massive domestic market and some of the largest companies in the world (Chapter 1), a testimony to both

The Era of Chinese Multinationals, https://doi.org/10.1016/B978-0-12-816857-8.00003-3

the speed and potency of its policy shifts and subsequent economic growth, especially after the Global Financial Crisis (GFC).

China's growth took off in the 1980s as the country adopted specific reforms to enhance economic performance, deepening its integration in international markets and expanding its technology and innovation capabilities. Since the mid-1990s, emerging markets as a whole have gained ground on the global stage (Box 3.1). However, China stands apart from that group, becoming a heavyweight on its own.

Box 3.1 Emerging economies and the E20

IFC economist Antoine van Agtmael coined the term "emerging market" in 1981. Fund managers at the time used the term "emerging market" to describe equity, bond, or currency markets in developing countries with strong growth potential, and also with high risk and volatility. While no universal definition for an emerging market exists, the term is now a broader economic concept usually referring to countries or economies at the cusp of becoming significant global players but with higher volatility than long-standing global leaders. Various definitions take into an account an economy's wealth, its growth trajectory, its finances, its weight in the global economy, and even its political system and institutions. For the purposes of this work, we have created a list of emerging economies that we refer to as the E20.

A number of market research institutions and international organizations have set up their own emerging markets/economies lists. Both the IMF and the United Nations Conference on Trade and Development (UNCTAD) have lists of emerging economies, as do several financial analysis agencies. The Emerging Market Index by MSCI, for instance, includes 24 economies, and the FTSE Emerging Market Index has 22 economies. Unsurprisingly, some countries are consistently included on all of these lists.

In developing the E20 list of the Emerging Market Institute (EMI) (Casanova & Miroux, 2016), we took into account the above-mentioned rankings and considered an economy's size measured by GDP, its demographics, and its role in global trade and FDI. The E20 includes 3 economies from Africa (Egypt, Nigeria, and South Africa), 10 from Asia (China, India, Indonesia, Iran, Malaysia, the Philippines, Saudi Arabia, South Korea, Thailand, and Turkey), and 5 from Latin America (Argentina, Brazil, Chile, Colombia, and Mexico)—which together represent about two-thirds of all developing economies' GDP—as well as Poland and the Russian Federation. The E20 experienced two decades of rapid growth from 1995 to 2015 (at an average annual rate of 7.4%, more than twice the rate of the G-7) and, by 2018, they accounted for nearly half of the world GDP on a PPP basis. That year, 9 of the 20 largest economies in the world were E20 economies.

Today, emerging economies not only serve as centers of production or trading hubs for advanced economies, but also as a massive consumer market. In a 20-year span, they tripled their share of exports and doubled their share of imports to reach about a third of the world total in each case. In 2016, 7 of the 15 largest

> **Box 3.1 Emerging economies and the E20—cont'd**
>
> countries by manufacturing value added were E20 emerging countries, a testimony to the progress that emerging economies have made in manufacturing, including in the high-tech sector. Another major engine of growth for emerging economies was their intensified role as FDI recipients and outward investors (Casanova & Miroux, 2016, 2017). In addition, the changing demographics of the E20—a growing young and more affluent population—suggest a significant spending shift away from the Western middle class, whose consumer spending could fall from nearly two-thirds of global spending in 2009 to only 30% by 2030 (Kharas, 2010).
>
> *Source:* Authors based on Casanova, L., & Miroux, A. (2016). Emerging market multinationals report. The China surge. Cornell S.C. Johnson College of Business, Cornell University and Casanova, L., & Miroux, A. (2017). Emerging market multinationals report. Emerging multinationals in a changing world. Cornell S.C. Johnson College of Business, Cornell University.

3.1 China, an economic powerhouse

3.1.1 Unprecedented economic growth

China is a unique case, both from a global and from an emerging market perspective. In less than three decades, it successfully upended itself from a mostly rural, self-contained, and inward-looking economy into a global economic power, second in size only to the United States. Whereas agriculture accounted for 27% of China's GDP in 1990, by 2018 it accounted for less than 8%. With a growth rate reaching nearly 10% a year on average between 1979 and 2017, the fastest sustained expansion by a major economy in history according to the World Bank, China's economic gains lifted more than 850 million people out of poverty. Real per capita incomes increased 16-fold from 1978 to 2018, and the extreme poverty rate (proportion of citizens living on less than $1.90 purchasing power parity (PPP) per day) dropped from 88% in 1981 to an estimated 0.5% in 2018, an achievement observed in no other country (World Bank, 2018). China's economic growth has been particularly marked since the early 2000s, as the country's GDP increased from about $1 trillion in 2000 to more than $13 trillion in 2018. During that period, China made significant strides to catch up with the United States (see Fig. 3.1), and Chinese firms emerged forcefully on the global scene (see Chapters 1 and 2).

The annual growth of China's GDP has slowed since 2013.[1] Still, its more recent growth rate of about 6.6% in 2017–18 remains impressive when compared with a

---

[1] A debate has emerged as to the reliability of Chinese GDP data. Some observers believe that the country's high growth rates—especially during 2000–10—were inflated, and have posited much lower actual values. This chapter uses only official data from international organizations, mostly the World Bank and the IMF.

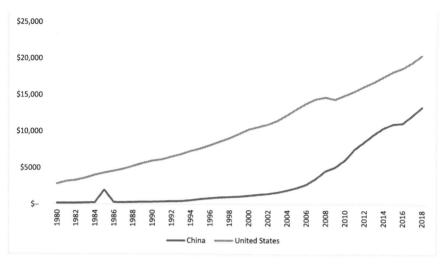

Fig. 3.1 Nominal GDP for China and the United States from 1980 to 2018, in billion US$.
Source: Authors based on data from the World Bank, available at https://databank.worldbank.
org/data/reports.aspx?source=world-development-indicators, and IMF, World Economic
Outlook databases 2019 for 2018, https://www.imf.org/external/pubs/ft/weo/2019/01/weodata/
index.aspx, (Accessed April 2019).

number of major developed economies that hover around 2%. (To keep things in perspective, in 2018 China's nominal GDP was the same as the U.S.'s in 2004—U.S.
growth that year was 3.8%, while China's in 2018 was 6.5%.) China is the largest
single contributor to world growth: in 2017, it touted an 18.3% share of global GDP
on a PPP basis, up from 2.3% in 1980, while the United States share fell from 24.3%
to an estimated 15.3% (see Fig. 3.2). China's economic rise is particularly notable
considering that, in 1980, its GDP (on a PPP basis) was only 10% of the United States.

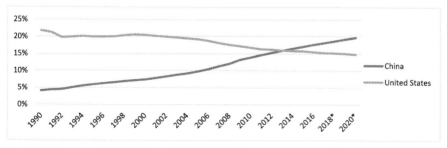

Fig. 3.2 Chinese and United States GDP (PPP basis) as a percentage of global GDP from
1990 to 2018, and projections through 2020.
Source: Based on data from IMF, World Economic Outlook databases 2019, https://www.imf.
org/external/pubs/ft/weo/2019/01/weodata/index.aspx, (Accessed April 2019).

China has also become the world's largest manufacturer. The UN estimated that, as early as 2006, the gross value-added manufacturing[2] in China surpassed that of Japan, the world's second largest manufacturing country at that time. By 2010, China had overtaken the United States and reached the top position, a rank it has maintained since then. Unlike other major economies, which typically turned into service economies, manufacturing became a key feature of China's economy. In 2016, China's gross valued-added manufacturing was equal to 29% of its GDP, compared to 12% for the United States and 21% for Japan, according to the World Bank data.

By 2018, China had also become the world's top exporter and second largest importer. It stands as the largest trading partner of about 120 countries and is a major player in global FDI. In international transactions, the renminbi is playing a larger part in the global economy as a result of China's increasing role in trade and finance (Prasad, 2017). The inclusion of the renminbi in the IMF special drawing rights (SDR) currency basket in 2016 was an exceptional development for China, given that no new currency had been introduced in the basket since the euro inclusion in 1999. Replacing parts of the shares accounted for by the euro, the British pound, and the Japanese yen in the IMF currency basket, the renminbi became the third largest currency in that basket, after the US dollar and the euro. The full impact of this move has yet to be borne out. As observed by experts, the renminbi's prospects as a global currency will ultimately be shaped by China's broader domestic policies (Prasad, 2016). In the meantime, the renminbi's inclusion in the SDR basket has already afforded China new international status.

China was able to reach many of these new milestones as a result of increased productivity, which stemmed partly from the flow of labor from agriculture to manufacturing and services. When productivity growth ebbed in the mid-1990s, estimates indicate that capital accumulation contributed to around half of China's economic growth (Yueh, 2015). In 2016, gross fixed investment as a percentage of GDP was much higher in China (42%) than in many large developed economies, such as Japan (23%) and the United States (16%). Sustaining such high levels of capital investment to maintain growth will prove increasingly challenging. In this context, productivity increases will gain priority in the future, which explains Chinese authorities' focus on innovation and technological development.

China is in some ways an outlier vis-à-vis both emerging and developing economies, making it difficult for analysts to pigeonhole the country in one category or the other. Categorization, however, has a number of important implications, such as determining China's access to development funds across multinational financial institutions. Despite significant increases, China's nominal GDP per capita—at $9600 in 2018 (IMF, 2019)—is only 15% that of the United States at $62,606 (see Fig. 3.3), with 55 million Chinese residents below the poverty line[3] (World Bank, 2018). In China's 11th Five-Year Plan (2006–10) Chinese authorities deemed that an 8% growth rate was necessary to raise the standard of living of Chinese citizens and address inequality. No country, however, has yet managed to maintain such high growth rates for an extended period.

---

[2] Expressed in US dollars. Gross value-added data (country output minus intermediate consumption) represents the value of manufacturing that actually takes place in the country.

[3] Defined as below PPP $3.10 per day (World Bank, 2018).

		China	United States
Economy	GDP	13,407,398 million USD	20,494,050 million USD
	GDP per Capita	9,608 USD	62,606 USD
	Exports	2,263.3 billion USD	1,546.7 billion USD
	Imports	1,841.9 billion USD	2,342.9 billion USD
	Primary Sector GDP Output (Share of GDP)	7.90%	1.05%
	Secondary Sector GDP Output (Share of GDP)	40.50%	20.03%
	Tertiary Sector GDP Output (Share of GDP)	51.60%	78.92%
	No. of Fortune 500 Companies in 2017	111	126
	Military Expenditures	151.4 billion USD	818.2 billion USD
Natural Resources	Arable Land	103.44 million hectares	174.45 million hectares
	Water Resources	2,81 billion cubic meters	2,82 billion cubic meters
	Petroleum Production	4.31 million barrels/day	14.46 million barrels/day
	Natural Gas Production	14.3 billion cubic feet/day	71.6 billion cubic feet/day
	Coal Production Total	3.52 billion tons	0.72 billion tons
Social Resources	Population	1.4 billion	330 million
	Total Land Area	9.32 million km^2	9.14 million km^2
	Water Area	0.27 million km^2	0.47 million km^2
	Average Life Expectancy	75.7 (ranking 102)	80 (ranking 43)
	Median Age	37.4	38.1
	Birth Rate (per 1000 of population)	12.30 (ranking 161)	12.58 (ranking 158)
	Immigrant	—	13.5% of Population
	Labor Force	780 million	163 million
	Number. of World Top 100 Universities	2	42
	Number of University Graduates 2017	8.2 million	1.8 million
	Number of Master's Graduates 2017	600,000	780,000

Fig. 3.3 Facts and figures: China vs the United States, 2018.
Source: IMF. (2019). World Economic Outlook Database. https://www.imf.org/external/ datamapper/datasets/WEO/1. (Accessed June 2019) and World Bank. (2019). World Development Indicators. https://datacatalog.worldbank.org/dataset/world-development- indicators. (Accessed June 2019).

China's government has embraced the country's slower growth rate as the "new normal" in the service of a growth model that puts emphasis on private consumption on one hand, and on innovation and technological development on the other. Against this background, the "Made in China 2025" plan, launched in 2015, seeks to modernize China's manufacturing. Focusing on high tech sectors, the plan aims to make China a major global player in 10 key sectors such as aerospace, information technology and robotics as well as agricultural machinery, green energy and green vehicles, medicine and medical devices, ocean engineering, new materials, power equipment, and railway equipment (see Chapter 4).

As of 2019, China has staved off the economic crises and currency volatility that have plagued other emerging markets. Many observers contend that China needs to address a number of long-term challenges through significant reforms to avoid stagnating growth. Among such challenges, it is often pointed out that China's economy heavily relies on the state, whose enterprises (SOEs) still dominate a number of sectors despite reforms and a decline in the overall number of Chinese SOEs. Additionally, China's debt levels, while comparable to those of the United States and lower than those of the European Union (EU), have grown significantly, driven in particular by the corporate sector. The debt of the corporate sector grew sixfold, for instance, from 2008 to 2017 (reaching $18 trillion), a warning sign of structural economic vulnerability.

Demographics played a key role in China's economic success but could pose a problem for its future. China's population was about 1.4 billion in 2018, 18% of the total world population. China's cheap cost of labor made it particularly attractive to foreign investors, especially as the working age population (15–64 years old) steadily increased from the 1980s to 2000s. By 2010, the country had nearly 1 billion workers. Ten years later, China's demographic growth has decelerated, and its population is aging. If this trend prevails, 25% of China's population could be older than 60 by 2030, up from only 7% in 1980. Meanwhile the ratio of working age people compared to the general population is expected to decline from a high of 72% in 2015 to 60% by 2040 (UNDESA, n.d.). By then, China's economy will have to contend with many challenges, including growing social expenditures and changed consumption patterns. Workers aging out of the labor force will likely contribute to increased wages, possibly eroding China's attractiveness in that respect.

Even still, China's population represents the biggest consumer market in the world, made up of a sprawling middle class that is expected to play an increasing role in global consumer spending. The Chinese middle class has already significantly impacted the Chinese tourism industry and contributed to the success of Chinese telecom equipment companies like Huawei, and e-commerce firms like Alibaba. For all of these examples, and more, China's demographics continue to offer a springboard for expansion. Chinese consumption is expected to grow by about $6 trillion from 2018 through 2030, equivalent to the consumption growth expected from the United States and Western Europe combined over the same period (McKinsey, 2019).

3.1.2 China's expanding role in global foreign direct investment[4]

As China's share of the global economy has grown, it has also increased its share of foreign direct investments (FDI). China first became one of the top FDI recipients and, later on, one of the largest global investors itself. Its emergence in global FDI, together with a number of other emerging economies, drastically transformed the FDI landscape.

(a) China as a top FDI recipient

During the 1980s, advanced economies received about 80% of all FDI inflows, led by the United States, which alone accounted for a little more than 45% of global FDI inflows in 1984 (see Fig. 3.4). That share fell through the 1990s, and since 2000 the US share has hovered between 10% and 25%. By 2017, the share of advanced economies in global FDI flows dropped to 49%.

---

[4] FDI data in this chapter is from UNCTAD statistics unless otherwise indicated.

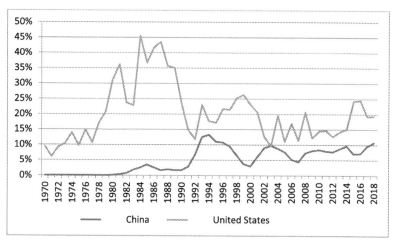

Fig. 3.4 Inward FDI flows for China and the United States as a percentage of the world flows.
Source: Authors' analysis based on UNCTADstats, at https://unctadstat.unctad.org and
UNCTAD. (2019). World investment report: Special economic zones. New York and Geneva:
United Nations, (Accessed June 2019).

FDI into emerging economies soared during that time, led by China, whose stakes
in global FDI inflows rose from less than 1% in 1980 to around 8%–10% since 2010,
with a peak around 12% in the mid-1990s[5] (see Fig. 3.4). From 1990 to 2017, China
alone accounted for about a third of the FDI flows to emerging economies and increased its FDI inflows from less than $4 billion in 1990 to $139 billion in 2018 (see
Fig. 3.5). Hardly visible before 1990 on that scene, by 2009 China had become the
second global FDI destination behind only the United States and has remained in the
top two or three since then (see Fig. 3.6).

(b) China, the second largest global investor

China began outward foreign direct investment (OFDI) in earnest later than its
strides in inward FDI, but the country's growth in OFDI has been no less striking.
From 2000 to 2018, Chinese OFDI alone accounted for about a third of the outflows
of the E20, significantly increasing Asia's prominence in the global FDI landscape.

Chinese outward FDI accelerated in the aftermath of the GFC, growing at a rate of more
than 20% per year on average from 2008 to 2015. During that period, Chinese OFDI came
closer to that of the United States, the leader in global OFDI since the 1970s. Though still
a major source of global OFDI, the United States is less prominent today, whereas China's
OFDI has risen nearly continuously (see Figs. 3.7 and 3.8).[6] In 2000, China's OFDI stock
was negligible, but by 2018, it had risen to nearly $2 trillion (UNCTAD, 2019).

---

[5] Statistics on Chinese FDI flows need to be read with caution. They may be inflated due to "round tripping," when OFDI from a country comes back to be reinvested in that country, often to take advantage of
financial incentives offered to foreign investors. With the abolition of most financial incentives for inward
investment in China, round tripping should be diminishing.
[6] In 2018, the US registered negative outflows (−$64 billion) as US firms repatriated foreign earnings, a
move largely prompted by US. tax reforms.

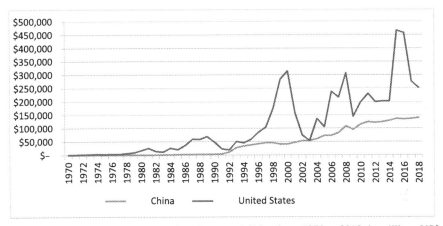

Fig. 3.5 Inward FDI flows for the United States and China from 1970 to 2018, in millions US$. *Source:* Authors' analysis based on UCTADstats, at https://unctadstat.unctad.org, and UNCTAD. (2019). World investment report: Special economic zones. New York and Geneva: United Nations, (Accessed June 2019).

Though the gap with the United States remains, since 2010 China has been the second or third largest investor in the world (see Fig. 3.9). In 2015, it became a net FDI exporter (with $145 billion outflows vs $135 billion inflows). In 2016, its outflows surged by 35% to $196 billion, due to an exceptional volume of overseas acquisitions, and outpaced the OFDI growth of virtually all other countries. Chinese OFDI then accounted for a peak 13% of global flows; a dramatic achievement considering that in 2000 it contributed less than 0.5% to the world total. In 2017, Chinese OFDI declined from this peak for the first time in 16 years—but, at about $158 billion, they clearly exceeded prepeak year levels, and China still ranked third as a global investor. This decline continued in 2018, with an estimated decrease of 18% (which did not prevent China from ranking second as a global investor after Japan). It remains to be seen whether the decline in China's OFDI will persist. In that respect, drastic changes in the global environment since early 2017, such as growing protectionism, may have a dampening effect on Chinese outward investment in the future. Yet, even if its OFDI does not grow as fast as in the past 10 years, China is likely to remain among the world's top global investors (see Chapter 4).

3.2 China as a rising soft power

As China's economic sphere of influence has expanded, so has its political influence, including an assertive soft power strategy, in line with directives set by Chinese government authorities. China's role in founding two multilateral development banks—the Asian infrastructure investment bank (AIIB) and the New development bank (NDB)—as well as its landmark launch of the Belt and Road Initiative (BRI) are evidence of the growing priority granted by China to this dimension of global influence.

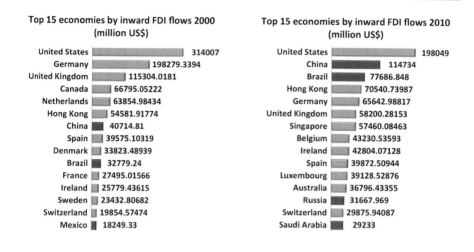

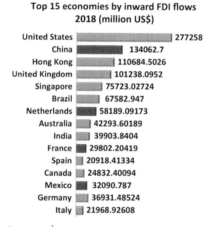

Fig. 3.6 Top 15 FDI host economies.
Source: Authors' analysis based on UNCTADstats, at https://unctadstat.unctad.org, and
UNCTAD. (2019). World investment report: Special economic zones. New York and Geneva:
United Nations, (Accessed March 2019).

3.2.1   The new development banks: AIIB and NDB

Upon their launch, the AIIB and the NDB shifted power away from long-
established global finance institutions: their governance structures and voting
share distributions significantly differ from those of the World Bank and the
International Monetary Fund (IMF). China was a critical force behind the creation of the AIIB and the NDB, and the country holds at least 20% of the voting
shares in both banks.

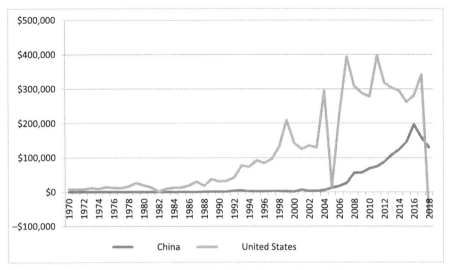

Fig. 3.7 China and United States OFDI flows, 1970–2018, millions US$.
Source: Authors' analysis based on UNCTADstats, at https://unctadstat.unctad.org, and UNCTAD. (2019). World investment report: Special economic zones. New York and Geneva: United Nations, (Accessed June 2019).

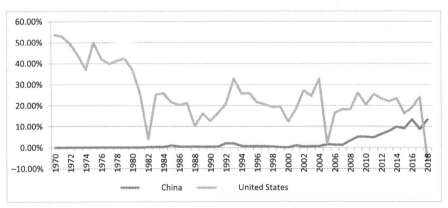

Fig. 3.8 China and United States OFDI flows as percentage of global flows, 1970–2018.
Source: Authors' analysis based on UNCTADstats, at https://unctadstat.unctad.org, and UNCTAD. (2019). World investment report: Special economic zones. New York and Geneva: United Nations, (Accessed June 2019).

AIIB was established in 2014 in Beijing to develop infrastructure in energy, transportation, telecommunications, rural infrastructure, water supply, sanitation, urban development, and logistics. As of June 2019, 74 countries are AIIB members. China holds 27% of the voting rights, far exceeding its 4.4% share in the World Bank, and other Asian regional members hold an additional 48% of the AIIB voting rights.

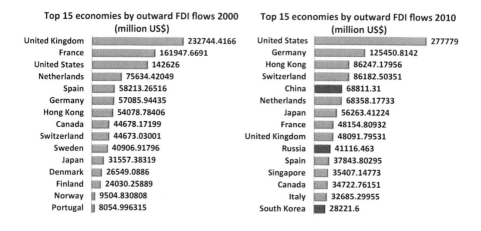

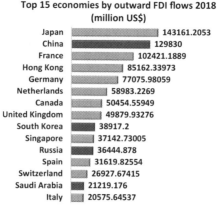

Fig. 3.9 China amid the top 15 global investors by country in 2000, 2010, and 2018.
Source: Authors' analysis based on UNCTADstats, at https://unctadstat.unctad.org, and
UNCTAD. (2019). World investment report: Special economic zones. New York and Geneva:
United Nations, (Accessed June 2019).

Despite initial outside skepticism, the AIIB has proven to be a broad-based multilateral institution. Beyond Asia, it has extended its membership to 24 countries in
Europe, 5 in Africa and Canada, and 26 countries from Africa and Latin America
were prospective members as of June 2019. Five AIIB members are from the G-7.
In addition, the AIIB signed partnership agreements with two key regional multilateral lenders, the Inter-American Development Bank (IADB) and the African
Development Bank (AfDB), which should facilitate expansion into Latin America
and Africa. In 2018, the Islamic Development Bank (IsDB) also announced an AIIB
partnership to fund infrastructure development in Africa as well as in other developing regions.

Due to China's majority voting rights and heavy involvement in the bank's launch, some analysts believe that China is using the bank to support the country's BRI. Negotiations at the time of the bank's creation, however, led to a series of compromises in terms of governance practices. To a number of observers, the Bank—that cooperates with peer development institutions such as the World Bank and the Asian Development Bank (ADB) in joint financing operations—largely conforms with existing development financing norms and practices (Australian Institute of International Affairs, 2017). The financing of the Trans-Anatolian Natural Gas Pipeline (TANAP), connecting Azerbaijan and Europe, is an example of its cooperation with peer development institutions, which involved a $600 million AIIB loan in 2016.

The NDB, founded by BRICS (Brazil, Russia, India, China, and South Africa) in 2015, is also headquartered in China, with an African Regional Center in Johannesburg. The BRICS countries (Brazil, Russia, India, China, and South Africa) share equal voting rights in the bank (20% each), though membership may expand over time. The NDB prioritizes infrastructure and sustainable development projects across emerging and developing economies; its charter specifies that emerging and developing economies will always keep at least 80% of voting rights, with the BRICS retaining at least 55% (NDB, Articles of Agreement, n.d.). Like AIIB, NDB has cooperation agreements with a number of other development banks (e.g., IADB, European Bank for Reconstruction and Development, World Bank Group and ADB, among others).

Both institutions began operations in 2016. Their potential influence stems from their focus on infrastructure—while other development banks tend to have much more diverse portfolios—and the size of their lending activity. Given that infrastructure bottlenecks have the potential to stall economic development in many countries, these banks can provide a crucial lifeline in the form of large-scale financing that is required to meet such needs. According to the OECD, for instance, global infrastructure spending will need a total of $71 trillion through 2030, while the ADB estimates that the Asia-Pacific region alone will need $26 trillion (ADB, 2017; OECD, 2015).

Given the magnitude of infrastructure projects, the banks' lending activity is understandably substantial. The AIIB's loan portfolio more than tripled in just 2 years of operation to reach $5.4 billion by June 2018. Meanwhile, the NDB quickly amassed a portfolio of $4.9 billion for BRICS country projects. Admittedly, both loan portfolios are smaller than those of legacy development banks. During the same 2-year period, the World Bank lent $26 billion to Asia in International Bank for Reconstruction and Development (IBRD) loans, while the ADB lent $64 billion between 2016 and 2017. However, on a country-by-country basis, the new banks carry some weight relative to their more established counterparts. For instance, the AIIB loan commitments to Pakistan, Philippines, and India were 19%, 26%, and 27%, respectively, of the World Bank commitments (IBRD loans) for 2016–17. The value of NDB's loans to China and India meanwhile was equivalent to about 20% and 36% of that of the World Bank (ADB, n.d.; AIIB, n.d.-a, n.d.-b; NDB, n.d.; World Bank, n.d.-a, n.d.-b, n.d.-c).

As alternatives to traditional development finance institutions, the AIIB and NDB can serve emerging economies—and China in particular—in the same way that the Bretton Woods system complemented the soft power strategies of major developed economies.

3.2.2 The Belt and Road Initiative

The Belt and Road Initiative (BRI) lies at the heart of President Xi Jinping's grand strategy to make China a global power again. With its ambitious spending program and wide geographical scope, the BRI is reshaping long-standing global alliances and steering some Western allies toward a rapprochement with China.

The One Belt One Road Initiative (OBOR), later known as the BRI, is one of the largest infrastructure projects in history. Unveiled in September 2013, the Chinese infrastructure development plan was meant to promote maritime and inland trade roads along the former Silk Road and to link South East Asia, Europe, and Africa (see Fig. 3.10). The Chinese government's vision for the BRI includes providing more efficient resource allocation, deepening market integration and economic policy coordination, as well as fostering in-depth regional cooperation (Belt and Road Forum, 2015). As stated in the "Vision and Action" document issued in 2015 by the Chinese Government, the BRI "...is a positive endeavor to seek new models of international cooperation and global governance..." (Belt and Road Forum, 2015). Chinese leadership enshrined the project as a top priority in 2017 by writing the BRI into the Communist Party Constitution during the 19th National Congress of the Chinese Communist Party.[7]

The BRI has both land- and sea-based components. The land component (known as the Silk Road Economic Belt) is composed of a network of large infrastructure projects such as bridges, railways, roads, pipelines, hydroelectric dams, and logistic hubs across Asia and Europe. Its sea-based component (known as the Maritime Silk Road) comprises a matrix of shipping ports, hydrocarbon refineries, and industrial parks. While the Belt portion contains six distinct on-land corridors (Fig. 3.10), the Maritime Road will connect China not only to Africa and Europe through the Indian Ocean and the South China Sea, but also to the South Pacific through the South China Sea. An additional land corridor was proposed in 2018 linking Nepal to both China and India.

The contours of the BRI are not precisely defined. Its geographical scope has expanded since its inception and there is no official list of participating countries. The Chinese government's 2015 Vision and Action plan for the BRI stated that the project would not be strictly limited to the area of the historic Silk Road but would be open to all countries. The list of BRI participants, which began with around 60 members grew to 125 countries by the end of March 2019, according to an official report on the BRI

[7] Resolution of the 19th National Congress of the Communist Party of China on the Revised Constitution of the Communist Party of China, October 24, 2017 available at http://www.xinhuanet.com//english/2017-10/24/c_136702726.htm. The resolution states "The Congress agrees to include into the Party Constitution the following statements: The Communist Party of China shall...work to build a community with a shared future for mankind; follow the principle of achieving shared growth through discussion and collaboration; and pursue the Belt and Road Initiative."

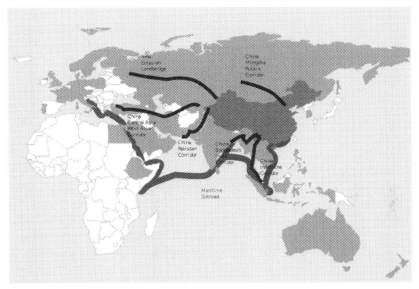

Fig. 3.10 Corridors of the BRI. *Note:* The Belt Road is in *black*, the Maritime Road in *dots*.
The corridors are as follows: the China-Mongolia-Russia Economic Corridor (CMREC), the
New Eurasian Land Bridge (NELB), the China-Central and West Asia Economic Corridor
(CCWAEC), the China-Indochina Peninsula Economic Corridor (CICPEC), the China-
Pakistan Economic Corridor (CPEC), and the Bangladesh-China-India-Myanmar Economic
Corridor (BCIMEC).
Source: Authors based on Wikimedia Commons.

progress, (Office of the Leading Group for Promoting the Belt and Road Initiative,
2019). Members include countries that have signed an agreement with China on the
initiative but may not yet have BRI projects planned.

The initial vision of corridors between Asia, Eurasia, and the eastern coast of Africa
has expanded progressively to include connections to West and Central Africa as well
as to Latin America and the Caribbean. In Africa, in addition to Djibouti, Egypt,
Ethiopia, Tanzania, and Zambia—key BRI partners on the direct path of the Maritime
Silk Road—about 30 other countries have signed memorandums of understanding
with China to join the BRI (as of March 2019, according to the Belt and Road Portal).
A number of these agreements were concluded following visits by Chinese President
Xi Jinping during China-Africa Cooperation Forums. A limited number of projects are
already in place (such as the flagship railway line from Addis Ababa to Djibouti, or the
port facilities in Djibouti, Lagos, Lomé, and Abidjan), but there are several important
projects planned or under construction falling under three main priority areas: (1)
railway lines (e.g., from Dakar to Bamako, or across Nigeria, Tanzania, Kenya, and
Zambia); (2) pipelines (e.g., from Tanzania to South Africa along the coast); and (3)
ports (e.g., Walvis Bay, Beira, Maputo, Libreville, São Tomé, Mombasa, and Conakry,
among others). Several of these projects will connect Africa's hinterland to key ports
on the eastern and western coasts of the continent.

The BRI grew its footprint later in Latin America. Panama paved the way for it when it signed a memorandum of understanding in December 2017, with agreements including investment in the Colón mega-port for containers and rail. In January 2018, China's Foreign Minister Wang Yi extended an invitation to other Latin American countries at the China-CELAC (Community of Latin America and the Caribbean) conference, indicating that the BRI would open up new prospects for cooperative partnerships. A total of 19 LAC members have since joined the initiative, including 10 from the Central America and Caribbean region alone (Belt and Road Portal). Though the size of many of these investments is relatively small in some of the countries involved (such as the Bahamas, Barbados, Antigua, and Barbuda), they can have a significant impact on local economies in the Caribbean. As of June 2019, large Latin American economies such as Brazil, Argentina, and Mexico have not joined the initiative.

Finally, several Western developed countries have joined the BRI. Particularly notable is Italy, a founding EU member, which became the first G-7 member to sign a BRI agreement in March 2019. Others include Austria, Greece, Luxemburg, New Zealand, Portugal, and Switzerland.

The estimated financing resources required by the BRI are nothing short of enormous. Many of the projects are still in the planning phase, which makes it hard to assess the initiative's true scale. As of early 2019, most estimates point to around $1 trillion, but much higher figures were hypothesized in earlier stages of the BRI, mentioning several trillion dollars (Deloitte, 2018; Hillman, 2018). Financing will come from multiple sources, including the AIIB, which is expected to be a key financier. Other development banks, as well as foreign financial institutions and capital markets are expected to participate. China's Sovereign Wealth Fund, established in 2007, and the Silk Road Fund, founded in 2014 are both expected to play a role. However, the largest financial contributors are projected to be the two Chinese state-owned institutions, the Export-Import Bank and the China Development Bank (the latter pledged $800 billion over the course of several years), as well as other Chinese state-owned commercial banks (South Asia Journal, 2018).

Another motivation for China to pursue the BRI is to provide alternatives to the existing maritime routes that are outside of Chinese control. New ports, railways, roads, and pipelines on the Indian subcontinent, such as those along CPEC, would allow China to bypass passages such as the Strait of Malacca (between Malaysia and Indonesia), through which 80% of China's crude oil imports passes. A deepwater port development project in Gwadar, Pakistan, would alleviate some of the burden, as would new port infrastructure projects in Sri Lanka. Pipelines to China transporting oil offloaded at terminals in the Indian Ocean (such as the one opened in Myanmar in 2017) would also reduce China's energy import vulnerability.

The BRI also has the potential to bring development to West and Central China, which would lessen the regional disparity between China's fast growing urban eastern coastline and its western interior. Projects along the corridors would strengthen the development prospects of inland China by further connecting China's landlocked west to key maritime trade routes. Some interior cities such as Xi'an are already establishing economic zones to facilitate trade across China, Central Asia, and the Middle East.

BRI infrastructure projects could also prove a boon to domestic firms, especially Chinese multinationals in energy, transport, and logistics industries that are well positioned to benefit from investment opportunities in the BRI recipient countries (see Chapter 4). Several Chinese firms—all SOEs—are now global leaders in those sectors at the core of BRI (see Chapter 1) and benefit from state financial backing. SOEs like China National Petroleum Corporation, China Merchants Group, China Ocean Shipping Company (COSCO), and China Railway Rolling Stock Corp are well positioned to lead upcoming BRI projects. Based on the information from the State-Owned Assets Supervision and Administration Commission of the State Council, for instance, by early 2019, Chinese central SOEs undertook more than 3000 projects in countries along the BRI (Belt and Road Portal, 2019a, 2019b).

Furthermore, Chinese authorities have established a specific payment system, the China International Payment System, to facilitate cross-border renminbi transactions for BRI-related purposes. This may spur international use of the renminbi.

Responding to many countries' unfulfilled need for investment, the BRI is also enabling China to expand its zone of influence. In Africa, for instance, the construction of major railway lines and ports bolsters China' foothold in the continent. China has long lacked the soft power that some other nations possess. Vis-à-vis other countries and continents, it did not benefit from a commonality of culture, or political or other ties inherited from colonization, and its clout through donor agencies and the Bretton Woods institutions remained limited. Financing globe-spanning infrastructure projects through the BRI is providing it with opportunities to quickly make gains in that respect. Indeed, with infrastructure, BRI is touching a hot spot, a sensitive issue between advanced economies and multilateral development institutions on the one hand and many Latin American, Asian, and African countries on the other. Infrastructure financing is a high-risk, long-term investment and sources of finance are limited. Financing, particularly from development institutions, national or international, has long given rise to protracted processes of checking and approval. Even then, ultimate financial decisions have sometimes proved to be politically motivated. In the meantime, populations are left waiting for vital infrastructure. The number of people in the world without access to clean water, electricity, or transportation is still enormous. Under these circumstances, a new and alternative source of infrastructure development—from China—was bound to meet the interest of many.

Even in some advanced economies, financing from China may also be a potential rescue line for financially distressed governments. In the EU, where infrastructure financing has been starved in the name of budgetary rebalancing, Chinese financing could provide a crucial lifeline, as illustrated by Chinese investments made since 2016 in Greece's Port of Piraeus. Portugal is another example: as noted by the country's Prime Minister Antonio Costa, in the crisis years only China was willing to put money into the EU periphery (Financial Times, 2019).

A project of the size and ambition of the BRI naturally carries its load of economic risks and financial challenges. Delays, like those experienced during the construction of the rail line between Jakarta and Bandung in Indonesia, escalate costs beyond those originally envisioned. In addition, some BRI countries are particularly vulnerable to ballooning debt. The IMF issued warnings that countries with high levels of public debt should proceed with caution in order to protect both the local and Chinese governments from later financial complications. In Sri Lanka, for instance, the fate of Hambantota Port was called into question, as the country was unable to service its contracted debt for the project. Sri Lanka entered in a debt equity swap with China, relinquishing control over the port as well as strategic land around it to China. Some countries took action to address the situation. For instance, in 2018, Malaysia's newly elected government suspended two projects (a rail line from Malaysia to Thailand and a pipeline), citing their high cost. In early 2019, the Malaysian rail line project was finally approved following an agreement with China, substantially reducing the cost of the project for Malaysia. New leadership in the Maldives also pushed back in an effort to reduce the country's debt exposure, while Sierra Leone cancelled a planned Chinese-funded airport in late 2018.

Some analyses, however, challenge the debt-trap argument put forward by some critics (Bräutigam, 2018; Broder, 2019). A study by the Center for Global Development in 2018, while observing that the BRI could increase debt sustainability problems in eight countries, found that the majority of BRI countries will likely avoid problems of debt distress due to BRI projects (Hurley, Morris, & Portelance, 2018). A study of China's external debt renegotiations by the Rhodium Group also revealed that, despite its economic weight, China's leverage in such renegotiations is limited. Asset seizures (as in the case of Hambantota port) are rare and many of the renegotiation cases examined in the study involved an outcome in the borrower's favor (Kratz, Feng, & Wright, 2019). Finally, some experts also consider that the majority of BRI projects are economically viable for the host governments (Bluhm et al., 2018; Broder, 2019).

Internal economic headwinds may impact the BRI. For instance, China's economic growth rate is lower than when the BRI was first announced. Its foreign reserves, although still by far the largest in the world, have declined from an estimated $4 trillion in 2013 to $3 trillion in 2018, and a number of the country's large SOEs are highly leveraged.

Other challenges include security issues and public perception of the projects in recipient countries. Some of the BRI's proposed routes pass through unstable regions or terrorism-affected area. In Pakistan, for instance, extremists have targeted some CPEC construction sites. Support has wavered in some countries, such as Laos, as locals objected to contract opportunities that went to Chinese companies and employees rather than Laotians.

Finally, geopolitical issues make up serious risks facing the BRI's expansion. Some analysts argue that China is looking to establish a military presence, for instance, in certain BRI areas where infrastructure facilities need to be secured. Meanwhile, India fears that the CPEC could undermine its territorial claims in the Kashmir region. The EU, too, has concerns as China reaches out to Eastern Europe with initiatives such as the "16 + 1" Summits, a platform initially bringing together China and 16 Central and Eastern European countries. In May 2019, Greece joined the platform. 12 of its member countries are now from the EU, and the EU is worried about the impact that such moves might have on its unity. The signature of a BRI cooperation agreement with Italy, a founding member and the third largest economy of the EU, has only heightened such worries. The United States, on its side, is concerned by the consequences of China's influence over US naval leverage and alliances in Asia, and potential military implications (Council on Foreign Relations, 2018).

Just 5 years after its launch, the BRI has become a visible reality. Taking center stage in international debate, it has also given rise to a number of concerns. At the Second Belt and Road Forum held in Beijing in April 2019, China addressed some of them, regarding financing and environment sustainability for instance. It unveiled new initiatives, such as the creation of a debt sustainability framework. While the true extent and impact of this adjustment remains to be seen, it shows that China has heard these concerns and criticism. That being said, Chinese authorities are determined to make the BRI a pillar of the country's power and influence. They will learn and adapt to respond to the challenges, they may redirect and scale down as required, but, clearly, they will not give up.

3.3   The path forward: US-China collision course?

The inroads made by Chinese multinationals in the global corporate world are a vivid illustration of the growing weight of China in the global economy. For citizens in developed markets, these inroads are the visible face of China's dramatic transformation from a poor and mostly rural country to the second most powerful economy in the world. Backed by increased economic might, China has also increased its soft power. Through a number of initiatives—the AIIB, the NDB, and the BRI among the most visible—China has bolstered its international profile.

Yet, some of the conditions that contributed to China's rapid growth have waned. Since 2015 in particular, China has faced a variety of challenges including rising protectionism and, especially since 2018, a trade war with the United States, which has had ripple effects beyond either country's borders. Protectionism has become a reality, even among former trade partners. In 2018, the United States first imposed tariffs on all its steel and aluminum imports, followed by two more rounds of tariffs ultimately affecting $250 billion of Chinese imports. China responded to each announcement by imposing its own tariffs on a total of $110 billion of imports from the United States. By late 2018, the two countries had imposed tariffs on each other that covered more than half of their bilateral trade (UNCTAD, 2018). The US-China trade war has also heightened the tensions between the U.S. and some of their traditional trade partners such as Canada, which was particularly concerned by potential new US tariffs on steel and aluminum, and the EU, because of threats to its automobile exports to the United States in particular.

These tariffs could have a broad impact on the global economy, not only for the countries directly participating, but also through indirect effects on third parties. The trade war between the United States and China, for example, may expose markets in Europe and Latin America to increased trade imbalances if Chinese shipments previously destined for the United States are diverted to those markets. Moreover, given the global nature of supply chains, the blow to Chinese exports could ripple through other emerging and developing economies, especially Asian ones that supply the Chinese manufacturing sector as parts of such value chains, for example, Cambodia (a third of its intermediate goods exports go to China), Korea (almost 30%), Thailand and Vietnam (more than 20%), and Malaysia (18%). A slowdown in China as a result of the challenging trade environment could also seriously affect commodity producers as Chinese demand contracts, but other markets may step in to fill the vacuum. On the other hand, if global value chains relocate from China to skirt US-imposed tariffs, other economies could benefit from new market opportunities.

As of February 2019, China and the United States initiated negotiations to prevent further escalations. By mid 2019, this was still a work in progress. Whatever the outcome of such negotiations, one of the most far-reaching, and perhaps damaging, effects of the current trade war is the loss of confidence in the global trading system. Drastic changes in trade policy, erratic announcements, as well as tit-for-tat attitudes have dramatically disrupted the rule-based system of international trade that took decades to form. Founding principles—such as the World Trade Organization's "most-favored-nation (MFN) principle" by which "countries cannot normally discriminate between their trading partners" (WTO)—have been seriously undermined. Protectionism and escalating trade tensions have unleashed one of the most serious threats to the international trade system, fueling a climate of growing uncertainty. Similarly, since early 2018, a number of host country governments have increased scrutiny and restriction on investments, affecting Chinese OFDI in particular (Chapter 4).

Competition in the technology area, a key to global leadership, is also the source of tensions between the United States and China. A number of US tariffs imposed in 2018, for instance, affected Chinese imports in industries targeted by the "Made in China 2025" plan. Tensions intensified in May 2019 when the US President declared a national emergency, signing an executive order forbidding US companies from using foreign telecom services that could pose a national security threat. The executive order did not name any nation or company, but it will particularly impact Chinese multinationals such as Huawei, the world leader of telecommunications equipment (Chapter 2). In 2018, Huawei was already the target of a number of measures effectively blocking its telephone sales in the US market. In May 2019, the company was put on the US "Entity List," meaning that US firms must obtain a special license to sell technology equipment to Huawei—an unlikely event given the current climate. Huawei is not the only firm prevented from selling phones in the United States: China Mobile was also blocked in April 2019 from selling international telephone services on the US market on national security grounds.

All these developments are suggestive of a drastic paradigm shift, transitioning away from a world in which emerging economies such as China could rely on an open global environment as a source for growth and a basis for global expansion.

None of the previous US rivalries, such as the Soviet Union in the 1950s and 1960s, or Japan in the 1970s, reached the dimension and scope of the US-China trade dispute of the late 2010s. It is the authors' view that the impulse to abandon the legacy system for zero-sum saber-rattling benefits no one. Moving forward, reform is necessary, but China must be included as a key player in the design.

References

Asian Development Bank [ADB]. (2017). *Meeting Asia's infrastructure needs.* https://www.adb.org/sites/default/files/publication/227496/special-report-infrastructure.pdf (Accessed September 2018).

Again Development Bank (ADB). (n.d.). *Annual reports.* https://www.adb.org.

Asian Infrastructure Investment Bank [AIIB] (n.d.-a) Our work. https://www.aiib.org/en/about-aiib/who-we-are/our-work/index.html (Accessed September 2018).

Asian Infrastructure Investment Bank [AIIB] (n.d.-b) *Approved projects.* http://www.aiib.org/en/projects/approved/index.html (Accessed September 2018).

Australian Institute of International Affairs. (2017). *What does China want from the Asian Infrastructure Investment Bank?* Australian Outlook. http://www.internationalaffairs.org.au/australianoutlook/what-does-china-want-from-the-aiib.

Belt and Road Forum. (2015). *Vision and actions on jointly building Silk Road Economic Belt and 21st century Maritime Silk Road.* National Development and Reform Commission, Ministry of Foreign Affairs, and Ministry of Commerce of the People's Republic of China. http://www.beltandroadforum.org/english/n100/2017/0410/c22-45.html.

Belt and Road Portal. (2019a). *Report on the BRI progress, contributions and prospects* Office of the Leading Group for Promoting the Belt and Road Initiative. https://eng.yidaiyilu.gov.cn/zchj/qwfb/86739.htm (Accessed April 2019).

Belt and Road Portal. (2019b). *China's central SOEs lead way in B&R construction.* https://eng.yidaiyilu.gov.cn/qwyw/rdxw/79294.htm (Accessed May 2019).

Bluhm, R., Dreher, A., Fuchs, A., Parks, B., Strange, A., & Tierney, M. (2018). *Connective financing: Chinese infrastructure projects and the diffusion of economic activity in developing countries.* AidData Working Paper #64 Williamsburg, VA: AidData at William & Mary.

Bräutigam, D. (2018). *U.S. politicians get China in Africa all wrong.* https://tinyurl.com/y9k75uqw (Accessed April 2018).

Broder, J. (2019). *China's belt and road initiative.* https://library.cqpress.com/cqresearcher/document.php?action=print&id=cqresrre2019012500 (Accessed January 2019).

Casanova, L., & Miroux, A. (2016). *Emerging market multinationals report. The China surge.* Cornell S.C. Johnson College of Business, Cornell University. https://www.johnson.cornell.edu/wp-content/uploads/sites/3/2019/04/2016-EMR-Updated-EMR-Consolidated.v3.pdf.

Casanova, L., & Miroux, A. (2017). *Emerging market multinationals report. Emerging multinationals in a changing world.* Cornell S.C. Johnson College of Business, Cornell University. https://www.johnson.cornell.edu/wp-content/uploads/sites/3/2019/04/EMR-2017-FINAL-FINAL-4dec2017.pdf.

Council on Foreign Relations. (2018). *Geostrategic and military drivers and implications of the Belt and Road initiative, prepared statement by Ely Ratner.* https://www.uscc.gov/sites/default/files/Ratner_USCC%20Testimony%20CORRECTED.pdf.

Deloitte. (2018). *Embracing the BRI ecosystem in 2018.* https://www2.deloitte.com/insights/us/en/economy/asia-pacific/china-belt-and-road-initiative.html.

Financial Times. (2019). https://www.ft.com/content/8c52f2ca-401f-11e9-9bee-efab61506f44 (Accessed March 2019).

Hillman, J. (2018). *How big is China's belt and road?* Center for Strategic and International Studies. https://www.csis.org/analysis/how-big-chinas-belt-and-road.

Hurley, J., Morris, S., & Portelance, G. (2018). *Will China's belt and road initiative push vulnerable countries into a debt crisis?* Center for Global Development, March 5, 2018. https://www.cgdev.org/blog/will-chinas-belt-and-road-initiative-push-vulnerable-countries-debt-crisis. and Examining the debt implications of the Belt and Road Initiative from a policy perspective, *Center for Global Development*, CGD Policy Paper 121. https://www.cgdev.org/sites/default/files/examining-debt-implications-belt-and-road-initiative-policy-perspective.pdf.

IMF. (2019). *World Economic Outlook Database.* https://www.imf.org/external/datamapper/datasets/WEO/1 (Accessed June 2019).

Kharas, H. (2010). *The emerging middle class in developing countries.* OECD Development Center Working Paper, No 285.

Kratz, A., Feng, A., & Wright, L. (2019). *New data on the "debt trap question.* Rhodium Group. https://rhg.com/research/new-data-on-the-debt-trap-question (Accessed April 2019).

McKinsey. (2019). *China brief: The state of the economy.* https://www.mckinsey.com/featured-insights/china/china-brief-the-state-of-the-economy.

NDB. Articles of agreement n.d. https://www.ndb.int/data-and-documents/ndb-core-documents/ (Accessed September 2018).

OECD. (2015). *Fostering investment in infrastructure.* https://www.oecd.org/daf/inv/investment-policy/Fostering-Investment-in-Infrastructure.pdf.

Office of the Leading Group for Promoting the Belt and Road Initiative. (2019). *Report on the BRI progress, contributions and prospects.* https://eng.yidaiyilu.gov.cn/zchj/qwfb/86739.htm (Accessed April 2019).

Prasad, E. (2016). *China's efforts to expand the international use of the renminbi.* Brookings Institution.

Prasad, E. (2017). *Gaining currency: The rise of the renminbi.* New York, NY: Oxford University Press.

South Asia Journal. (2018). *China's belt and road initiative, ambition and opportunity.* http://southasiajournal.net/chinas-belt-and-road-initiative-ambition-and-opportunity/.

UNCTAD. (2018). *Key statistics and trends in international trade.* Geneva: United Nations.

UNCTAD. (2019). *World investment report: Special economic zones.* United Nations: New York and Geneva.

UNDESA Population Division (n.d.), World population aging, United Nations ST/ESA/SER.A/390, UN, New York.

World Bank. (2018). *China systematic country diagnosis 2017, towards a more inclusive and sustainable development, Report.* Washington: The World Bank Group.

World Bank (n.d.-a). Health nutrition and populations statistics.

World Bank. (n.d.-b) China Overview, https://www.worldbank.org/en/country/china/overview (Accessed April 2019).

World Bank. (n.d.-c) IBRD statement of loans. https://finances.worldbank.org/Loans-and-Credits/IBRD-Statement-of-Loans-Latest-Available-Snapshot/sfv5-tf7p (Accessed June 2019).

Yueh, L. (2015). *China's growth: A brief history.* https://hbr.org/2015/12/chinas-growth-a-brief-history.

Further reading

Belt and Road Portal. (n.d.) https://eng.yidaiyilu.gov.cn.

Breuer, J. (2017). *Two Belts, One Road? The Role of Africa in China's Belt & Road initiative.*

China Daily. (2019). *SOEs bring integrity and responsibility.* http://www.chinadaily.com.cn/a/201904/28/WS5cc4dcb5a3104842260b8cab.html.

IMF. (2015). *Press Release No. 15/540.*

IMF. (2017). *World Economic Outlook.* https://www.imf.org/en/News/Articles/2018/04/11/sp041218-belt-and-road-initiative-strategies-to-deliver-in-the-next-phase.

Jolly, D. R. (2011). *Ces entreprises qui font la Chine.* Paris: Eyrolles Editions d'Organisation.

NDB. (2018). *List of all projects.* www.ndb.int/projects/list-of-all-projects (Accessed September 2018).

UNCTAD. (n.d.) Statistical data for FDI and OFDI. United Nations: New York and Geneva. https://unctadstat.unctad.org/EN/.

World Bank. (2019). *World Development Indicators.* https://datacatalog.worldbank.org/dataset/world-development-indicators (Accessed June 2019).

WTO. (n.d.) Understanding the WTO: Principles of the trading system. https://www.wto.org/english/thewto_e/whatis_e/tif_e/fact2_e.htm.

Yueh, L. (2013). *China's growth: The making of an economic superpower.* Oxford University Press. xviii + 347 pp.

Forty years of opening up: Policy support and Chinese OFDI expansion

China's economy is full of strength and resilience. The long-term positive trend has not changed and will not change. We are sure to be able to cope with various risks and challenges, including Sino-U.S. economic and trade frictions.

President Xi Jinping, May 2019

Acronyms

BRI	Belt and Road Initiative
BRICS	Brazil, Russia, India, China, and South Africa
CDB	China Development Bank
CFIUS	Committee on Foreign Investment in the United States
ExIm	China Export and Import Bank
FDI	Foreign direct investment
FIRRMA	Foreign Investment Risk Review Modernization Act
OBOR	One Belt, One Road initiative
OFDI	outward foreign direct investment
SOEs	state-owned enterprises
NDRC	National Development and Reform Commission
DRC	Development and Reform Commission
MOFCOM	Ministry of Commerce
MOFTEC	Ministry of Foreign Trade and Economic Cooperation
ROAs	return on assets
SAFE	State Administration of Foreign Exchange
SEZs	special economic zones
SGCC	State Grid Corporation of China
WTO	World Trade Organization

China's economic success has largely relied on the close collaboration between business and government. The latter undertook a number of significant institutional and economic reforms aimed at boosting China's business sector, and encouraged the development of national champions, seen as pillars for strong economic growth. It is within this broader context that China's outward foreign direct investment (OFDI) policy developed. Over the course of four decades, the government policies moved from outright prohibition to liberalization, and eventually to active support and encouragement, making the country one of the very few emerging economies that adopted such a proactive OFDI policy.

The Era of Chinese Multinationals. https://doi.org/10.1016/B978-0-12-816857-8.00004-5

China's "Go Global" strategy—also known as *Zou Chuqu*, launched in 2000—foreshadowed the emergence of Chinese multinationals on the world stage. In several phases, Chinese government policy had direct or indirect influence on the country's subsequent OFDI surge. Supported by the emergence of new development banks and encouraged by other government-led programs such as China's 12th Five-Year Plan (2011–15) and the Belt and Road Initiative (BRI), China became the emerging market leader in outward investments. In this chapter, we describe these successive phases of Chinese outward investment policies and examine the potential obstacles that China's OFDI expansion may encounter as the world economy moves into more uncertain territory.

4.1   Phase one (1978–92): From a closed to open economy

Chinese Premier Deng Xiaoping instigated a turning point for China with his speech titled "Emancipate the mind, seek truth from facts, and unite as one in looking to the future" at the Third Plenum Meeting of the Communist Party in 1978. The premier's lofty words prefigured a more open economy and helped trigger decades of reform that would transform China from one of the poorest countries in the world to the second largest economy. In time, "Reform and Opening" became the country's mantra. Among its many modifications, the government decentralized power in a number of institutional and political reforms. Ultimately, decentralization provided a significant opportunity for the private sector to flourish in certain market segments. Early successes fueled momentum for what would become an unprecedented—though gradual—process of opening the state economy.

The launch of the "open door policy" marked the first steps to open up China to foreign trade and investment. At the time, the "opening up" meant attracting foreign capital and technology. In 1979–1980, China created its first four special economic zones in the southeastern coastal region in a bid to attract foreign enterprises. These zones offered tax benefits and other incentives to foreign firms and gave local governments the power to make infrastructure decisions without an initial green light from the central government. The special economic zones (SEZs) led to an infusion of new capital, technology, and skill sets into China's economy. At the same time, Chinese enterprises were sheltered from international competition in the domestic market. As a result, idea exchange thrived in southeast China and product quality improved as foreign enterprises mingled with Chinese firms in these SEZs. Chinese enterprises, especially state-owned firms, soon flourished in the regions.

However, no regulation or specific framework for establishing outward investment operations overseas was initially enacted. Foreign investment was limited to state-owned enterprises (SOEs) and "provincial and municipal cooperation enterprises" under state control (Buckley, Cross, Tan, Liu, & Voss, 2010). The Chinese State Council highly regulated investment projects, which were only approved on a case-by-case basis (Chen, 2015). Even as inward FDI increased in the early 1980s, China's overseas investment barely budged, reaching only $90 million in 1983, compared to the $10 billion of the United States.[1]

By the mid-1980s, the Chinese government finally debuted regulations that established principles and administrative processes governing investment by Chinese enterprises. In a key move, the government extended the right to apply for approval to enterprises other than state-owned foreign trade companies. Local governments took advantage of new regulations to help enterprises set up activities abroad.[2] Yet, all OFDI still required government examination and the approval procedures remained strict and relatively complicated. As a result, while Chinese OFDI increased during the second half of the 1980s, it never exceeded $850 million, far below the US level (which was $37 billion in 1989 alone).

The last years of this phase were fraught with turbulence in China. The number of overseas investment failures increased, while unchecked speculative overseas investments led to serious state asset losses (Wenbin & Wilkes, 2011). As a result, the Chinese government enacted tighter approval requirements and reinforced already strict foreign exchange control, especially to ensure outward large-scale investment was for "genuinely productive purposes."

4.2 Phase two (1992–99): Building national champions amid "opening and reform"

After 3 years of policy retrenchment, Premier Deng Xiaoping relaunched the idea of economic reform during his 1992 tour of Southern China. In his South speeches, the Chinese premier explicitly stated that the SEZs would be permanent, and that the success of Chinese firms abroad was an important part for enhancing China's overall competitiveness (Hong & Sun, 2006). These assertions further encouraged local governments to support and promote overseas investment by enterprises under their supervision and gave new momentum to Chinese OFDI. Shortly after 1992, Chinese OFDI outflows increased sharply from an estimated $900 million in 1990 to about $4 billion in 1993. Outflows remained volatile, however, backsliding to below $2 billion in 1999, while that year US OFDI flows reached $200 billion.

The end of the 1990s, however, marked another transition in China's OFDI policy. As China began to understand the critical role that outward investment could play in driving its domestic economic development, the government's attitude shifted from a stance of allowance to one of direct support and encouragement. For example, in this new outlook, the government specifically supported OFDI projects in activities

---

[1] In this chapter, FDI statistics are from UNCTAD unless otherwise indicated.

[2] The following regulations were of particular importance: "Notice about principles and the scope of authority for examination and approval of establishing non-trading enterprise in foreign countries, Hong Kong and Macao" (1984), and the "Interim regulations on the administrative measures and procedures of examination and approval of establishing non-trading enterprises abroad" (1985), (OECD, 2008).

requiring the purchase of Chinese inputs.[3] Incentives took the form of export tax rebates, foreign exchange facilities, and other types of financial assistance. In line with its strategy to create and nurture national champions in strategic sectors, the government focused its support on large overseas investments of the SOEs in a bid to increase the country's competitive edge.

Overall, Chinese OFDI policy during the 1990s was contradictory—with both stricter control mechanisms and increasing support for industry-specific OFDI. These seemingly opposing forces, however, enabled China to simultaneously support and encourage OFDI, yet maintain a close watch on capital outflow.

4.3 Phase three (2000–08): Soaring growth and increasing internationalization

In 2000, then Chinese Premier Zhu Rongi formalized this policy of encouragement with the launch of China's "Going Out" Strategy at the Fifth Plenary Session of the 15th Congress of the Communist Party. The Chinese government solidified this strategy with China's 11th Five-Year Plan in 2001 (Sauvant & Chen, 2014). The plan outlined specific policy directions for Chinese overseas investment, setting the trend for the decade to come. Symbolizing China's commitment to internationalizing, the new policy marked a fundamental shift. Rather than focusing on attracting FDI to China, the Chinese government began to actively encourage Chinese firms to invest abroad to enhance China's competitiveness. By including overseas investment in its development strategy, China responded to the demands of entrepreneurs for a more sustainable model of business expansion and assuaged concerns of export dependence. In an effort to find additional avenues for economic growth, the Chinese government began work to amend the constitution to include guarantees on private property in 2004; by 2007, a private property law fully acknowledged the important role private business could play in China's economic transformation.

China solidified its journey on the path to liberalization by joining the World Trade Organization (WTO) in 2001. Combined with increased privatization, as well as the restructuring of the financial sector (see Chapter 5), this move enhanced China's credibility to foreign investors, economic partners, and international organizations. Subsequently, more foreign companies poured into China's market, further contributing to the learning and subsequent internationalization process of Chinese companies (Tian & Deng, 2007).

The "Go Global" policy expanded over time as the government added measures enabling Chinese companies to expand into international markets. These measures included streamlining approval procedures, simplifying application requirements as well as relaxing restrictions on foreign exchange, among other types of assistance.

---

[3] See, for instance, the 1999 State Council "Opinion on encouraging companies to carry out overseas material processing and assembly."

The year 2004 was a key year, signaling a transition from "control" to "encouragement and facilitation." In particular, the State Council's Decision on Reforming the Investment System adopted that year marked the end of the old "examination and approval" system that had characterized OFDI policy since the late 1970s. Instead, a more transparent system based on "verification and approval" and "record-filing" replaced it. The 2004 State Council Decision effectively initiated a new era in Chinese OFDI development (Chen, 2015). Financing became easier to access, as did certain tax incentives and interest-subsidized loans for priority OFDI project investments (e.g., in natural resources, infrastructure, or manufacturing projects leading to exports). New information services also provided guidance on, inter alia, foreign business environments, market conditions, and opportunities. A guidance catalog on Countries and Industries for Overseas Investment, issued in 2004 by the Ministry of Foreign Trade and Economic Cooperation (MOFTEC, which later became the Ministry of Commerce (MOFCOM) following a reorganization) and the National Development and Reform Commission (NDRC) identified specific targets for China's OFDI expansion. A wide network of ministries and institutions provided administrative, financial, and commercial support including, the Ministry of Commerce, the National Development and Reform Commission, the Export-Import Bank of China (China Exim Bank), the China Development Bank (CDB), and the China Export and Credit Insurance Corporation. The Chinese government issued 17 OFDI-related policies per year on average from 2004 to 2008 compared to about four from 1990 to 1998 (Wenbin & Wilkes, 2011), which testifies to the importance of the issue for the Chinese authorities.

As a result, Chinese OFDI increased significantly, reaching more than $55 billion in 2008, 20 times as large as in 2004 (see Fig. 4.1).

4.4 Phase four (2009–16): The global financial crisis as a turning point

The Global Financial Crisis (GFC) marked the beginning of a major surge in Chinese OFDI. Postcrisis, Chinese firms took advantage of opportunities that financially distressed firms in developed economies offered (Casanova & Miroux, 2017, and Chapter 2). Given the number of favorable measures adopted in preceding years, and the Chinese government's willingness to continue its support to OFDI, the policy environment in China was propitious, enabling Chinese firms to acquire European and US assets whose values had fallen. In 2009, the government issued two important sets of regulations: the Administrative Measures on Outward Investment (by MOFCOM) and the Administrative Measures on Foreign Exchange Used by Domestic Organizations for Outward Investment (by the State Administration of Foreign Exchange, SAFE). The former measure decentralized OFDI regulation to provincial authorities and also simplified procedures for projects smaller than $100 million (with a few exceptions). The latter measures consolidated previous policies and expanded the foreign exchange available to Chinese firms for overseas investment.

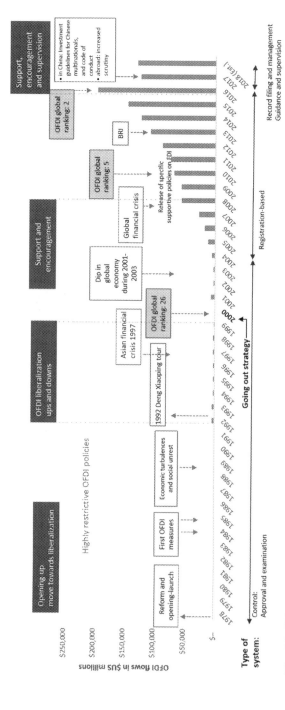

Fig. 4.1 Chinese OFDI policies from 1970 to 2018.
Sources: Authors; FDI data is from UNCTADstats.

In 2014, the NDRC and MOFCOM further relaxed the regulatory environment for OFDI with the following measures, respectively: the Measures for the Administration of Approval and Registration of Overseas Investment Projects (NDRC) and the revised Administrative Measures for Overseas Investment (MOFCOM) (Wang & Gao, 2018). Under these regulations, official approval was only necessary for Chinese investment projects exceeding $1 billion, or for projects in certain sensitive countries or specifically designated industries. For the other projects—the vast majority of Chinese OFDI in fact—only registration with the provincial NDRC was required. In addition, regulations made reinvestment abroad by Chinese overseas enterprises even easier. In sum, the Chinese system was moving toward a "registration-based and approval-supplemented system" (as characterized by Wang & Gao, 2018), aimed at facilitating, encouraging, and guiding the outward expansion of Chinese enterprises.

Combined with the aftereffects of the GFC and China's massive foreign reserves, China's OFDI policy triggered a dramatic increase in its OFDI flows. Consisting mostly of US government debt accumulated since the early 2000s, China's reserves generated a low return on investment. Post-GFC, many Chinese companies acquired firms in developed markets as an alternative to purchasing financial assets abroad. As a result, Chinese firms became leading global acquirers, buying many distressed foreign firms. This spike in Chinese M&A activity in developed countries contributed significantly to the remarkable surge in Chinese outbound investment. Between 2008 and 2016, OFDI flows rose from more than $55 billion to almost $200 billion (see Fig. 4.1), solidifying China's place as the second largest investor in the world after the United States. By 2015, China's OFDI exceeded its inward FDI for the first time in the country's history (see Chapter 3).

In addition to the above-mentioned economic measures, diplomatic efforts supported China's outgoing strategy. For instance, the Chinese Premier went on various tours of Latin America and Africa since 2013. That year, China's launch of the BRI was another key initiative expected to fuel the expansion of Chinese enterprises overseas.

Meant initially to promote maritime and inland trade routes to Asia, Europe, and Africa, and extended to Latin America, the BRI is one of the largest infrastructure projects in history (see Chapter 3). Supporting the expansion of Chinese enterprises is not a direct and explicit objective of the BRI. Yet, Chinese firms are likely to benefit from foreign investment opportunities as a result. As detailed in Chapter 3, the initiative will involve massive amounts of investment in infrastructure development in BRI countries. As governments often coordinate such large infrastructure projects, SOEs with industry expertise and substantial financial resources are likely to play a large role in the initiative.

By its very nature, the BRI is deeply linked to China's "Going Out" strategy. The role of Chinese firms, especially SOEs, will likely remain significant as the BRI has become a high priority of the Chinese government. The fact that the 2017 "Guidelines on Overseas Investment" (see Section 4.5) specifically encourages investments that promote the BRI is also indicative of the close link between the BRI and China's "Going Out" strategy.

Taken together, the central government's strategies worked to increase Chinese OFDI. The BRI in particular contributed to the massive flood of outflows. Between 2013 and 2017, for instance, Chinese OFDI in countries along the BRI amounted to more than $80 billion (MOFCOM, 2018). Even with the broad-based slowdown in Chinese OFDI after 2016, flows to BRI countries remained robust; in fact, they have assumed greater importance, with their share in total Chinese FDI outflows rising from 7.6% to more than 12% between 2016 and 2018.

4.5   Phase five (2017–present): OFDI support remains, with some road blocks

With OFDI flows soaring by almost 40% in 2016 alone, concerns emerged that such massive outflows could destabilize the yuan, and in turn the entire economy. While government policy remained supportive of outward FDI expansion on the whole, authorities took steps to rein the remarkable outflows of capital amid the flurry of large outbound M&As (mergers and acquisitions) (Chapter 2). Authorities feared that a number of private company acquisitions were motivated by the desire to transfer money abroad—especially in the case of acquisitions outside the buyer's core area of business. To stem the outflows, the government began taking some measures by the autumn of 2016: it announced tighter regulations for M&A deals worth more than $10 billion (or $1 billion if the acquisition was outside the investor's core business area) and restricted real estate purchases abroad by SOEs worth more than $1 billion (Casanova & Miroux, 2017). Then, in August 2017, to discourage "unfavorable" investment and promote "favorable" ones, Chinese authorities issued guidelines on overseas investment categorizing investment into "prohibited," "restricted," and "encouraged" categories (see Box 4.1).

The release of a 36-point "Code of conduct for private companies investing abroad" by the National Development and Reform Commission in December 2017 was another important move in the same vein. The code calls upon private firms to "invest in line with their own conditions and abilities," avoid high-leverage financing and stay within their core area of activities; they should also respect local laws and regulations, protect the environment, and fulfill their social responsibilities. Highly leveraged and risky outbound acquisitions by large Chinese conglomerates—such as Wanda, Fosun, HNA (Hainan Airlines), and Anbang—likely motivated this particular code, as the government saw these acquisitions as threats to the companies' and country's financial stability. The new guidelines also require firms to report investment plans to the government and seek approval for investments in sensitive countries or industries.

In addition to OFDI policy changes, the Chinese government tightened credit and pursued a financial clean-up campaign, which tempered the fever of acquisitions. The government introduced a number of measures to control rising leverage in the financial system, making it more difficult to obtain financing. A number of major Chinese investors that drove much of the 2015–16 surge were forced to reverse course and sell off overseas assets. This led to a wave of divestments affecting mostly real estate,

---

Box 4.1   China's 2017 guidelines on overseas investment.

In August 2017, the State Council issued the "Guidelines on Further Guiding and Regulating Overseas Investment" put forward by the NDRC, the Ministry of Commerce, the Ministry of Foreign Affairs, and the People's Bank of China. In line with the national economic and strategic interests of China, the guidelines classify overseas investments into three main categories: (1) *prohibited investments*, (2) *restricted investments*, and (3) *encouraged investments*.

Prohibited investments include, inter alia, investments in gambling and "lewd industries" as well as those that provide access to sensitive sectors such as core military.

Restricted investments include, among others, real estate, hotels, entertainment, and sport clubs—industries in which Chinese authorities flagged a number of deals as questionable regarding their true objectives and actual economic rationale. Outdated industries and projects in countries with no diplomatic relations with China or in regions suffering from high degrees of instability have also been restricted.

On the other hand, firms are *encouraged* to actively engage in investments that promote the BRI (in particular, infrastructure and connectivity projects), as well as in investments that "strengthen cooperation with overseas high-tech and advanced manufacturing companies." They are especially incentivized to establish R&D centers abroad. For encouraged investments, the Chinese government intends to adopt a number of measures to provide, among others, tax, exchange rate, insurance, and customs benefits.

Source: Authors based on "Guidelines on Further Guiding and Regulating Overseas Investment," General Office of the State Council, August 4, 2017 (unofficial translation).

---

hospitality, and entertainment assets. The Chinese airline conglomerate HNA, for instance, sold off major real estate properties in the United States, Hong Kong, and Australia, and some of its equity stakes in Deutsche Bank, among other assets (see Chapter 10).

The "Administrative Measures for Outbound Investment by Enterprises," was another important regulation released by the NDRC in December 2017. These new measures provided clearer and more streamlined regulations. They effectively completed the shift to a filing and reporting system for investment in nonsensitive industries, even relaxing reporting requirements for investments below $300 million (see Table 4.1). They strengthened monitoring and supervision during and after transactions and clarified disciplinary actions for violations and misconduct, bringing China closer to a postinvestment monitoring and supervision system. Furthermore, these measures applied to a broader scope of entities, covering overseas enterprises controlled by Chinese firms in addition to entities incorporated in China.

The policies and measures adopted during this last phase should not be seen as evidence of diminished governmental support for OFDI per se. Rather, they indicate a

Table 4.1   NDRC approval requirement for Chinese investment.

	Investment in nonsensitive industries	Investment in sensitive industries
Less than $300 million	Nothing required (no approval, registration or reporting required)	Approval required
More than $300 million	Only reporting required	Approval required

Source: Authors based on "Administrative Measures for Outbound Investment by Enterprises," NDRC, December 2017.)

will to better control outflows (given the risk of capital flight) and enhance supervision in the postinvestment phase.

The regulations also marked a change in China's approach toward OFDI. At the beginning of the "open door" policy, Chinese OFDI policy was primarily determined by political objectives. However, commercial interests acquired increasing importance as the system simplified—progressively shifting from exante "examination and approval" to a system largely based on filing and expost monitoring and supervision—gradually leaving the investment decision to the enterprise itself, at least regarding nonsensitive investments.

Notwithstanding such an evolution, Chinese authorities still reserved the capacity to strategically guide China's outward investment. First, the government has retained close supervision of overseas investment in sensitive industries by maintaining the need to obtain investment approval. Second, it has kept a watchful eye on large M&As in an effort to stamp out any ripple effects that could harm the broader country's economy. Third, financial support and foreign exchange controls remain firmly a government responsibility. Fourth, SOEs continue to play a major role in Chinese OFDI, even though private firms have gained importance.

Without a doubt, the Chinese government has been the primary factor determining Chinese outward investment over the past few decades. But as Chinese OFDI surged, host countries also had their part to play in influencing OFDI destinations. The characteristics of Chinese outward investments, such as a pronounced interest for technology sectors, triggered widespread scrutiny in host countries, and sometimes outright opposition to Chinese OFDI.

While many countries instituted mechanisms to screen foreign investments, several developed countries strengthened these measures after 2017. In Germany, for instance, the Chinese acquisition of robotics firm Kuka in 2016 signaled a wakeup call among politicians and EU representatives. The following year, a German Foreign Trade and Payments Ordinance enabled the government to more easily block foreign acquisitions based on security grounds. In addition, since December 2018, a new policy is expected to subject more transactions by non-EU buyers to government scrutiny: it allows the German government to review, and potentially block, purchases of stakes as low as 10% (vs 25% before). In France, a 2018 decree expanded the list of sectors requiring the Ministry of Economy's approval for foreign investment; and further measures may be adopted in the future. The UK Parliament also introduced legislation in

2018 to reinforce the ability of the state to scrutinize investments in innovative sectors. Likewise, in 2018, Australia, a major provider of natural resources to China, tightened sales of agricultural land and electricity infrastructure to foreigners.

The EU as a whole began to take a firmer position vis-à-vis Chinese investment, in spite of the differing viewpoints among member countries. China became a welcome source of financing for EU countries (such as Greece, Portugal, and Hungary) while other members were concerned by the potential threats Chinese investment may pose to sensitive sectors and crucial infrastructure in the EU. By February 2019, the European Parliament adopted a framework for screening FDI inflows into the EU in relation to investments in critical infrastructure and sensitive technologies. This mechanism provides the European Commission the power to request information and issue opinions to member states on whether to approve deals that are likely to affect security and the public order; the country concerned, nonetheless, still makes the final decision. If the member country chooses not to comply with the commission's recommendations, it is required to justify its decision. The new framework has not created a very strong EU-wide investment screening mechanism but is likely to have a profound impact for a number of reasons. For instance, the risk assessment is based on broad criteria. In addition, the list of sectors earmarked for increased scrutiny is likely to expand. Second, the regulation encourages member states to look into intra-EU investments involving non-EU ultimate buyers, such as acquisitions by Chinese-owned EU firms. Third, through monitoring and reporting requirements, the regulation has created an incentive for states without investment screening mechanisms to monitor and analyze foreign acquisitions

Finally, the United States has enacted the most comprehensive approach for screening to date with its 2018 Foreign Investment Risk Review Modernization Act (FIRRMA). Considered the most significant overhaul of the Committee on Foreign Investment in the United States (CFIUS) since 1988, FIRRMA has enlarged the scope of foreign investment transactions reviewable by the CFIUS on national security grounds while lengthening the review period. It extends the authority of CFIUS to real estate acquisitions in proximity to facilities sensitive to national security interest, and to minority investments in any US business involved in critical technologies, critical infrastructure, or with access to sensitive personal data. It also expands the scope of what comprises national security, for instance, by including in the critical technologies category certain "emerging and foundational technologies," as determined by the Departments of Commerce, Defense, State, and other federal agencies.

Illustrating host country hostility, five mega deals (worth $100 million or more) involving the acquisition of US companies by Chinese buyers were withdrawn or prohibited between 2017 and mid-2018, for explicitly stated national security concerns: the acquisitions of Lattice Semiconductor Corporation, Here International B.V. (an IT-related firm), MoneyGram International (financial services), Fluent Inc. (a data-driven marketing services firm formerly known as Cogent), and Xcerra Corporation (semiconductor testing equipment, later on bought by the US firm Cohu Inc.). Outside of the United States, the Australian government also rejected high-profile transactions on national security grounds, such as the sale of a majority stake in Ausgrid, an electricity provider, to State Grid Corporation of China (SGCC) in 2016. For the first time in

Europe, in 2018, a Chinese transaction was de facto blocked: the sale of the German specialized machines and equipment manufacturer Leifeld collapsed following the German government's threat of a veto.

All of the factors above contributed to an observed decrease in Chinese outward investment in 2017 and 2018. M&As felt the brunt of the effects, declining in both 2017 and 2018 after years of increase (see Chapter 2). Despite these downturns, China has remained a top global investor. In the medium term, the net effect of increased scrutiny at home and restrictive measures abroad remains to be seen. While speculative deals will likely face higher hurdles, the underlying economic motivations for increased Chinese outbound investment remain. For Chinese companies, these motivations include not only access to resources, but also increasingly access to markets, international brands, technology, and know-how, as well as better return on assets (ROAs). In addition, in a global environment characterized by increased trade barriers, setting up activities overseas enables firms to jump local barriers and preserve and develop markets in line with traditional FDI theory. The Chinese government, on its side, remains determined to continue growing its economy with a focus on innovation and high value-added sectors, as illustrated by "Made in China 2025," its strategic plan aimed at upgrading Chinese industrial capabilities (Chapter 3).

4.6   Conclusion

China's OFDI support policy was integral to the expansion of Chinese multinationals; such a policy formed part of a broader strategy aimed at boosting the Chinese business sector, through the creation and nurturing of national champions.

As China's government made its radical change from restriction to liberalization and then active support and encouragement, its approach to OFDI support varied widely. From a relatively eclectic or even "half-hearted approach" early on in the reformation process, the Chinese government ultimately shifted to pragmatic and determined support policies. Key to this transition was the government's efforts to relax foreign investment controls and prohibitions and streamline the approval system. The subsequent surge in China's OFDI flows, especially after 2008, was a direct result of China phasing out restrictions and phasing in supportive policies.

Despite flourishing even as many developed economies floundered post-GFC, China's trajectory is anything but straightforward. In light of tighter external financing conditions and spreading protectionism in many developed economies, growth opportunities may become more limited. On the other hand, a number of Chinese firms now rank among the largest in the world, and in 2019 about 20% of the firms in the Fortune Global 500 are Chinese. For many Chinese firms, internationalization has become an imperative, largely shared by the Chinese government. Given current policy headwinds, the growth of Chinese OFDI may not be as dramatic as in the past. Yet, the drive toward outward expansion will remain, fed in particular by the overall objective of transforming China into an innovation- and technology-driven economy around high value-added and strategic sectors. Against this background, the Chinese government is likely to continue encouraging OFDI, while subjecting it to enhanced supervision.

References

Buckley, P. J., Cross, A., Tan, H., Liu, X., & Voss, H. (2010). Historic and emergent trends in Chinese outward direct investment. In *Foreign direct investment, China and the world economy*. London: Palgrave Macmillan.

Casanova, L., & Miroux, A. (2017). *Emerging market multinationals report: Emerging multinationals in a changing world*. Emerging Markets Institute. S.C. Johnson School of Management. Cornell University. https://www.johnson.cornell.edu/wp-content/uploads/sites/3/2019/04/EMR-2017-FINAL-FINAL-4dec2017.pdf.

Chen, J. (2015). *Chinese law: Context and transformation*. Leiden, The Netherlands: Brill Nijhoff.

Hong, E., & Sun, L. (2006). Dynamics of internationalization and outward investment: Chinese corporations' strategies. *The China Quarterly, 187*, 610–634.

MOFCOM. (2018). *National Bureau of Statistics of the Republic of China*. . Statistical Bulletin of China's Outward Foreign Direct Investment.

OECD. (2008). *Investment Policy Reviews: China 2008 – Encouraging responsible business conduct*. Paris: OECD.

Sauvant, K., & Chen, V. (2014). China's regulatory framework for outward foreign direct investment. *China Economic Journal, 7*(1), 141–163.

Tian, Z., & Deng, X. (2007). The determinants of corporate political strategy in Chinese transition. *Journal of Public Affairs, 7*, 341–356.

Wang, B., & Gao, K. (2018). Outward direct investment: Restricted, relaxed and regulated stages of development. In R. Garnaut, L. Song, & C. Fang (Eds.), *China's 40 years of reform and development: 1978–2018* (pp. 619–636). Acton ACT: ANU Press.

Wenbin, H., & Wilkes, A. (2011). *Analysis of China's overseas investment policies*. Working Paper 79. Bogor, Indonesia: CIFOR.

Further reading

Davies, K. (2013). China Investment Policy: An update. *OECD Working Papers on International Investment, 2013/01*. OECD Publishing.

UNCTAD. (2018). World investment report: Investment and new industrial policies. New York and Geneva: United Nations.

Yelery, A. (2014). *China's 'going out' policy: Sub-National Economic Trajectories, ICS Analysis, No 24, December 2014*. Delhi: Institute of Chinese Studies.

ICBC—The global bank

Seizing the historic opportunities arising from the transformation of domestic economic development…the Bank strived to overcome the adverse impact of the international financial crisis, firmly promoted structural adjustment and development mode transformation, and preliminarily built an intensive and sustainable development path featuring balanced assets and capital, quality and benefits, and cost and efficiency.

Excerpted from ICBC's Corporate Strategy

Acronyms

ABC	Agricultural Bank of China
AMCs	Asset Management Companies
ADBC	Agricultural Development Bank of China
BOA	Bank of America
BOC	Bank of China
BOCOM	Bank of Communications
BRI	Belt and Road Initiative
CBRC	China Banking Regulatory Commission
CBIRC	China Banking Insurance Regulatory Commission
CCB	China Construction Bank
CDB	China Development Bank
CSRC	China Securities Regulatory Commission
ExIm	Export-Import Bank of China
ICBC	Industrial and Commercial Bank of China
FOCAC	Forum on China-Africa Cooperation
GDP	gross domestic product
GFC	Global Financial Crisis
IMF	International Monetary Fund
IPO	initial public offering
MOF	Ministry of Finance
NPL	nonperforming loans
PBOC	People's Bank of China
ROAs	return on assets
ROE	return on equity
SBA	Standard Bank Argentina
SOE	state-owned enterprise
UNEPFI	United Nations Environment Program Finance Initiative
WTO	World Trade Organization

The Era of Chinese Multinationals. https://doi.org/10.1016/B978-0-12-816857-8.00005-7

5.1   The Chinese banking sector

The ascension of Industrial and Commercial Bank of China (ICBC) is a paradigmatic case for China's relatively young banking system. The country established its first modern bank, the People's Bank of China (PBOC), in 1948. Based on a mono-bank model, PBOC took charge of all state policy, lending, and commercial operations. In the early 1980s, the country transitioned to a multiownership system, out of which the PBOC implemented monetary policies and regulated financial institutions, while other banks partook in commercial credit and savings business. These became known as the "big five" specialized state-owned banks—that is, the Agricultural Bank of China (ABC), China Construction Bank (CCB), the ICBC, the Bank of Communications (BoCom), and the Bank of China (BOC). By 1994, the Chinese government established three more: the Agricultural Development Bank of China (ADBC), the China Development Bank (CDB), and the Export-Import (ExIm) Bank of China.

Chinese banks held $37 trillion in assets by 2018, an increase of 7.1% with respect to the previous year. These assets amounted to nearly 300% of China's gross domestic product (GDP), and surpassed those of the US banking system and the European Union (EU) in 2010 and 2016, respectively. The five specialized banks controlled about $13.4 trillion (90.4 trillion yuan), or approximately 35.5% of these assets. By 2018, ABC, CCB, ICBC, and BoCom became among the five largest banks in the world by assets (Fortune, 2018). Yet, 95% of the assets of Chinese banks remain domestic as of 2018—China is the eighth largest country based on cross-border lending (BIS, 2017). Still, China has deepened trade relations and increased its international exposure by way of loans and investments all over the world. It has become the most important lender for a number of African countries, as well as emerging and frontier markets in Asia (IBIS World, 2018).

The mainstays of the industry are corporate deposits/loans, personal deposits/loans, currency in circulation, fiscal deposits, and financial bonds. From 2012 to 2017, the sector's revenue grew at an annualized rate of 4.4% to an estimated $573.5 billion and touted 3858 commercial banks in China, employing 3.63 million people, with wages of $83.8 billion. Most profits in the Chinese banking sector come from lending sourced from core deposits, which account for approximately 85% of bank funds (IBIS World, 2018). Together, they represented 61.3% of lending in 2017, up from 56.4% in 2008. Other credit uses were foreign exchange purchases and portfolio investments (IBIS World, 2018).

Analysts forecast that revenue growth in the banking sector will slow in China due to weak demand for new medium- and long-term loans, a narrowing interest spread, and intensified competition. Chinese domestic banks have faced pressures to upgrade operations management, and optimize asset and credit risks since the country officially opened its banking sector in 2006, which permitted foreign banks to conduct RMB business (IBIS World, 2018). The financial sector is continuing to open further as of 2018–19.

Competition at home in China will only intensify, encouraging domestic companies to improve their operational efficiency and modernize their products in order to compete successfully with new rivals. Rural Chinese markets stand as one of the few high-growth domestic opportunities. Corporate institutions have partnered with rural credit cooperatives since 2007, when the China Banking Regulatory Commission (CBRC) relaxed the market-entry policies for banking institutions in rural areas. This development has saturated rural markets, however, and Chinese commercial banks will increasingly look for development opportunities abroad or in other banking sectors within the country.

5.1.1   Chinese banking structure and regulation

Many other banks have launched since the first state-owned banks were founded: from a dozen joint-stock commercial banking institutions and over 100 city-based commercial banks to financial institutions dedicated to rural regions of the country. The Chinese government has likewise permitted foreign banks to establish branches in China and allowed foreign strategic minority investments into many state-owned commercial banks.

The main regulatory body that oversees the Chinese banking system is the China Banking Insurance Regulatory Commission (CBIRC), which replaced the CBRC in April 2018. The CBIRC determines the regulations that govern China's banking and insurance sectors. The commission also oversees banks and insurers, collects and publishes statistics on the banking system, approves the establishment or expansion of banks, and resolves potential liquidity, solvency, or other issues that might arise at individual banks.

The PBOC has considerable authority over the Chinese banking system. Aside from determining monetary policy and representing the country internationally, the PBOC's role is to reduce overall risk and promote stability. The PBOC regulates lending and foreign exchange among banks and supervises the country's payment and settlement system.

5.1.2   ICBC's domestic competition

ICBC stands out as the clear leader among China's "Big Four" banks. The CCB focuses more on medium- to long-term credit for specialized construction projects, whereas ABC deals mainly with small farmers and large agricultural wholesale companies. The smallest of the "Big Four" is BoC. It initially performed all essential bank operations for the Chinese market, but eventually spun off a portion of the bank to become what is now ICBC.

The largest banks in China are HSBC (United Kingdom), JPMorgan Chase & Co. (United States), and BNP Paribas (France), with $2.57 trillion, $2.45 trillion, and $2.4 trillion in assets, respectively in 2018. While ICBC has heavily invested in its investment banking capabilities, reaching a top 10 spot in 2018 as an M&A advisor, increased competition from US-based banks, especially from their trading/distribution network, has challenged ICBC's ascension in M&A activity in Asia (see Fig. 5.1). Equity capital markets have also been one of ICBC's core businesses. The bank's presence in the top 20 book runners in Asia demonstrates its intention to capture a leading market share (see Fig. 5.1). It still has a long way to go, however, before its rankings in Asian M&As and equity markets match its assets and market capitalization.

Asia M&A league tables – 2018 – USD millions			
Rank	**Advisor**	**Amount ($)**	**Deals**
1	Morgan Stanley	75,492	32
2	JP Morgan	72,714	22
3	Goldman Sachs	65,504	27
4	China International Capital	62,955	50
5	Citi	60,565	29
6	UBS	56,602	21
7	CITIC	49,649	65
8	Ernst & Young	42,391	65
9	**ICBC**	**32,633**	**152**
10	Bank of America Merrill Lynch	23,309	18

Asia equity league tables – 2018 – USD millions			
Rank	**Book runner**	**Proceeds ($)**	**Issues**
1	Goldman Sachs	14,060	61
2	Morgan Stanley	11,986	58
3	Citi	10,017	62
4	Credit Suisse	7681	50
5	JP Morgan	7665	46
6	Bank of America Merrill Lynch	7599	23
7	UBS	6131	39
8	China International Capital	5432	28
9	CITIC	3558	31
10	Deutsche Bank	2986	25
…			
19	**ICBC**	**1823**	**16**

Fig. 5.1 Asia (ex. Japan) 2018 M&A/equity capital markets league tables.
Source: Authors based on data from Capital IQ, (Accessed February 2019).

5.2   ICBC'S journey to the top

By 2007, ICBC clawed its way up into the number one spot in the Fortune Global 500, ousting US-based Citibank (founded in 1812). Since then, the company has been ranked first in the world in terms of assets, deposits, loans, customers, and employees. In 2018, with $4.1 trillion in assets, the bank earned $105.42 billion in operating income and $43.43 billion in net profit, the highest in the global banking industry (see Fig. 5.2).

As for the bank's other financial metrics, the return on equity (ROE) was between 15% and 17%, the net interest margin was 2.3% and the return on assets (ROAs) was around 1%. ICBC's 2018 market capitalization of $345 billion made it the second largest bank in the world after JP Morgan, with a capitalization of $390 billion. With more than 453,000 employees, 5.7 million corporate customers (7033 of them big companies) and 607 million individual customers, ICBC operated more than 16,800 Chinese domestic institutions and 400 overseas institutions in 2018.

In USD millions, except for percentages	2018 ($)	2017 ($)	+/– ($)	Growth (%)
Net interest income	83,233	77,268	5965	7.7
Noninterest income	21,124	22,730	–1606	–7.0
Operating income	**105,418**	**99,998**	**5420**	**5.4**
Less: Operating expenses	28,233	27,557	676	2.5
Less: Impairment losses	23,493	18,910	4,583	24.2
Operating profit	**53,693**	**53,531**	**162**	**0.3**
Shares of profits of associates and joint ventures	447	437	10	2
Profit before taxation	54,142	53,968	174	0.3
Less: Income tax expense	10,674	11,424	–750	–7
Net profit	**43,429**	**42,543**	**886**	**2.1**
Attributable to: equity holders of the parent co.	43,276	42,336	940	2.2
Noncontrolling interests	151	207	–56	–27

Fig. 5.2 Key income statement items, 2017–2018. *Note:* Original data in 2018 Annual Report is in renminbi and authors have converted in US$. The average exchange rate for the 2017 period was US$ 1 = RMB 6.7567. The exchange rate used for 2018 was USD 1 = RMB 6.8785. Growth rates calculated in USD using average rates for the period.
Source: Authors based on data from ICBC Annual report. http://www.icbc-ltd.com/ICBCLtd/Investor%20Relations/Financial%20Information/Financial%20Reports/, (Accessed February 2019); Capital IQ.

Beyond China, the bank has over 17,000 offices in 51 territories (24 in Asia, 17 in Europe, 5 in North America, 3 in South America, and 2 in Oceania). According to its 2018 annual report, pretax profits outside China were $4.12 billion, an increase of 5% with respect to 2017, on $380 billions in assets. Despite this impressive performance, foreign activities represent only 9.5% of ICBC's total, even as the bank supports the Belt and Road Initiative (BRI, see Chapter 3).

ICBC's main operating segments are corporate banking (49.2% of the total operating income), personal banking (36.7%), and treasury operations (13.4%) (see Fig. 5.3). In addition, ICBC also offers wealth management services. The share of ICBC's profit before taxation derived from corporate banking decreased 1.2% points in 2018 from 2017. This change signaled increased competition facing the company. The bank's product strategy is to increase the participation of mortgages, consumer loans, credit cards, and personal banking in its domestic market (see Fig. 5.4).

ICBC was the first Chinese bank to adhere to the Equator Principles, a number of social and environmental standards it adopted in 2003. In concert with other banks, it also contributed to the Principles for Responsible Banking launched by the United Nations Environment Program Finance Initiative (UNEPFI), which provides guidance on how banks can embed sustainability into their businesses. The draft principles were debuted in November 2018. Transparency and accountability are at the heart of this initiative aimed at rebuilding trust in the financial industry. As of 2018, both The Banker and Brand Finance ranked ICBC as the most valuable banking brand in the world for the third year in a row (see Fig. 5.5).

In USD millions, except for percentages	2018		2017	
	Amount ($)	%	Amount ($)	%
Operating income	**105,418**	**100.0**	**99,998**	**100.0**
Corporate banking	51,444	48.8	49,176	49.2
Personal banking	39,760	37.7	36,692	36.7
Treasury operations	13,445	12.8	13,409	13.4
Others	767	0.7	721	0.7
Profits before taxation	**54,141**	**100.0**	**53,968**	**100.0**
Corporate banking	22,056	40.7	22,625	41.9
Personal banking	20,976	38.7	20,401	37.8
Treasury operations	11,024	20.4	10,762	19.9
Others	85	0.2	179	0.3

Fig. 5.3 ICBC operating segment information. The average exchange rate for the 2017 period was US$ 1 RMB 6.7567. The exchange rate used for 2018 was US$ 1 = 6.8785 RMB.
Source: Authors based on data from ICBC Annual report. http://www.icbc-ltd.com/ICBCLtd/Investor%20Relations/Financial%20Information/Financial%20Reports/, (Accessed February 2019); Capital IQ.

Fig. 5.4 Personal and corporate banking customer increase (2015–18).
Source: Authors based on data from ICBC Annual report. http://www.icbc-ltd.com/ICBCLtd/Investor%20Relations/Financial%20Information/Financial%20Reports/, (Accessed February 2019).

In December 2017, Wang Zhaoxing, vice-chairman of the China Banking Regulatory Commission, indicated that it behooved commercial banks to innovate and extend their coverage in rural areas (Reuters, 2017). This prompted ICBC to expand its operations to attend new market segments, especially small and micro businesses. According to ICBC's chairman Yi Huiman (who resigned in January 2019 to be the head of the banking regulatory body in China), ICBC established its Inclusive Finance Department in part to align its corporate strategy to national strategies.

ICBC's initial public offering (IPO) represented a major milestone, forcing the bank to modernize its corporate governance and improve its transparency. On October 16, 2006, the company offered its first public shares to investors in mainland China,

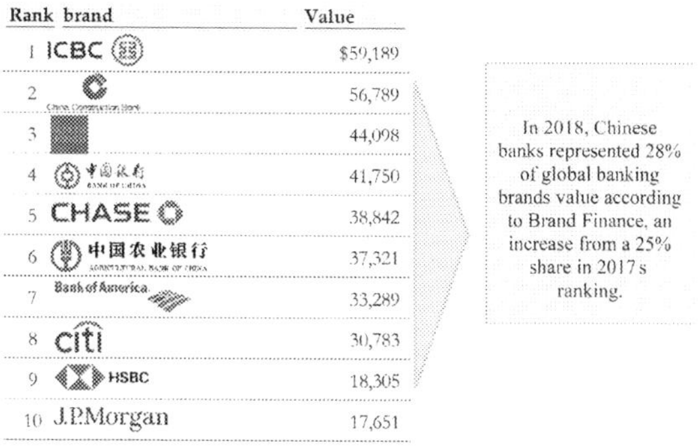

Rank brand	Value
1 ICBC	$59,189
2 China Construction Bank	56,789
3	44,098
4 中国银行 BANK OF CHINA	41,750
5 CHASE	38,842
6 中国农业银行 AGRICULTURAL BANK OF CHINA	37,321
7 Bank of America	33,289
8 citi	30,783
9 HSBC	18,305
10 J.P.Morgan	17,651

In 2018, Chinese banks represented 28% of global banking brands value according to Brand Finance, an increase from a 25% share in 2017s ranking.

Fig. 5.5 Most valuable banking brands 2018 (in million US$).
Source: Authors based on data from https://brandfinance.com/knowledge-centre/reports/brand-finance-banking-500-2019/, (Accessed February 2019).

as well as the Shanghai and Hong Kong Stock Exchanges, thereby becoming the first Chinese company to trade on both exchanges concurrently. The initial issuance brought in a record high of $21.9 billion. On October 27, ICBC successfully listed on both the Shanghai and Hong Kong Stock Exchanges and closed the day with a combined share value of $141.9 billion. ICBC immediately ranked fifth among other global listed banks. Its IPO broke 28 records in the process and was named "The IPO of the Century."

Before ICBC's IPO, the Chinese government was the company's main source of corporate financing. For example, in 2005, the government provided $1 billion in capital. The Ministry of Finance (MOF) also allocated 124 billion RMB, or $17.8 billion for ICBC's later use. Around 2005, in order to improve the country's banking operations and cultivate more independent corporate governance, China's State Council had opted for the adoption of international banking standards and the restructuring of traditional ownership. ICBC became a joint-stock limited company that year in October when Huijin, a state-owned investment company, acquired half of the ordinary shares (see Fig. 5.6).

Even as its growth ballooned, ICBC has retained its general structure. It divided its operations into segments, separating the head office from the various branches. The bank continued to refine its company structure by developing a collaborative marketing system and encouraging transversal collaborations from within. In 2013, ICBC implemented the "big corporate banking" strategy and incubated a "customer manager + product manager + service solution" integrated model to better address customer needs. The bank also established four lines of financial products, namely aircraft financing, ship financing, global syndication, and export buyer's credit.

5.3 ICBC'S metamorphosis

ICBC's transformation from a state-owned bank to a major global player in the banking industry began in the early 1990s, when the Chinese government embarked on sweeping financial system reforms in response to operational inefficiencies.

Class A shareholders	# Shares held	% of total A shares	% of total A+H shares
Central Huijin	123,717,852,951	45.9	34.7
Ministry of Finance	123,316,451,864	45.7	34.6
Ping an Life Insurance	3,687,330,676	1.4	1.0
China Securities Finance	2,416,131,564	0.9	0.7
Wutongshu Investment	1,420,781,042	0.5	0.4
Central Huijin Asset Management	1,013,921,700	0.4	0.3
China Life Insurance	1,000,845,252	0.2	0.3
Others	13,384,131,277	5.0	3.8
Total A shares	**269,957,446,326**	**100.0**	**75.8**
Class H shareholders	86,151,664,334		24.2
Total A&H shareholders	**356,109,110,660**		**100.0**

Fig. 5.6 ICBC's shareholding structure.
Source: Authors based on data from Bloomberg, published June 2018 and ICBC's website, published by December 2017, ICBC annual report, http://www.icbc-ltd.com/ICBCLtd/Investor%20 Relations/Financial%20Information/Financial%20Reports/, (Accessed February 2019).

Numerous bottlenecks contributed to a massive concentration of nonperforming loans (NPLs), as state-owned banks without managerial independence provided financial services to state-owned enterprises (SOEs). As late as 1995, SOEs received 90% of all lending for fixed investment (Lardy, 1998).

By 1997, however, the Chinese government was negotiating China's entrance as a new member of the World Trade Organization (WTO). To join, China needed to institute deep reforms to its banking sector that would improve competitiveness by: (1) strengthening balance sheets; (2) establishing specific criteria for state-owned banks to make loans to SOEs; (3) improving SOE financial management; and (4) refining corporate governance. In 1998, the MOF issued $32.6 billion in bonds to improve capital adequacy in response to outstanding NPLs. One year later, China's State Council established four asset management companies (AMCs), which paired with CCB, ABC, BoC, and ICBC, assumed as much as $208 billion (about 1.4 trillion RMB) of the NPLs (Luo, 2016). These measures proved useful, as NPL ratios fell after China fully joined the WTO in 2001, and by 2005 the ratio had plunged to 4.5%.

5.3.1 Corporate governance

ICBC had to evolve in its corporate governance practices as a result of its expansion. Early on, the bank set its sights on becoming a modern, world-class financial enterprise, and it has not been shy about transforming its business as part of a broader development strategy. As noted in other chapters, the Global Financial Crisis (GFC) did not impact China harshly; Chinese banks took advantage of the crisis to balance assets and capital, improve quality of service and benefits to customers, as well as make cost and efficiency improvements. ICBC enhanced its operations and built a more flexible framework to promote further business transformation and development. The bank then began to explore internationalization, testing out cross-border and cross-market service capabilities.

ICBC's corporate governance evolution has closely tracked Chinese economic reforms (see Chapter 4). As China's markets evolved and competition increased, ICBC became more agile and better suited for globalization. Today, ICBC's board of directors comprises 13 members, 2 of them act as executive directors, 5 as nonexecutive directors, and 6 as independent nonexecutive directors. The board's attention to detail, openness to discussion, and interchange of ideas certainly contributed to ICBC's success. According to sources, the board meetings are more operational than those in regular Western banks, and show little formality.

In addition to its particular board of directors' meetings, ICBC ushered in an integrated corporate governance structure that leverages the Communist Party's participation in communication, monitoring, and decision-making. In addition to its board of directors, ICBC submits to a supervisory board that implements general oversight to prevent misconduct and abuse of power. ICBC over time switched to a stakeholder-oriented corporate governance approach, which integrated Western practices into its system. The bank adopted a hierarchical structure for shareholder meetings and included independent directors and committees in decision-making processes. ICBC's hybrid approach to corporate governance has been widely rewarded, from the likes of the Corporate Governance Asia Journal to Best Overall Investor Relations from IR Global Rankings, as well as other accolades.

In January 2019, ICBC's Chairman Yi Huiman was appointed the head of China Securities Regulatory Commission (CSRC) with the mandate to globalize China's capital markets and increase the participation of foreign investors, who owned only 3% of China's total market capitalization. Yi had been at ICBC for more than 30 years and served as its president since 2013. In April 22, 2019, Chen Siqing (chairman of BoC since 2017) was appointed the new ICBC chairman.

While ICBC's long-term strategy focused on stability, minor structural adjustments and innovation, the bank set out on three major short-term projects in 2019, namely:

- reconstructing its credit management foundation;
- comprehensively disposing of non-performing loans; and
- improving its enterprise risk management.

5.4 Domestic and international expansion

In its first decade, ICBC focused on supporting large- and medium-sized SOEs. After making significant progress in deposits, loans, and foreign exchange, the bank expanded into credit cards, international business, and other emerging businesses, as cause and effect of the government's "opening-up policy."

5.4.1 Domestic development

By 1984, ICBC took steps to give its branches six independent rights that mirrored reforms passed by the CPC Central Committee: business operation, credit fund allocation, interest rate floating, appointment and dismissal of employees, decision-making for labor organizations, and disposal of retained profit. The bank tried to balance branches' power, responsibility, interest, and incentives by focusing on "target-oriented operation" and "retained profit," launching a self-disciplined capital manage-ment system and a responsibility system for loan risk management. It established an accounting management and financial budget system, focusing on economic benefits and cost calculation. The bank also shaped its audit management foundation and set up strict management and business inspection systems.

These changes combined with the rapid growth in ICBC's main businesses set the stage for tremendous expansion. Deposits increased 420% within the first 10 years of development, while the company's loans portfolio grew 350%, making ICBC China's largest bank. ICBC began to build a culture revolving around its employees' education and service quality. It improved its public image, and these efforts allowed ICBC to achieve a 710% growth in fixed asset balance.

In 2000, ICBC transitioned to become a state-owned bank, and in the process trans-formed the way information was gathered and stored throughout the bank. ICBC intro-duced an internally monitored system controlled by the head office. By the early 2010s, ICBC expanded into local urban markets. The bank continued to refine its national development strategy and reform its various branches for increased market competi-tiveness. The bank also focused on the online space, improving its e-banking service.

5.4.2   Expanding into regional and other emerging markets

ICBC entered external markets by the mid-2000s. It introduced various strategic (long-term) investors, setting up the Strategic Investment Promotion Working Group in close partnership with potential investors. After lengthy negotiations, ICBC identified the Goldman Sachs Investment Group as its first strategic investor, signing a strategic investment and cooperation agreement in Beijing in 2006. As per the agreement, the Goldman Sachs Investment Group invested $3.78 billion into ICBC. Such shareholder agreements laid the foundation for ICBC to go public and provided the bank with enough resources to make its foray into the international capital markets.

Several years later, after its successful IPO, ICBC used its reserves to weather the GFC. Throughout the crisis, ICBC continued to optimize its internationalization strategy, building its network of overseas institutions between 2005 and 2014. It also founded numerous subsidiaries, including for instance ICBC Credit Suisse Asset Management, ICBC Financial Leasing, and ICBC International. The company utilized greenfield entry into foreign markets, a winning overseas strategy, which it called the "branches + specialized product lines" approach.

In addition to its greenfield strategy, ICBC acquired local banks as a means to enter markets in other regions. In 2000, it acquired Union Bank and, by 2004, Fortis Bank Asia, both were based in Hong Kong. ICBC also acquired Thailand-based ACL Bank, rebranding it into ICBC Thai. Overall, the company has been China's most active bank in international expansion. To date, ICBC has set aside $7 billion for acquisitions in Asia, South Africa, and America, and its largest M&A transaction was a nearly $5.5 bil-lion deal for a 20% share of Standard Bank in South Africa. Such partnerships have been especially lucrative as ICBC expands its sphere of influence beyond the Chinese market.

ICBC went on to accomplish the major milestone of expanding into South America, before moving into Europe and the Middle East. In 2011, ICBC reached an agreement with the Standard Bank of South Africa on the sale of an 80% stake in Standard Bank Argentina (SBA) for $600 million. This was the first time a Chinese bank acquired ownership of a commercial bank outside Asia. At the time of the transaction, SBA ranked 25th among Argentina's 80 banks. SBA operated a network of nearly 100 branches and 700+ ATMs serving 910,000 personal customers, 30,000 small and medium enterprises, and 1500 corporate clients. As of 2018, ICBC Argentina expanded to 119 branches and 877 ATM in 18 provinces with 3700 employees. With 1 million personal accounts, 40,700 SMEs, and 1821 corporate clients, the bank's total assets reached $4.9 billion. Performance metrics indicated a strong ROAs profile (2.4%) and a bad loans rate of only 1.2%. After the takeover, ICBC became the largest Chinese bank in Latin America, with the biggest business scale and most extensive branch network. ICBC later opened offices in Brazil, Peru, and Mexico. Beyond Asia and Latin America, ICBC also opened branches and offices in Europe (Austria, France, Germany, Italy, Luxemburg, Poland, Spain) and the U.S. among others as well as in the Middle East (Abu Dhabi, Kuwait, Qatar, and Saudi Arabia). By 2015, ICBC purchased Turkey's TekstilBank and formed its ICBC Turkey subsidiary. ICBC entered Russia in 2016, and Switzerland in 2017.

ICBC's international expansion was a natural step in its growth and search for global leadership. As local markets matured, demand for loans fell, and ICBC looked for new growth markets abroad. ICBC's close ties with the Chinese government often influenced the bank's expansion. One prominent example is ICBC's push for international expansion after the Chinese government implemented the "Going Global" strategy. Beginning in the early 2000s, the government encouraged the country's four largest banks to move into overseas markets knowing that Chinese banks would provide financial services to Chinese businesses that had also begun operations in foreign markets (see Chapter 2).

5.5   Drivers for going global

ICBC's international expansion grew the market for China's renminbi. With government support, the company was the first major Chinese bank to introduce renminbi-based products internationally. The increasing global prominence of the renminbi afforded the Chinese government more influence with the WTO and the International Monetary Fund (IMF), a goal for the Chinese government, due to the renminbi's underrepresentation in global trade relative to China's level of involvement. Meanwhile, Chinese banks were better positioned to address the needs of Chinese companies in other regions, easing the transfer of money between mainland China and international locations. Lastly, as outbound tourism from China thrives, ICBC has yet another incentive to expand into those markets.

ICBC was able to leverage its value chain to spur the company's international growth. As the Chinese government expanded the finance industry, ICBC was quick to grasp the importance—and differences—between the various members in its value chain. ICBC has carefully managed three major stakeholders: the Chinese government, Chinese companies, and the general Chinese public. It needed to ensure complete compliance with strict government protocols and had to tailor its strategies according to the government's vision for the finance industry. Early on, ICBC recognized that it would also need to closely ally with the Chinese companies it relied on for business and mirror their international expansion. This ensured a long-lasting mutually beneficial relationship.

ICBC's management was integral to the company's success. In the bank's nascent years, efficiency was key in all of its operations, without concern for elaborate offices (a different strategy from other banks, which tend to use luxury offices as an indicator of the bank's strength), effectively optimizing its limited resources. As ICBC expanded internationally, the company struck the delicate balance between independence and state ownership. It emphasized building a strong business culture from within, while also refining its asset portfolio.

Post-IPO, ICBC improved its management system for balance sheet consolidation risk and country-specific risk. In doing so, it gradually implemented a reputation risk management system to establish and improve the bank's all-around risk management organizational structure and mechanism. These improvements enabled the company to juggle operation principles of capital constraints and balance risk and return. It also set in motion additional controls for ensuring group-wide compliance.

5.6   E-banking innovation

ICBC pioneered internet banking in China. Through "operation quick loan," it granted credits to 600,000 small and micro enterprises amounting to $14 billion. Likewise, it heralded the "e-mortgage quick loan" which approves mortgages in 2 days. By 2017, the bank introduced ICBC Easy Loan, a credit-based personal loan product that disbursed $14.5 billion in new loans during the year. The product won the "Top 10 Internet Financial Innovation Product Award" from Chinese Banker magazine. The company received several awards including the Best Internet Bank in China from Asian Banker and the Best Mobile Bank award from Financial Money magazine, to name a few.

According to McKinsey & Company, about 40% of Asian mass affluent customers now prefer online or mobile banking to in-person banking; in the under-40 years of age bracket, around half prefer digital banking, a share that is growing. Digital banking is expected to reach 1.7 billion Asian consumers by 2020, and ICBC is poised to capture much of the market (see for instance the increase in the number of mobile banking users in ICBC platform in Fig. 5.7). And yet, ICBC faces strong competition from mobile payments leaders Tencent's WeChat Pay and Alibaba's Alipay, which together account for 90% of total mobile payments in China. In 2015, both companies created their own mobile banks: WeBank and MyBank.

5.7   Moving forward

Bold ambition, key strategic expansions, and effective management catapulted ICBC to its position as a global leader. Like many other Chinese firms, ICBC benefited

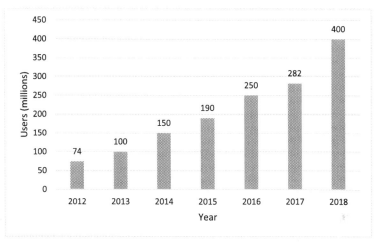

Fig. 5.7 Mobile banking users in ICBC's platform.
Source: Authors based on data from 2018-State-of-the-Industry-Report-on-Mobile-Money-1.
pdf, 2018 ICBC Annual Report, (Accessed February 2019).

from the Chinese domestic market's rapid growth, leveraging government policies to support parallel growth into foreign markets. Further, ICBC embraced an explicit strategy of learning from competitors, thereby innovating with new products and services.

With its vast resources, ICBC weathered the GFC as an opportunity rather than a setback. Leaning into the resilience of the Chinese economy, the bank was able to continue its international expansion while other global leaders were retrenching internationally. While ICBC is loath to make long-term predictions, the company's leadership is confident that it has the skills and resources to overcome future challenges as they arise. These include ongoing trade tensions that may decelerate national and global growth, the rise of new technologies like blockchain and artificial intelligence that have the potential to disrupt some aspects of banking relationships, and the liberalization of interest rates on deposits and loans, which is expected to narrow interest rate differentials.

As of 2019, ICBC views overseas expansion as an important area of growth. In particular, supporting China's BRI will boost ICBC's portfolio of loans in target countries. The bank expects the renminbi to become a more generally accepted international currency, but China's domestic market still retains its tremendous growth potential, which the company is well positioned to continue to tap.

Acknowledgments

We gratefully acknowledge the support of César Bustillos, MBA'19 at S.C. Johnson School of Management at Cornell University, as well as ICBC executives, for their assistance in this chapter.

References

Bank of International Settlements [BIS]. (2017). *Quarterly report.*
IBIS World. (2018). *IBIS world industry report. Commercial banks in China.* (Retrieved 1 July 2018) from IBIS World database.
Fortune. (2018). *Fortune Global 500 directory.* http://fortune.com/fortune500/ (Accessed May 2019).
Lardy, N. (1998). *China's unfinished economic revolution.* Brookings Institution Press.
Luo, D. (2016). *The development of the Chinese financial system reform of Chinese commercial banks.* Palgrave Macmillan.
Reuters. (2017). *China's commercial banks need to focus more on small businesses: Regulator.* https://uk.reuters.com/article/us-china-banking/chinas-commercial-banks-need-to-focus-more-on-small-businesses-regulator-idUKKBN1E004Q. (Accessed July 2018).

Further reading

Allen, F., Huang, D., Qian, J., & Zhao, M. (2011). *The initial public offering of the industrial and commercial bank of China (ICBC).* http://finance.wharton.upenn.edu/~allenf/download/Vita/ICBC-Final-27nov11.pdf. (Accessed April 2019).
Barquin, S., & Vinayak, H. V. (2015). *Digital banking in Asia: What do consumers really want?*
Bartel, J., & Huang, Y. (2000). *Dealing with the Bad Loans of the Chinese Banks John Bartel and Yiping Huang.* Discussion Paper No. 13. https://www8.gsb.columbia.edu/apec/sites/apec/files/files/discussion/boninhuang.pdf. (Accessed April 2019).
Casanova, L., & Miroux, A. (2018). *Emerging markets report: Emerging markets reshaping globalization.* Emerging Markets Institute, S.C. Johnson School of Management, Cornell University. https://www.johnson.cornell.edu/wp-content/uploads/sites/3/2019/04/EMR2018_V3_FIN-11Jan.pdf.
Cerutti, E., & Zhou, H. (2018). *The Chinese banking system: Much more than a domestic giant.* https://voxeu.org/article/chinese-banking-system. (Accessed June 2019).
Forbes. The world's largest public companies. (n.d.) https://www.forbes.com/global2000/list/#header:profits_sortreverse:true (Accessed June 2019).
Fortune. Fortune Global 500 directory. (n.d.). http://fortune.com/fortune500/ (Accessed May 2019).
Geng, X., Yang, X., & Janus, A. (2009). China's new place in a world in crisis. In *State-owned enterprises in China reform dynamics and impact.* https://www.jstor.org/stable/pdf/j.ctt24hcrw.16.pdf. (Accessed June 2019).
GSMA. (2019). *State of the Industry Report on Mobile Money 2018.* http://2018-State-of-the-Industry-Report-on-Mobile-Money-1.pdf. (Accessed June 2019).
Industrial and Commercial Bank of China Limited [ICBC]. (2006). *Hong Kong offering memorandum October 20, 2006.*
Industrial and Commercial Bank of China Limited [ICBC]. (2017). *Annual report 2017.* http://v.icbc.com.cn/userfiles/Resources/ICBCLTD/download/2018/720180423.pdf. (Accessed June 2019).
Industrial and Commercial Bank of China Limited [ICBC]. (2018a). *Annual report 2018.* http://v.icbc.com.cn/userfiles/Resources/ICBCLTD/download/2019/2018AnnualReport20190425.pdf. (Accessed June 2019).

Industrial and Commercial Bank of China Limited [ICBC]. (2018b). *Corporate strategy*. http://www.icbc-ltd.com/icbcltd/About%20Us/Corporate%20Strategy/. (Accessed June 2019).

Industrial and Commercial Bank of China Limited [ICBC]. (2018c). *ICBC SEC filings*. https://www.sec.gov/litigation/admin/2018/34-83251.pdf. (Accessed June 2019).

International Monetary Fund. (2017). *People's Republic of China: Financial system stability assessment*. Country Report No. 17/358. https://www.imf.org/~/media/Files/Publications/CR/2017/cr17358.ashx. (Accessed June 2019).

Lu, A. (2012). *Industrial and commercial Bank of China: Governance lessons from east to west*.

Pan, G. (2019). *Visiting scholar IMF presentation. strategic transformation: Chinese banking in a dynamic and mature economy*. https://www.brookings.edu/wp-content/uploads/2012/04/0519_pan_presentation.pdf. (Accessed June 2019).

Reinhart, C. (2017). *The curious case of the missing defaults*. Project Syndicate.

Sun, Y., Jayaram, I., & Kassir, K. (2017). *Dance of the lions and dragons JUNE 2017 How are Africa and China engaging, and how will the partnership evolve?* McKinsey Report June 2017.

The Banker. (n.d.). Top 1000 World Banks 2018: Top 5 by Tier 1: Global. http://www.thebanker.com/Top-1000 (Accessed June 2019).

Part II

Strategic advantages and challenges for Chinese firms

State grid, powering China and the world

China's strides in Ultra High Voltage technology are a 'Sputnik moment' (the Soviet Union's 1957 launch of first earth-orbiting space satellite, ahead of U.S.) for the U.S.

Steven Chu, former U.S. Secretary of Energy

Acronyms

ADMIE	Independent Power Transmission Operator S.A.
BRI	Belt and Road Initiative
CCP	Chinese Communist Party
CSR	corporate social responsibility
EBITDA	Earnings before interest, taxes, depreciation, and amortization
EDP	Electricidade de Portugal
GDP	gross domestic product
GEI	Global Energy Interconnection
GEIDCO	Global Energy Interconnection Development and Cooperation Organization
GSEP	Global Sustainable Electricity Partnership
IEA	International Energy Agency
IEC	International Electrotechnical Commission
NGCP	The National Grid Corporation of the Philippines
REN	Redes Energeticas Nacionais
SASAC	State-owned Assets Supervision and Administration Commission
SGCC	State Grid Corporation of China
SGSPAA	SGSP Australia Assets Pty Ltd.
SOE	state-owned enterprise
SPI	Singapore Power International
UHV	ultrahigh voltage
WBCSD	World Business Council for Sustainable Development

From smart cities to electrified transportation, the energy sector is becoming increasingly relevant to larger swathes of the world economy, encompassing innovations beyond the production and transmission of power. The explosion in demand for electrical power against the looming backdrop of climate change has revealed the tremendous challenges related to transitioning to clean and efficiently produced energy. To power human activity worldwide, energy demand is expected to rise 28% by 2040 (EIA, 2017). Further, the energy sector also presents a historical market opportunity, particularly as the middle class grows in size across emerging markets, generating unprecedented need for the energy sector in the coming years.

The Era of Chinese Multinationals. https://doi.org/10.1016/B978-0-12-816857-8.00006-9

China has grappled with increased energy needs for over a decade. In 2011, it became the largest energy consumer in the world (EIA, n.d.). In 2016, it accounted for about 18 % of the world energy consumption. To meet the growing challenges of its rising energy demand, the country founded State Grid Corporation of China (SGCC) in 2002. The State Power Corporation of China was broken into 11 smaller power generation and distribution companies. SGCC was by far the larger of two resulting transmission companies, and effectively operates as a monopoly across nearly 90% of the nation. SGCC is now a pioneer in the development of clean energy and the protagonist behind the "Global Energy Interconnection" (GEI), a project whose mandate entails the creation of a global electric grid powered by clean renewable energy (Power Magazine, 2016).

SGCC, a Chinese state-owned enterprise (SOE), has overseen the construction and operation of power grids within China, as well as across far-flung regions of the world. SGCC's mission is to promote re-electrification and to meet the power demand with clean and green alternatives. The Chinese SASAC (State-owned Assets Supervision and Administration Commission) classified the company as an A-Class enterprise based on its operation performance for 13 consecutive years. By 2018, SGCC provided energy to over 1.1 billion people, employed more than 1.6 million people, and reported $372 billion in revenues (see Fig. 6.1).

As of 2019, SGCC is a powerhouse energy provider, the world's largest energy and utilities company, and the second largest company in the world (based on revenues) in the 2018 Fortune Global 500 list. SGCC has positioned itself as a technology innovator, a policy entrepreneur, and an expanding international company with a clear goal: to champion GEI in the 21st century. While SGCC's success is increasingly

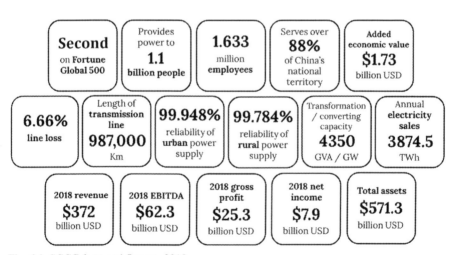

Fig. 6.1 SGCC facts and figures, 2018.
Source: Fortune Global 500 (2018 list); Standard & Poor's Capital IQ, (Accessed March 2019); State Grid Corporation of China [SGCC]. (2017). Corporate social responsibility report 2017. http://www.sgcc.com.cn/html/files/2018-08/29/20180829165036376453337.pdf (Accessed May 2019); Conversion RMB to US$ 6.8 (Capital IQ May 2019).

self-evident based on its extraordinary rise, it is still relatively unknown and little understood. Its success is a product of at least four major trends as follows.

First, like many other Chinese national champions, SGCC benefited from the tremendous growth of the domestic market. Its coverage area includes all of China, with the exception of only five provinces in Southern China (covered by China Southern Power Grid). This privilege affords the company the bandwidth to invest in innovation and prioritize long-term strategies, over short-term profits.

Second, SGCC negotiated favorable terms in its partnership with the Chinese government. The company's managerial team persuaded authorities to implement controversial energy projects in ultrahigh-voltage (UHV) technology in the name of universal electrification, a response to China's lack of interconnectivity and its enormous power shortages, especially in rural areas. The company has been well positioned to translate its ideas into solutions and even into federal policies, thereby playing an active role in key decision-making processes. SGCC opened the world's first 1100-kV UHV transmission line in January 2009.

Third, SGCC has prioritized investment in cutting-edge scientific research in UHV technology, technical innovation, and green energy development. Building on policies introduced in 2006 to boost R&D (research and development) in China, it allocated resources toward teams of experts focused on technological innovation, especially in clean and renewable sources. The company's competitive advantage is attributed to its capacity to match its research and manufacturing capabilities. For instance, given that pollution is one of China's perennial challenges, SGCC implemented an ambitious electricity replacement program to decrease emissions, which positioned the country on course to meet its targets set by the Paris Agreement (2016 United Nations Framework Convention on Climate Change).

Fourth, the company made significant strides beyond its domestic market. As of 2018, it owns and operates assets in Brazil, Australia, the Philippines, Portugal, Italy, Greece, and Hong Kong. This expansion shows its growing commitment to the GEI, launched by Chairman Liu Zhenya at the 2014 Global Sustainable Electricity Partnership (GSEP) Moscow summit. GEI envisions a global smart grid with UHV technology to generate, transmit, and distribute energy worldwide. SGCC's internationalization process runs parallel to China's attempt at developing a global grid. As such, the company's rapid internationalization is both the means and the end for the company to secure its place as a leader in the energy sector, the importance of which grows every year.

This chapter tracks the rise of SGCC as a major emerging multinational in both the Chinese ecosystem and beyond. It begins with SGCC's journey and the conditions that enabled its ascent. The chapter then analyzes the company's current status and ongoing strategy in the service of internationalization. Finally, it explores the challenges that SGCC faces as it aspires to champion the GEI.

6.1 The development of the electricity sector in China

China's electricity sector has evolved in three distinct phases (see Fig. 6.2). The first phase (1949–78) was characterized by the use of small unit provincial power grids that distributed low-voltage electricity.

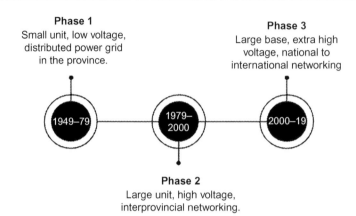

Fig. 6.2 The evolution of China's electricity sector.
Source: Authors based on SGCC CSR reports.

But by the 1970s, China's rapid economic growth was powered by coal, a fuel source that eventually yielded negative environmental externalities for the Chinese population.

The government faced power shortages heading into the second phase (1979–2000). The country could not keep up with rising demand, despite various attempts to decentralize the energy supply by permitting local governments and foreign companies to build their own energy generating facilities. By 1997, however, Beijing changed course by introducing a more market-based approach to the sector.

The third phase (2000–19) was marked by the advent of national networking. Regulatory reform designed in 2002 reinforced this new direction. The "Plant-Grid Separation" formally separated the generation and transmission assets of the State Electric Power Corporation into two grid companies: SGCC and the China Southern Power Grid Company (Gee, Zhu, & Li, 2007). SGCC subsumed the transmission assets (Ni, 2008).

6.2 Policy entrepreneurship

As an SOE, SGCC has actively promoted and implemented state reform efforts, including coordination with related state-level departments, as well as local party committees and officials. To date, SGCC has organized over 16,670 party centralized promotions, 36,627 centralized study activities, and 13,370 theme party classes (SGCC, 2017). Notwithstanding such support, according to scholar Xu Yi-Chong (2017), the company maintains a degree of autonomy from the CCP, which has enabled SGCC to centralize most of their subsidiaries under common governance. As a result, SGCC was empowered to diversify into financial services (banks, securities, insurance, etc.), which expanded financing sources and lowered costs.

6.3   Corporate social responsibility

In 2006, SGCC was the first Chinese SOE to issue a Corporate Social Responsibility (CSR) report (Marquis, Dai, Yang, & Wu, 2010). Since then, the company has issued a CSR report each year. Its main objective is to rally the public's support behind SGCC's work in global sustainability and China's development. Their CSR reports define 13 priorities: (1) party building (i.e., policy entrepreneurship), (2) quality development, (3) intrinsic safety, (4) excellent management, (5) innovation-driven strategy, (6) excellent service, (7) promoting rural development, (8) employee development, (9) mutually beneficial win-win cooperation, (10) corporate citizenship, (11) green development and environmental protection, (12) serving and promoting the Belt and Road Initiative (BRI), and (13) transparent operation (see Fig. 6.A1; SGCC, 2017).

According to its corporate responsibility report in 2017, SGCC has transported over 900 TWh from sustainable sources. In doing so, the company has reduced its emissions of CO_2 by 820 million tons, SO_2 by 1.40 million tons, NOx by 1.41 million tons, and of smoke and dust by 220,000 tons. The result of the large-scale adoption of UHV is culminating in a "super grid" that will connect China's six regional grids and distribute clean energy (wind, water, and solar), produced mainly in the northern and western parts of China.

6.4   Innovation and R&D: Smart grid innovation and UHV

SGCC attaches great importance to building strong and smart power grids. It has made a series of breakthroughs in grid technology. Since 2004, SGCC has made major progress in UHV theory, technology, standards, equipment, project construction, and operation (see Fig. 6.3). The company has mastered UHV power transmission technology with independent intellectual property rights and promoted Chinese UHV technology and equipment to go global.

UHV is a technology that enables large-capacity, long-distant power transmission with high efficiency and reduced line loss. (UHV refers to +1000 kV and ±800 kV power transmission.) With cables enabling power to be transported over vast distances at costs lower than traditional transmission lines, major power projects become in creasingly feasible, such as the construction of dams in remote areas and transmission

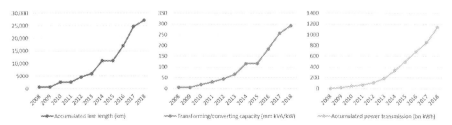

Fig. 6.3 SGCC UHV projects.
Source: http://www.sgcc.com.cn/ywlm/index.shtml, (Accessed May 2019).

of their electricity to far away cities. While German Siemens and Swedish-Swiss ABB also use UHV cable technology, SGCC became the first company to deploy the technology on a grand scale, and also contribute to the development of new global industry standards. Indeed, UHV technology has tremendous potential to help manage peaks and lows of energy consumption, one of the main challenges of the electricity sector. The longer, high-capacity lines make it possible to balance out the dimming sun in one time zone with, say, wind, hydroelectric, or geothermal energy several zones away.

In 2017, SGCC invested over \$1.1 billion in R&D (see Fig. 6.A2), a sum intended to underwrite the energy sector's transformation into sustainability. In particular, the firm invested in the development of clean energies, such as the electric vehicle (EVs) industry, electrical charging stations, renewable energy, new-generation power system, and smart grids with UHV technology. The latter innovation reduced the line loss percentage up to 6.7% each year, which translated into lower energy prices for consumers as operational costs were reduced. By 2017, SGCC accomplished the world's first $\pm 1100\,kV$ UHV DC (direct current) wall.

In 2017, demonstrating a yearly increase of 30%, SGCC integrated 280 GW of renewable energy capacity, which accounted for 19% of total installed capacity. Furthermore, the capacity of newly installed wind power and photovoltaic power was 13.44 and 48.77 GW, respectively. In 20 Chinese provinces and regions, renewable energy has become the first and second largest energy source. Renewable energy production amounted to over 10% of the amount of consumed electricity in 10 provinces and districts (SGCC, n.d.-a).

To date, the company has earned 69 National Awards for Science and Technology, including 2 grand prizes, 7 first prizes, and 60 second prizes. The company has obtained 91 China Patent Awards, including 7 Chinese Patent Gold Awards and 25 China Standards Innovation and Contribution Awards, in which 7 are first prizes. Additionally, the company has received 597 China Power Science and Technology Awards, including 59 first prizes. SGCC also ranked first among central SOEs for patent ownership and invention patent applications for 7 consecutive years (see Fig. 6.4). As of 2017, it had filed 73,350 patents.

6.5   Global energy interconnection

In 2014, SGCC proposed a network, the GEI, to stitch together the global electricity systems across borders and oceans, in alignment with BRI. The GEI envisions a global grid network with the means to transmit clean energy (hydropower, wind power, and solar power) from one continent to another in accordance with production and consumption capacities (Figs. 6.5 and 6.6). By 2050, SGCC seeks to develop large energy bases around the world with a grid network based on UHV transmission technologies, all at a proposed price tag of \$50 trillion. Moreover, the GEI was conceived as a strategy to tackle climate change and world energy security through the replacement of 80% of carbon-based global energy with renewable sources, reducing 66.7 billion tons of CO_2 emissions (SGCC, 2014).

The GEI plan is divided into three phases: (1) domestic interconnection (up to 2020), the objective of which is to consolidate the development of renewable energies

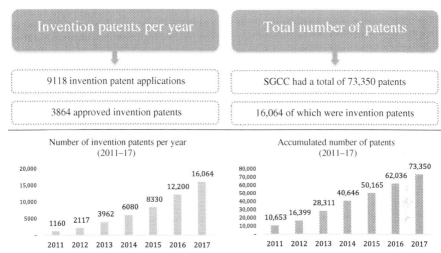

Fig. 6.4 Patents filed and accumulated by SGCC.
Source: SGCC company website, http://www.sgcc.com.cn/html/sgcc_main_en/
col2017112726/column_2017112726_1.shtml (Accessed May 2019).

and smart grids within its borders; (2) intracontinental interconnection (2020–30), in which SGCC plans to connect different grids across Asian countries and within other continents through efficient clean energy allocation; (3) intercontinental interconnection (2030–50), which consists of boosting wind power production in the Artic and solar power along the Equator. At this stage, the intention is to transmit energy across continents, bringing the main purpose of the GEI to fruition.

To meet its ambitious goals, in 2016, SGCC founded the Global Energy Interconnection Development and Cooperation Organization (GEIDCO), in cooperation with the United Nations "Sustainable Energy for All" program. GEIDCO is tasked with designing a framework of technical standards for the development of the GEI, organizing and coordinating the efforts of different actors in research and international cooperation, as well as providing consulting services for the development of the GEI. Around 100 organizations, government sectors, businesses, institutions, and universities from over 30 countries are members of the GEIDCO.

The GEI has gained extensive support from international organizations (e.g., IEA, WBCSD, and IEC) and from leaders such as former UN Secretary-General Ban Ki-moon to former World Bank Group President Jim Yong Kim. The Global Infrastructure Connectivity Alliance Initiative was launched at the 2016 G20 Summit. The GEI was included as a policy recommendation for world development as a means toward sustainable energy access for all, responsiveness to regional gaps, and support for South-South and North-South cooperation. As of 2018, the GEIDCO chairman is Liu Zhenya, former CEO of SGCC.

To date, SGCC has built up 10 cross-border power transmission lines between China and neighboring countries such as Russia, Mongolia, and Kyrgyzstan with a total power trade volume of more than 20 TWh. SGCC is also engaged in the early stages

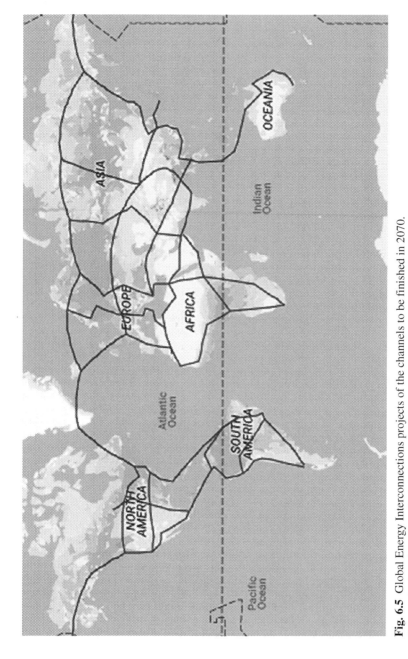

Fig. 6.5 Global Energy Interconnections projects of the channels to be finished in 2070.
Source: Authors based on Global Energy interconnection Development and Cooperation Organization GEIDCO 2018, https://en.geidco.org/journal/english/ (Accessed June 2019).

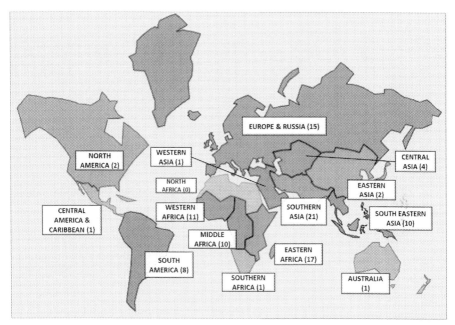

Fig. 6.6 Chinese announced investments in electricity grids.
Source: Authors based on various sources.

of the construction of China-Mongolia, China-Russia, China-Nepal, China-Pakistan, and other grid interconnection projects, and is exporting power to these countries. A series of power infrastructure connectivity projects are likewise underway. For instance, the Ethiopia-Kenya DC Power Transmission Project was operational at the end of 2018 and the Turkey-Iran Grid Interconnection back-to-back Project has started construction.

6.6   Internationalization strategy post-2004

Supported by the Chinese government's "Going Out" policy of internationalization, SGCC seized upon opportunities overseas. Encouraged by open markets, low acquisition costs, favorable international relations, and tax arbitrage abroad, SGCC spent over $7 billion from 2007 to 2014 in overseas acquisitions related to local infrastructures, equipment exports, standard setting, and international energy cooperation.

Beyond SGCC, Chinese investments in electricity grids are enormous. Since 2013, the country invested $102 billion for building or acquiring power transmission infrastructure in 83 projects across the world—in Africa (Nigeria, Eastern and Middle Africa, as well as South Africa), Europe, and Latin America (see Figs. 6.6 and 6.7). Inclusive of loans and investments in power plants, China spent a total of $452 billion in energy projects across the globe.

Fig. 6.7 SGCC's expansion from 2007 to 2016.
Source: Authors based on SGCC CSR reports.

Fig. 6.7 features major milestones in SGCC's expansion since 2007. In the following section, we highlight a selection of SGCC's overseas investments.

6.6.1 2007—Russia

SGCC began its internationalization in earnest in 2007, when it signed cooperation agreements with companies in Russia, which later became a power transmission project that would transform the Sino-Russia energy cooperation program.

6.6.2 2009—The Philippines

In 2009, a consortium of Monte Oro Grid Resources Corp., Calaca High Power Corporation, and SGCC bought the National Grid Corporation of the Philippines (NGCP) in 2009; SGCC's equity share was 40% (Capital IQ, 2018). The consortium now holds a 25-year concession (obtained in 2009) to operate the national power transmission network (see Table 6.1).

NGCP is a power system operator and transmission service provider that operates, maintains, and develops the state-owned power grid (NGCP, n.d.). By 2020, NGCP seeks to build a strong and unified power transmission network in the Philippines called "One Grid 2020" (BusinessWorld, 2018). Meanwhile, SGCC has supported NGCP in the development of strong grids to secure stable operations and to respond to natural disasters such as typhoons, tropical storms, and earthquakes (SGCC, 2013, 2016).

6.6.3 2010—Brazil

Due to the size of its landmass, Brazil is an ideal place to test the UHV grid. In addition, its concentration of electricity consumption in cities distant both from one another and from the power generators poses a unique challenge.

In 2010, SGCC bought seven transmission companies in Brazil for $1.7 billion (Bloomberg, 2018)[1] and secured 30-year operating rights, in the process becoming

---

[1] Expansion Transmissao de Energia Eletrica S.A., Expansion Transmissao Itumbiara Marimbondo S.A., Ribeirao Preto Transmissora de Energia Eletrica S.A., Itumbiara Transmissora de Energia S.A., Pocos de Caldas Transmissora de Energia Eletrica S.A., Serra Paracatu Transmissora de Energia S.A. and Serra da Mesa Transmissora de Energia Eletrica S.A.

Table 6.1 SGCC: Selected direct investments overseas.

Year	Country	Company	Stock hold (%)	Investment in million US$
2009	The Philippines	National Grid Corporation of the Philippines (NGCP)	40	$2370
2010	Brazil	Seven transmission companies	100	$1721.2
2010	Brazil	Two transmission lines	25	$125
2012	Brazil	Seven power lines	100	$941.96
2012	Portugal	Redes Energeticas Nacionais (REN)	25	$509.14
2012	Australia	ElectraNet South Australian Transmission Network	41.1	$522.33
2013	Australia	ElectraNet South Australian Transmission Network	5.65	NA
2013	Australia	Singapore Power International (Australia) Assets Pty. Ltd (SGSP)	60	NA
2013	Australia	AusNet Services Ltd.	19.9	$802.74
2014	Hong Kong	HK Electric Investments	21	NA
2014	Italy	Cassa Depositi e Prestiti Reti SpA (CDP RETI)	35	$2810.9
2015	Brazil	Atlántico & Montes Claros transmission lines	100	Undisclosed
2016	Brazil	CPFL Energia SA	94.74	$9981.9
2016	Greece	ADMIE	24	$356.82
2017	Australia	Darling Downs Pipeline Network	100	$292.12

Source: Standard & Poor's Capital IQ. (2018). Retrieved July 1, 2018 from Capital IQ database.

the fifth-largest transmission company in the country (SGBH, n.d.). Brazil Holding S.A. is an SGCC subsidiary founded in 2010. It contributes to the majority of SGCC's investments in Brazil, with revenues of $411 million, EBITDA at $225 million, and a net income of $32 million in 2016.

Also in 2010, SGCC bought 25% stakes in two other transmission lines for $125 million. This was followed by the purchase of seven power lines for $942 million in 2012 and of the Atlántico & Montes Claros transmission lines for an undisclosed amount in 2015 (Bloomberg, 2018). Two years later, SGCC acquired close to 95% of CPFL Energia SA in four different deals. By December 2017, SGCC completed the construction of the first phase of the Belo Monte hydropower UHV transmission project, the company's first overseas UHV project (SGCC, 2017).

As of 2019, SGCC operated nearly 6000 km of transmission lines in Southeastern Brazil covering Brasilia, Rio de Janeiro, São Paulo, and other large areas near loading centers. As a result of its $21 billion total investments in Brazil, SGCC is now the biggest power generation and distribution company in the country.

6.6.4   2012—Australia

In 2012, SGCC entered the Australian market by acquiring 41.1% of ElectraNet, an Australian company that operates the South Australian transmissions network, for $522 million. A year later, through its subsidiary State Grid International Development, it acquired 60% of Singapore Power International (SPI) (Australia) Assets Pty. Ltd from SPI. This acquisition established SGSPAA, which currently owns Jemena, an assets business company, and Zinfra, a services business company (Bloomberg, 2018; Capital IQ, 2018).

Jemena manages and operates energy infrastructure assets in the eastern states of Australia (New South Wales, Queensland), as well as gas and electricity distribution networks in Victoria for approximately 330,000 homes and businesses through approximately 6300 km of distribution network (Jemena, n.d.). Zinfra, meanwhile, is a leading service provider to the utility infrastructure sectors delivering a comprehensive range of engineering, operations, maintenance, and construction services nationally. Its services include engineering and design, project management, construction, civil, maintenance, and asset operations (Zinfra, n.d.).

Through its subsidiary State Grid International Australia Development Company, in 2013 SGCC bought almost 20% of AusNet Services Ltd. The deal was closed for $803 million, (Bloomberg, 2018; Capital IQ, 2018). By 2017, through its subsidiary SGSPAA, SGCC also bought the entire Darling Downs Pipeline Network from Origin Energy Ltd for $292 million (Bloomberg, 2018). SGCC now partly owns three of the five electricity distributors in Victoria: 20% of AusNet, 60% of Jemena and 34% of United Energy Electricity Distribution Victoria (United Energy, n.d.; Uhlmann, 2016).

6.6.5   2012—Portugal

In 2012, SGCC signed a strategic partnership with REN (Redes Energeticas Nacionais). It bought a 25% stake in the company for $509 million and became REN's largest shareholder. REN operates in two major business areas: (a) high-voltage electricity transmission and overall technical management of the National Electricity System and (b) transportation of high-pressure natural gas as well as overall technical management of the National Natural Gas System (REN, n.d.). The Portuguese government also granted a concession to operate a pilot area for generating electricity from sea waves to Enondas (Energia das Ondas. S.A) which is 100% owned by REN (REN, n.d.).

China Three Gorges, another Chinese state-owned firm, has also been seeking to increase its 23% stake in Electricidade de Portugal (EDP), which is the largest electricity company in Portugal, with the aim to control the 220,000 km-transmission lines and EDP's assets in Spain and also the company's assets in Brazil. Three Gorges' increasing control of EDP would complement SGCC's assets in Portugal. As of July 2019, the deal had not yet been completed.

6.6.6 2014—Italy

In 2014, SGCC bought a 35% stake of Cassa Depositi e Prestiti Reti S.p.A (CDP RETI) for $2811 million through its subsidiary State Grid Europe Limited (Bloomberg, 2018). CDP RETI, an Italian holding company, holds a close to 30% stake in Terna S.p.A., which manages the Italian transmission grid (the only transmission operator in the country and one of the largest in Europe). SGCC also procured a 30% stake in Snam S.p.A., which specializes in the construction and management of natural gas infrastructure via the Italian gas transportation network. Finally, SGCC owns a 26% stake in Italgas, the leading gas distribution network in Italy and the third largest in Europe (SGCC, n.d.-b; CDP, n.d.).

6.6.7 2014—Hong Kong

In 2014, SGCC acquired a 20% stake of HK Electric Investments (SGCC, 2014). The Hong Kong Electric Company Limited is the principal subsidiary of HK Electric Investments. It commenced operations in 1890 and is one of the longest established utility companies in the world. It is the electricity provider (generation, transmission, and distribution) to more than 570,000 commercial and residential customers in Hong Kong and Lamma Island (HK Electric Investments, n.d.). Clean energy generation has exceeded 30%. It has established smart power consumption and enhanced energy efficiency in public places (SGCC, 2016).

6.6.8 2016—Greece

In 2016, SGCC's subsidiary SIGD bought a 24% stake of Greece's ADMIE for $356.82 million. ADMIE runs and maintains the country's power transmission network (Bloomberg, 2018). The grid, which is integrated across many European countries, is a key power transmission corridor in Southern Europe. The purpose of ADMIE is to operate, control, maintain, and develop the Hellenic Electricity Transmission System (ESMIE) to ensure the country's electricity supply (ADMIE SA, n.d.).

In addition to the above-mentioned projects, SGCC has run projects in more than 20 countries including Cambodia, Equatorial Guinea, India, Indonesia, Iran, Kenya, Myanmar, Nigeria, Pakistan, Saudi Arabia, Sudan, Thailand, Venezuela, Vietnam, and Zambia.

6.7 Looking forward: Opportunities and challenges

SGCC is a major contributor to the development of electrical infrastructure in emerging markets. Their involvement has gained them a good reputation among other emerging and developing economies.

A number of areas offer growth opportunities to SGCC. For instance, to respond to the electricity needs of rural regions, SGCC is establishing an energy-services company to promote the distribution of clean energy to underdeveloped rural areas.

Another potential area for growth is related to the development of electric vehicles in China and the need for electric car charging stations. SGCC supports charging services for all kinds of electric vehicles, enabling consumers to install their own charging stations.

Smart network control presents another opportunity: SGCC is developing software to control the voltage and frequency at destination points throughout the network, enabling the system to react rapidly and automatically to shifting levels of supply and demand.

While SGCC aims to construct a worldwide energy network, the company may however face some setbacks. For instance, the differences in legal systems regulating global interconnecting energy transmission systems may constitute an obstacle to a global grid network. In addition, SGCC is poised to face increased hostility from Western countries regarding Chinese investments in critical infrastructure, such as energy. Heightened political and economic uncertainties since 2017 cast a shadow on the favorable regulatory environment. For instance, China Three Gorges has faced extended pushback; as of July 2019 it had not yet been able to take control of EDP, as mentioned above.

Furthermore, there may still be technological hurdles. For instance, while energy loss is reduced in UHV relative to alternative cables, there is still some loss, which could stymie plans for intercontinental grid integration.

The transition from fossil fuel to renewable energy is another challenge. China has not made full use of its existing renewable power plants. It is still heavily reliant on fossil fuel sources or nuclear power. Less than half of the UHV lines built or planned to date in China are intended to transmit electricity from renewable sources. This fact affects the company's objective of cutting greenhouse gas emissions and raises the question to what extent its long-distance lines can help clean up power generation.

SGCC is characterized by its success in UHV technology, as well as its ambitious and innovative proposals for building domestic and international interconnected grids. Such modern technology and speedy execution have catapulted China to electrifying the country in record time and with cost efficiency and move aggressively internationally. The creation of the world's first global electricity grid, however, will require international trust and cooperation. It remains to be seen whether SGCC can overcome political scrutiny and environmental challenges to ensure that the interconnected grid delivers on its promises.

Appendix

Fig. 6.A1 SGCC CSR report components.
Source: Authors' analysis of CSR Report 2017, http://www.sgcc.com.cn/ywlm/
socialresponsiility/pdf/csr2017_en.pdf, (Accessed July 2018).

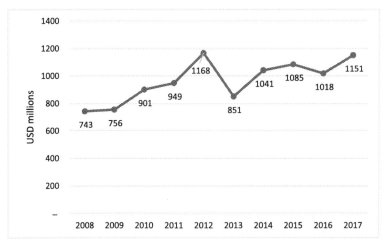

Fig. 6.A2 SGCC's R&D input over time, million US$. *Note:* Figure uses a 6.8 conversion rate from RMB to US$.
Source: SGCC, Corporate Social Responsibility Annual Reports, 2008–2017.

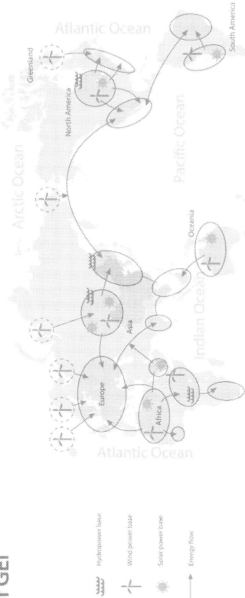

Fig. 6.A3 Sketch of the GEI's energy flow.
Source: State Grid Corporate Social Responsibility Report, 2015. http://www.sgcc.com.cn/images/ywlm/socialresponsiility/brief/2016/08/24/2F6590C1495CD544B95B193DC0982F8D.pdf. (Accessed July 2018).

References

ADMIE SA, (n.d.) www.admie.gr/en/company/ (Accessed June 2019).

Bloomberg, L. P. (2018). *Retrieved July 1, 2018 from Bloomberg database.*

BusinessWorld. (2018). *NGCP now expects unified power grid by 2020.* http://bworldonline. com/ngcp-now-expects-unified-power-grid-by-2020/ (Accessed July 2018).

Cassa Depositi e Prestiti [CDP]. CDP RETI. (n.d.) https://en.cdp.it/about-us/companies/cdp-reti.kl (Accessed July 2018).

Gee, R. W., Zhu, S., & Li, X. (2007). China's power sector: Global economic and environmental implications. *Energy Law Journal, 28,* 421.

HK Electric Investments. About us. (n.d.). https://www.hkelectric.com/en/about-us (Accessed July 2018).

Jemena. About us: Who we are. (n.d.). http://jemena.com.au/about/about-us/who-we-are (Accessed July 2017).

Marquis, C., Dai, N., Yang, D., & Wu, H. (2010). *State grid: Corporate social responsibility.* Harvard Business School, Case 410-141. June 2010. (Revised August 2010.) Harvard Business School Teaching Note 412-006, July 2011.

National Grid Corporation of the Philippines [NGCP]. (n.d.). https://www.ngcp.ph/corporate-profile.asp (Accessed June 2018).

Ni, C. C. (2008). *The Xinfeng Power Plant incident and challenges for China's electric power industry.* The Institute of Energy Economics, Tokyo, Working Paper (February 2007). https://eneken.ieej.or.jp/en/data/pdf/382.pdf (Accessed May 2019).

Power Magazine. (2016). *China rolls out proposal for worldwide grid.* February 25 http:// www.powermag.com/china-rolls-out-proposal-for-worldwide-grid/?pagenum=1 (Accessed May 2019).

REN. About REN: Company profile. (n.d.). https://www.ren.pt/en-GB/quem_somos/perfil_da_empresa/ (Accessed 1 July 2018).

Standard & Poor's Capital IQ. (2018). *Retrieved July 1, 2018 from Capital IQ database.*

State Grid Brazil Holding SA [SGBH]. http://www.stategridbr.com/about-us-en.html (Accessed July 2018).

State Grid Corporation of China [SGCC]. (2013). *Corporate social responsibility report 2013.* http://www.sgcc.com.cn/images/ywlm/socialresponsiility/brief/2014/10/23/2FE46B-3DA8D748AF3A0F1854CD73F75D.pdf (Accessed July 2018).

State Grid Corporation of China [SGCC]. (2014). *Corporate social responsibility report 2014.* http://www.sgcc.com.cn/html/files/2019-04/08/20190408100223322793249.pdf (Accessed May 2019).

State Grid Corporation of China [SGCC]. (2016). *Corporate social responsibility report 2016.* http://www.sgcc.com.cn/html/files/2018-07/28/20180728130448830583544.pdf (Accessed May 2019).

State Grid Corporation of China [SGCC]. (2017). *Corporate social responsibility report 2017.* http://www.sgcc.com.cn/html/files/2018-08/29/20180829165036376453337.pdf (Accessed May 2019).

State Grid Corporation of China [SGCC]. Power grid: Clean energy. (n.d.-a). http://www.sgcc. com.cn/html/sgcc_main_en/col2017112619/column_2017112619_1.shtml?childColumnId=2017112619 (Accessed May 2019).

State Grid Corporation of China [SGCC]. State grid corporation of China completed the acquisition of equity stake in CDP RETI. (n.d.-b) http://www.sgcc.com.cn/ywlm/mediacenter/corporatenews/11/311305.shtml (Accessed July 2018).

U.S. Energy Information Administration [EIA]. (2017). *International Energy Outlook 2017*. Retrieved from. https://www.eia.gov/outlooks/ieo/pdf/0484(2017).pdf.

U.S. Energy Information Administration [EIA]. (n.d.) International energy statics. https://www.eia.gov/beta/international/data/browser/#/?pa=0000002&c=41000000020000600000000 00000g0002000000000000000001&tl_id=2-A&vs=INTL.2-2-AFRC-BKWH.A&cy=201 5&vo=0&v=H&end=2017.

Uhlmann, C. (2016). Chinese investment in Australia's power grid explained. *ABC News*. http://www.abc.net.au/news/2016-08-21/chinese-investment-in-the-australian-power-grid/7766086 (Accessed July 2018).

United Energy. (n.d.). Company information. https://www.unitedenergy.com.au/our-story-and-vision/company-ownership/ (Accessed July 2018).

Xu, Y. C. (2017). *Sinews of power: The politics of the State Grid Corporation of China*. New York: Oxford University Press.

Zinfra. (n.d.). About us. http://www.zinfra.com.au/About-Us (Accessed June 2018).

Further reading

Brazilian Ministry of Planning, Development and Management. (2018). *Bimonthly Newsletter on Chinese Investment in Brazil—n° 5*. http://www.planejamento.gov.br/assuntos/internacionais/arquivos/bimonthly-newsletter-on-china-investment-number5.pdf/@@download/file/Bimonthly%20Newsletter%20on%20China%20Investment%20-%20number%205.pdf (Accessed July 2018).

Independent Power Transmission Operator [ADMIE SA]. Company. (n.d.). http://www.admie.gr/en/company/ (Accessed July 2018).

Kynge, J., & Hornby, L. (2018). China eyes role as world's power supplier. *Financial Times*. https://www.ft.com/content/bdc31f94-68aa-11e8-b6eb-4acfcfb08c11 (Accessed June 2018).

State Grid Corporation of China (SGCC), company website. http://www.sgcc.com.cn/html/sgcc_main_en/index.shtml

China, an innovation hub

7

China's history is marked by thousands of years of world-changing innovations: from the compass and gunpowder to acupuncture and the printing press. No one should be surprised that China has re-emerged as an economic superpower.

Gary Locke, US ambassador to China from 2011 to 2014

Acronyms

AI	artificial intelligence
AIDP	Artificial Intelligence Development Plan
AIRC	Artificial Intelligence Research Center
BYDs	Build Your Dreams
CATL	Contemporary Amperex Technology
CNNIC	China Internet Network Information Center
C-V2X	cellular-V2X
DJIs	Da-Jiang Innovations
DSRC	dedicated short-range communication
EVs	electric vehicles
FDI	foreign direct investment
GDP	gross domestic product
GII	Global Innovation Index
GPU	graphics processing unit
IMF	International Monetary Fund
IPO	initial public offering
MOE	China's Ministry of Education
NIIDT	The National Innovation Institute of Defense Technology
PC	personal computer
PCT	Patent Cooperation Treaty
R&D	research and development
S&T	science and technology
STEM	science, technology, engineering, math
USRC	Unmanned Systems Research Center
V2I	vehicle to infrastructure
V2N	vehicle to network
V2P	vehicle to pedestrian
V2V	vehicle to vehicle
V2X	vehicle-to-everything
WIPO	World Intellectual Property Organization

The Era of Chinese Multinationals. https://doi.org/10.1016/B978-0-12-816857-8.00007-0

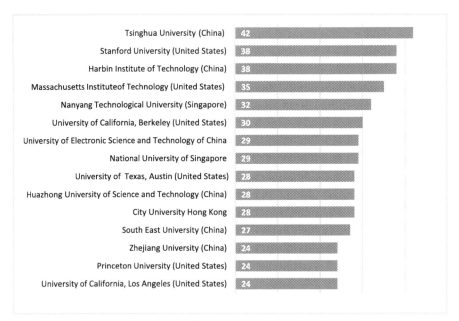

Fig. 7.1 Number of papers in the top 1% most highly cited in math and computing by university, papers published in 2013–16.
Source: Global Innovation Index. (2019). https://www.globalinnovationindex.org. (Accessed May 2019).

The global center of gravity for technology and innovation may be shifting to China. Tsinghua University in Beijing could well become the top-ranked science university in the world, having produced more of the top 1% most highly cited papers in mathematics and computing, as well as a greater share of the 10% most highly cited papers in science, technology, engineering, math (STEM) than any other university in the world (see Fig. 7.1). While many analysts had come to terms with China moving beyond its traditional position as a low-cost producer, few had taken stock of how far the country had come in the frontiers of science and technology (S&T) research.

China's rapid progress is most visible in its companies' success. Their global achievements would not have been possible without a disciplined effort to acquire new technology and a significant investment toward homegrown innovation. Today, leading Chinese firms such as Haier and Huawei produce consumer goods that demonstrate the technological progress underway, while the battle for future technological dominance intensifies.

This chapter details how S&T policy reform and innovation set China on a remarkable path in higher education and corporate research and development (R&D). We draw on The Global Innovation Index (GII, www.globalinnovationindex.org) published by Cornell University, INSEAD and the Geneva-based World Intellectual Property Organization (WIPO). The GII is widely recognized as the most comprehensive measure of a country's innovation capability. Based on the index, China has or is very close to reaching its 2020 national goal (set in 2012) to be recognized as a leading innovative nation. No other country has risen as rapidly in the GII rankings over the last decade as China, all while still classified as an emerging market with gross domestic product (GDP)/capita at $9,608 (International Monetary Fund (IMF), 2019).

In just three decades, China introduced a wide range of S&T policies, leading to a sprawling innovation ecosystem and a burgeoning educated workforce, laying a solid foundation for future development. This chapter unpacks the implications by highlighting key technological frontiers in which Chinese firms established strong leadership stakes: mobile payments, artificial intelligence (AI), and electric vehicles (EVs). Throughout, we demonstrate how the alliance of government, academia, and business has been the precipitating and driving force behind rapid progress.

7.1 Four phases of China's S&T policy evolution[1]

We turn first to the buildup of China's innovation capabilities. Since the late 1970s, Chinese S&T policy evolved in four phases, which vaulted China into the top tier of global innovators. These four phases include: (i) experimentation (1978–85), (ii) systemic reform (1986–95), (iii) deepening reform (1996–2006), and (iv) long-term planning (2007–14). Over the years, the ratio of R&D expenditure in China increased substantially, getting closer to the US ratio (see Fig. 7.2).

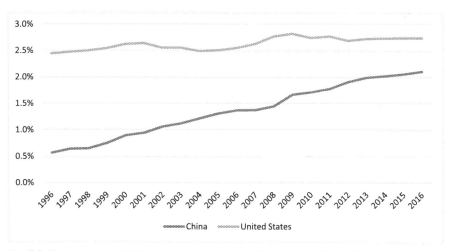

Fig. 7.2 Comparison of R&D expenditures between China and the United States measured as a percentage (%) of GDP.
Source: The World Bank, World Development Indicators. http://datatopics.worldbank.org/world-development-indicators/, (Accessed May 2019).

[1] This section is adapted from Chen, Zheng, and Guo (2018).

7.1.1   The experimental phase (1978–85)

In the early 1980s, China's economic foundation was weak, and its level of S&T research was far behind that of developed nations. It became clear that the Soviet model for S&T research, which China had adopted in the 1960s, had serious drawbacks and led to a yawning chasm between the research and industry. Initial policy reform focused, therefore, on spin-offs and selective privatization of the parts of public research institutions that were commercially viable. This separation promptly alleviated some of the financial burden of the holding institutions, whose newly privatized entities proved substantially valuable.

Some of the most successful technology companies in China today were established during this period, including the computer products and services company Lenovo Group Ltd. (formerly Legend Computer), a spin-off from the Computing Institute of the Academy of Sciences, and the conglomerate Founder Group Co. Ltd., a spin-off from Peking University. In the face of limited national S&T funding, the initial reform phase leaned on a bottom-up approach. At the national level, the Key National Research Projects (1984) and the Key National Laboratories launched important initiatives to better allocate limited funding for research groups based on performance.

7.1.2   Systemic reform (1985–95)

The Science and Technology System Reform Act in 1985 marked the advent of top-down national technology system reforms in China. The act's primary objective was to bridge the gap between research institutions and relevant industries. By emphasizing competitiveness and connections to the market, the act sought to gradually strengthen the economic impact of S&T funding. Its most significant reforms included the establishment of the National Natural Science Foundation of China, which promotes and finances basic and applied research, along with a number of new initiatives supporting applied and translation research.

By 1993, the government instituted the 211 Project to improve the country's higher education system by tying it to social development. The government allocated a special budget for leading universities selected from each province and from major cities such as Beijing. This budget was enacted in the country's 9th Five-Year National Budget Plan and was fully implemented by 1995. Meanwhile, the Hundred Talents Program of the Chinese Academy of Sciences was introduced to encourage Chinese scholars overseas to take up key teaching and research positions back in China.

7.1.3   Deepening reform (1996–2006)

The 9th Five-Year National Budget Plan and the Outline of the 2010 National Target ushered in a period of systemic reform in S&T, out of which China established a comprehensive national strategy for "rejuvenating the nation's economy with science and education." By 1996, the government passed the Act of Promoting Commercialization of S&T Discoveries and Inventions, which would (1) shift the drivers of innovation from public research organizations to industrial sectors, (2) improve the R&D and innovation capacity of industrial sectors, and (3) optimize the commercialization of academic outputs.

Meanwhile, four crucial shifts to the national innovation infrastructure took place as follows:

First, the 985 Initiative broadened the 211 Project to include major technology and engineering universities in the National Advanced Education Development Fund.

Second, the government implemented the Knowledge Innovation Initiative in the Chinese Academy of Sciences to improve research quality at its public institutions.

Third, the government encouraged large-scale R&D funding for basic research, with initiatives such as the 973 Program.

Finally, the Yangtze River Scholars Program was introduced to significantly enhance professors' wages to attract talent, domestically and beyond.

7.1.4   Long-term plan and policy optimization (2006–14)

The 2006 National Plan looked ahead to 2020, outlining four major guidelines for S&T development: (1) nurturing independent innovation, (2) fostering the capacity to leapfrog in key technology areas, (3) building major infrastructure, and (4) developing future global leadership. The plan emphasized sustainable economic growth, seeking innovation-driven growth strategies. The government wanted to prioritize effective policy design and implementation to overcome lingering coordination issues and lack of cohesiveness in prior policy-making.

By 2012, China set its sights higher, seeking to become a "top innovative nation" by 2020. The 18th Communist Party National Congress then established "innovation-driven growth" as a national development strategic priority. The congress called for setting clear targets: improving entrepreneurship, making industry the main driver behind innovation, and establishing market-oriented mechanisms to facilitate collaborative technology transfer from academia to industry. These changes aimed to spur China's global competitiveness in innovation.

The S&T reform privileged education by increasing the ratio of high school graduates enrolled in colleges and universities. This emphasis resulted in college and university graduates in the sciences ballooning from 1,337,300 students in 2002 to 6,081,600 in 2012—an average annual growth of 16.4%. The number of Master's and PhD graduates grew even more quickly from 80,800 in 2002 to 486,500 in 2012, at an average annual clip of 19.7%. As a result of the reforms, new talent cultivated by the strong scientific education system flowed through an ongoing pipeline of highly skilled, educated labor force, emboldening the rapid buildup of China's innovation system. Likewise, R&D personnel subsequently increased, from 1.1 million in 2004 to 3.3 million in 2012, at an annual rate of 10% or higher (National Bureau of Statistics of China, 2013).

7.1.5   Latest reforms (2015–present)

Since the ascension of President Hu Jintao during the 18th Communist Party Congress, China has gestured to further improvements in the form of yet another round of policy reforms.

•   First, an amendment to the National Act for Promoting Technology Transfer was proposed. Universities would be granted the right to license patents generated from public R&D funding, thereby ensuring that inventors share a greater percentage of the proceeds. The program was first piloted in 11 universities, and then broadly extended

- Second, in January 2015, the Chinese government issued the 2014–20 Action Plan on the Implementation of National Intellectual Property Strategy. The plan sought to ease market processes for transactions pertaining to intellectual property, including declassifying patents for civilian use and funding seed companies that specialize in intellectual property transaction services.
- Third, to improve efficiency in S&T funding, the Chinese government overhauled the entire S&T funding process, increasing accountability to stakeholders as a result.
- Fourth, China launched a special stock market (the National Equity Exchange and Quotations) to reward tech start-up companies (not yet profitable) with more avenues to raise capital and simplified rules and regulations to encourage mergers and acquisitions.
- Finally, in March 2015, the Chinese government published "A Guideline for the Development of Public Incubation Space to Promote Grassroots Entrepreneurship," promoting the participation of multilevel capital markets, including crowdfunding.

7.2   China in the Global Innovation Index

China's progress in the GII has been remarkable. The ranking provides detailed metrics for more than 120 countries each year, representing more than 90% of the world's population and more than 96% of the world's GDP (in current US dollars). The overall GII score is the simple average of the Input and Output Subindex scores.

The Innovation Input Subindex comprises five input pillars that capture elements of the national economy that enable innovative activities: (1) institutions, (2) human capital and research, (3) infrastructure, (4) market sophistication, and (5) business sophistication. The Innovation Output Subindex provides information about outputs that are the results of innovative activities within the economy. There are two output pillars: (6) knowledge and technology outputs, and (7) creative outputs.

From a rank of 34th in 2012, China has risen to the 17th overall position in 2018, 10th in the Innovation Output Subindex, and 5th in knowledge and technology outputs, the first time China entered a top 10 ranking in one of the main indices of the GII. As shown in Fig. 7.3, in absolute terms, China leads the world in number of patent applications by origin and scientific and technical publications, as well as number of researchers. In knowledge and technology outputs, the country proved robust in knowledge creation (4th), knowledge diffusion (22nd), and knowledge impact (2nd). These positive developments can be attributed in part to several strengths including scientific and technical publications, foreign direct investment (FDI) outflows, computer software spending, patents, and utility models by origin and high-tech exports.

The GII also measures the quality of innovation through a subset of key variables: (1) quality of local universities (QS World University Ranking, average score of top three universities); (2) internationalization of local inventions (patent families filed in three offices); and (3) the number of citations that local research documents receive abroad (citable documents H index). Fig. 7.4 shows how the scores of these three indicators add up and capture the top 10 highest performing high- and middle-income economies. China is ranked first among middle-income economies in the quality of innovation aggregate measure. While there is still a gap between China and the United States in terms of quality of innovation, it is shrinking year after year.

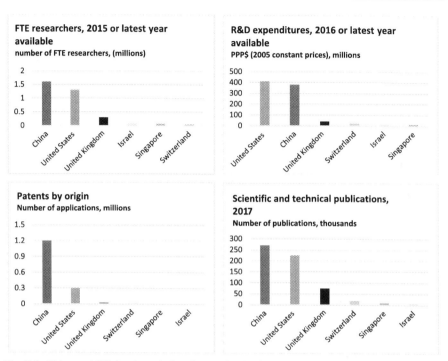

Fig. 7.3 China and US dominate in key innovation indicators. *Note:* FTE, Full-time equivalent.
Source: UNESCO Institute for Statistics (UIS) Database, WIPO Statistics Database, Clarivate Analytics, Thomson Reuters, Science Citation Index (SCI), Social Science Citation Index (SSCI).

By means of geocoding inventor addresses, the GII identifies the largest inventive clusters as measured by WIPO's Patent Cooperation Treaty (PCT) patenting activity, using advanced mapping techniques. In 2018, the identification of top S&T clusters rests on international patent filings, with the addition of metrics for scientific publishing activity. China has 18 clusters in the top 100 as compared to 26 clusters from the United States. It is noteworthy that Shenzhen-Hong Kong is ranked 2nd in the list after Tokyo-Yokohama (see Table 7.1). The launch of the Great Bay Area in December 2018, which comprises Guangzhou-Shenzhen-Hong Kong Macao, will likely boost this corridor to the top.

7.3 Innovation excellence in China

China is either leading or at the very top of many technological domains—notably, mobile payments, AI, and EVs. While not exhaustive of China's leadership, they are indicative of how the country's multinationals leverage innovation as they compete across the globe.

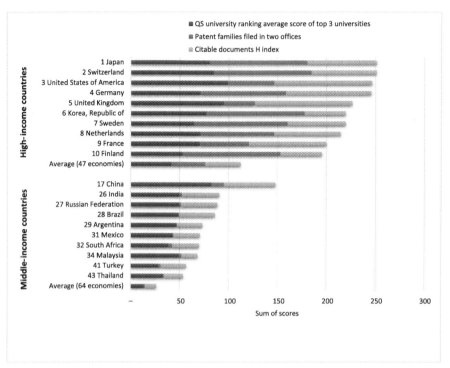

Fig. 7.4 Metrics for quality of innovation: Top 10 high- and middle-income economies.
Notes: Numbers to the left of the economy name are its rank in innovation quality. Economies are classified by income according to the World Bank Income Group Classification (July 2017). Upper- and lower-middle income categories are grouped together as middle-income economies.
Source: GII 2018 data. www.globalinnovationindex.org, (Accessed May 2019).

7.3.1 Mobile payments in China

China is at the vanguard in establishing a mobile-payment-driven cashless society. The lack of history of credit card use and the wide adoption of e-commerce facilitated the quick expansion of mobile payments in China. The two leading mobile payment companies are Alibaba, thanks to its dominance in e-commerce, and Tencent (see case study in Chapter 9), based on its mobile social media and messaging platforms (WeChat and QQ), with their respective e-wallet products, Alipay and WeChat Pay.

According to data published by China Internet Network Information Center (CNNIC), 802 million people actively used the Internet in 2018, 57.7% of the population. This dwarfs the 300 million Internet users in the United States. 788 million of the 802 million Chinese Internet users are mobile users, a whopping 98%, indicating China's efficiency at rolling out network coverage, as well as how indispensable mobile technology has become in everyday life in the country.

About 583 million Chinese used mobile payment in 2018, up 10.7% from 2017, and a total of 600 million people used online payment (including desktop) in 2018, a 13%

Table 7.1 The five largest and other selected inventive regional clusters, as measured by WIPO's PCT patenting activity.

Rank	Cluster name	Territory(ies)
1	Tokyo-Yokohama	JP
2	Shenzhen-Hong Kong	CN/HK
3	Seoul	KR
4	San Jose-San Francisco, CA	US
5	Beijing	CN/HK
9	Paris	FR
15	London	GB
17	Amsterdam-Rotterdam	NL
20	Cologne	DE
22	Tel Aviv-Jerusalem	IL
28	Singapore	SG
29	Eindhoven	BE/NL
30	Moscow	RU
31	Stockholm	SE
33	Melbourne	AU
37	Toronto, ON	CA
38	Madrid	ES
44	Tehran	IR
45	Milan	IT
48	Zurich	CH/DE

Source: Global Innovation Index (GII). (2018). https://www.globalinnovationindex.org. (Accessed May 2019).

year-on-year increase, according to the CNNIC (2018). When consumers shopped offline, they still preferred to use mobile wallets. About 67.2% of China's Internet users made mobile payments offline, up from 65.2% in 2017.

According to Ipsos' 2018 Q4 Third-Party Payment Industry Report, only 21% of Chinese rely on cash, and another 25% use credit and debit cards. The estimated annual third-party mobile payment transaction value in mainland China is approximately $22 trillion (RMB 152.77 trillion). The total number of annual transactions was 10.4 trillion, a 24% year-on-year increase. A majority of users (54%) use third-party mobile payment providers, a space dominated by WeChat Pay (Tenpay) and Alipay (see Fig. 7.5).

China not only leads the world in mobile payments, but it dwarfs the United States in terms of penetration and volumes. According to Simon-Kucher & Partners (2019), despite having a high smartphone penetration (close to 80%) in the world, nearly 90% of American customers prefer to use cash (27%) or debit/credit cards (61%), and less than 10% prefer to pay by mobile payments. While the use of mobile payments/e-wallets is projected to rise from 16% in 2018 to 28% in 2022 and overtake cash and credit cards globally, their use in North America is expected to double from 3% to 7%. This is a significant increase but still far below the global rate, and even further behind Chinese customers.

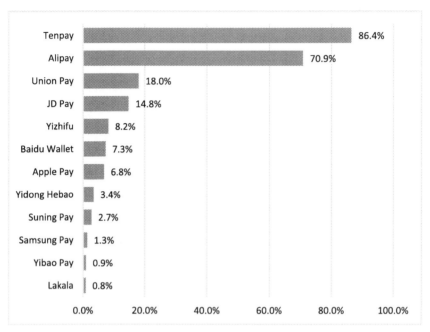

Fig. 7.5 Mobile payment user penetration (%) per company 2018.
Source: https://www.reportlinker.com/p02912885/China-Third-Party-Payment-Industry-Report.html?utm_source=PRN.

The history of the online payment industry in China can be divided into three phases. First came the personal computer (PC)-based payment service, designed by Alibaba to facilitate e-commerce. The second phase was marked by ubiquitous mobilization, largely spurred by WeChat Pay. In 2013, WeChat introduced a feature that enabled users to link their bank accounts and send money to their friends on WeChat. Consumers even used WeChat to honor Chinese traditions such as the "red envelope exchange" for holidays and special occasions. This buttressed the popularity of mobile payments, which was increasingly integrated into a supply chain with third-party apps as WeChat Pay and Alipay cultivated a market of Application Programme Interfaces (APIs).

WeChat soon enabled users to accept payment with only a QR code. This feature brought mobile payment from online applications to offline applications such as buying street food or paying bills in restaurants. Since vendors only needed to print the QR code, it was easy to adopt. Alipay followed by subsidizing users. As a result, a war of subsidies ensued that cost both companies hundreds of millions of dollars as mobile payment penetration skyrocketed.

Driven by strong demand from both the consumer and business side, thousands of third-party developers integrated WeChat Pay with enterprise information system and hardware. For example, instead of requiring users to scan the QR code, the cashier scanned the QR code on the users' smartphone with a barcode scanner. This was useful for venues such as supermarkets and fast food restaurants where customers desired fast checkout times. WeChat Pay and Alipay also integrated into the payment systems of hospitals, schools, turnpike tolls, tax collection service, commercial garages, among others.

Finally, online payments extended into financial services in the third phase. WeChat Pay and Alipay together processed 1.7 billion transactions per day in 2018. This means that every Chinese consumer used WeChat Pay or Alipay, on average, more than once per day. With copious amounts of transaction data at hand, the companies continuously learn about the trustworthiness of individuals. This in turn allows them to create specific credit profiles for lending. Indeed, Alipay and WeChat lend both to consumers and to small businesses. Before the age of mobile payment, it was difficult for financial institutions to learn about the revenues of small businesses when most transactions were done in cash. Now, however, WeChat Pay and Alipay have direct access to the details of payments accepted by many consumer-facing businesses, reducing their risk of fraud and cost of lending.

More recently, Chinese regulatory authorities have stepped up pressure on Alipay (rebranded as Ant Financial Services in 2014) to not venture aggressively into financial services, as their rapid growth was hurting the margins of state-owned banks. Ant Financial Services has refocused on technology services, and its credit-checking arm (Sesame credit) is only performing credit checks for nonfinancial purposes such as bike rentals and visa fees. While the relative roles of incumbent state-owned banks and new entrants such as Alipay and WeChat Pay in the Chinese payment ecosystem remains to be determined, it is clear that China has established a strong, and possibly unassailable lead in the global mobile payments space.

Both Alipay and WeChat Pay are expanding abroad aggressively, though with different strategies. In 2019, Alipay had users in more than 54 countries while WeChat Pay covered 17 currencies in 49 countries. Alipay has typically focused on making major acquisitions in key countries, such as its recent $700 million acquisition of UK-based payment group WorldFirst in 2019. Alipay also offers merchants a lower rate if they deal directly with Alipay as opposed to a local payment provider. Alipay is well positioned to offer international transfers to Chinese vendors as they expand globally thanks to its control of parts of global supply chains. By contrast, WeChat Pay encourages local merchants to work with local payment providers, a reflection of a difference in Tencent's business focus—media content and gaming. Alipay and WeChat Pay hold the potential to dominate the payments industry in many Asian countries, which are largely cash-based today, show low credit card penetrations, and are migrating into mobile payments through the rapid expansion of mobile phone penetration.

Ping An Insurance (Group) of China, a leading financial services provider in China, is another example of a company that has empowered its core business through technology and innovation (see Box 7.1).

7.3.2 Artificial intelligence

In July 2017, China's State Council issued the *New Generation Artificial Intelligence Development Plan* (AIDP). The ambitions of China's AI sector received significant and sustained attention from the highest levels of China's leadership, including

Box 7.1 Ping An's digital transformation from insurance to fintech and healthtech

Ping An Insurance (Group) Company of China is a leading financial services provider in insurance, banking, and securities in China with US$ 1 trillion in assets, US$ 157 billion in revenues, and US$ 16.5 billion in net profits as of 2018. In 2018, it ranked 29th in the Fortune Global 500 by revenues and first among global insurance groups.

Since 2008, Ping An has made research a priority and consistently invested over 1% of its revenue in Research and Development. As a result, the firm is number one in fintech patents, holding over 15,000 global patents and 40 global technology awards, such as Stanford SQUAD (NLP) and Global LUNA in medical imaging. The company has also established eight leading research institutes and over fifty laboratories, housing over 99,000 technology staff, 32,000 in researchers, and 2200 top scientists. Ping An has now 80% of its 4000 systems on the cloud. It sources its technological transformation from four ecosystems described below.

Financial Services: through its "Open Platform and Open Market" model, Ping An has incubated fintech companies including Lufax, an online wealth management and lending company with over 38 million users, US$ 55 billion of assets and US$ 56 billion of loans under management and OneConnect, a leading fintech TaaS (technology-as-a-service) company serving over 3700 financial institutions in China and 10 countries in Asia, with transaction volume over US$ 3 trillion.

Healthcare. Ping An has established a "patient–provider–payer" model, servicing through Ping An Good Doctor, Smart Health in Smart City and HealthKonnect. Good Doctor is the largest one-stop healthcare service, with over 280 million users and over 650,000 consultations per day. Smart Health provides leading healthtech solutions such as CDSS and disease prediction to 3000 healthcare institutions in over 20 provinces. Finally, Ping An HealthKonnect offers payment solutions such as smart social health insurance management and member services for over 280 cities.

Auto-Service. Autohome is the world's largest online platform providing car trade and car finance services with DAU to over 40 million. It now has coverage of over 90 Original Equipment Manufacturers (OEMs), 20,000 new car dealers, 30,000 second-hand dealers, and 70,000 repair shops.

Smart Cities. Ping An covers over 100 cities across 21 service lines in city management, business development, and citizen services. This ecosystem has three verticals: Smart Transportation which provides solutions that optimizes traffic handling and congestion, among other services, now deployed in over 20 cities. Smart Agriculture has developed end-to-end agricultural solutions for more efficient land, disaster management, and other functions. Smart Life draws on application to manage over 3000 citizen services across welfare, healthcare, transportation, a 70% increase in service efficiency.

Source: Authors, based on various sources including https://www.prnewswire.com/news-releases/ping-an-powering-ahead-with-world-leading-fintech-and-healthtech-300745534.html.

President Xi Jinping. Total Chinese national and local government spending on AI is not publicly disclosed, but it is estimated to be in the tens of billions of dollars. At least two Chinese regional governments have each committed to investing 100 billion yuan (~$14.7 billion).

Likewise, the National Innovation Institute of Defense Technology (NIIDT) has established two Beijing-based research organizations focusing on the military use of AI and related tech. These are the Unmanned Systems Research Center (USRC), led by Yan Ye, and the Artificial Intelligence Research Center (AIRC), led by Dai Huadong. Each organization was created in early 2018 with a research staff of over 100 (more than 200 total), making them among the largest and fastest growing government AI research organizations in the world. AIRC staff are engaged in basic research into dual-use AI technology, including applying machine learning to robotics, swarm networking, wireless communications, and cybersecurity.

China's July 2017 national AI strategy set a 2020 goal for the international competitiveness of China's AI industry to reach elite levels. By many accounts, China has already achieved this objective (in 2019). At the World Peace Forum, Tsinghua University's Xue Lan delivered a briefing on Tsinghua University's major report on the state of the AI sector in China. This study found that "China has secured a leading position in the top [AI] echelon in both technology development and market applications and is in a race of 'two giants' with the United States." It also found that China is No. 1 in both total AI research papers and highly cited AI papers worldwide, in AI patents and in AI venture capital investment; No. 2 in the number of AI companies and in the size of the AI talent pool.

Not only is China advancing state-of-the-art AI research, its companies are successfully developing innovative market-competitive products and services around AI applications. SenseTime, for example, is undisputedly one of the world leaders in computer vision AI and claims to have achieved annual revenue growth of 400% for three consecutive years. Shenzhen-headquartered Da-Jiang Innovations (DJIs) offers another example, leading the world in consumer drones with 74% market share.

In many cases, the products and underlying technologies between commercial AI and military/security AI products are identical or nearly so. DJI was recently selected as the sole drone provider to the New York Police Department, which will use DJI's consumer model drones. Similarly, SenseTime's consumer facial recognition systems share infrastructure and technology with its security systems, deployed by both Chinese law enforcement and intelligence organizations.

China's expertise in designing and integrating high-performance computing systems is a strong competitive advantage for Chinese AI companies. SenseTime, for example, revealed in December 2018 that its aggregate computing power is more than 160 petaflops, more than the world's top-ranked supercomputer at Oak Ridge National Laboratory. SenseTime's computing infrastructure includes more than 54,000,000 graphics processing unit (GPU) cores across 15,000 GPUs within 12 GPU clusters. Such numbers indicate that SenseTime has spent hundreds of millions of dollars on computing infrastructure.

China's success springs from its access to global technology research and markets. Many Chinese AI achievements are the result of combined efforts of multinational research teams and companies, and such international collaboration has been critical to China's research progress. According to the Tsinghua University study of China's AI ecosystem, Chinese AI researchers—the top tier of whom often received their degrees abroad—were coauthoring with non-Chinese individuals. Even purely "Chinese" successes often build upon open source technologies developed by international groups.

Partly as a result, leading Chinese technology companies show significant and sometimes underreported dependencies on the United States. DJI, for instance, is vertically integrated with nearly all design, manufacturing, and marketing done in-house. However, all of DJI's drone flight software development is performed at DJI's American office in Palo Alto, which predominantly employs US citizens as staff. Additionally, nearly 35% of the bill of materials in each of DJI's products comes from the United States, mostly reflecting semiconductor content.

The Tsinghua University China AI report noted that the global AI talent pool in 2017 comprised 204,575 individuals: the United States with 28,536 such individuals and China in second place with 18,232. However, China's ranks eighth in the world in terms of top AI talent, with only 977 individuals compared to 5518 of the United States. While acknowledging the disparity, venture capitalist Kai-Fu Lee argues that this is not a major barrier because "the current age of implementation [AI application commercialization] appears well-suited to China's strengths in research: large quantities of highly skilled, though not necessarily best-of-best, AI researchers, and practitioners."

However, the Chinese government is taking important steps to improve the size and quality of China's AI talent pool. In April 2018, China's Ministry of Education (MOE) launched its *AI Innovation Action Plan for Colleges and Universities*. Among other elements, the plan will create 50 world-class teaching materials for undergraduate and graduate studies related to AI applications for specific industries; 50 national-level high-quality online open courses; and establish 50 AI faculties, research institutions, or interdisciplinary research centers. In a separate initiative, the MOE also plans to launch a new 5-year AI talent training program to train an additional 500 AI instructors and 5000 students at top Chinese universities.

The field of AI integrates multiple foundations and is continuously evolving. China has several areas in which it needs to improve to solidify its leadership in the future of AI. One is the creation of machine learning software frameworks, many of which are open source and serve to speed up the development of AI systems. Popular machine learning frameworks include TensorFlow (Google), Spark (Apache), CNTK (Microsoft), and PyTorch (Facebook). Notably, none of the popular machine learning software frameworks were developed in China.

The absence of Chinese AI companies among the major AI framework developers and open source AI software communities is a weakness of China's AI ecosystem. Domestic AI products and applications are often based on AI frameworks from Google and Microsoft. SenseTime has devoted extensive resources to its own machine learning framework, Parrots, which is intended to be superior for computer vision AI applications. However, the company appears to have had limited success in promoting Parrots' adoption.

Another area of weakness for China is the design of custom AI chips. Custom-designed AI chips are essential for training large machine learning systems and for delivering real-time AI performance. Today, most of the expertise in the design of such chips lies outside of China. However, especially in light of the sanctions announced on Huawei in 2019, China is accelerating its efforts to reduce its dependence on foreign suppliers for advanced semiconductor chips. Huawei has demonstrated that it can design and assemble high quality and competitive chips such as the Kirin 980, which is one of the only two smartphone processors in the world to use 7-nm process technology—the other is Apple's A12 Bionic. Despite such progress, as of June 2019, significant gaps remain for Chinese companies with their American counterparts in advanced semiconductor design.

7.3.3 Electric vehicles

China is the world's largest automobile market with 23 million cars sold in 2018 (as compared to 17 million in the United States over the same time period). Domestic brands made up about 41% of the cars sold in China in 2018, with the rest mostly dominated by European, Japanese, and American brands. Chinese domestic automobile manufacturers have faced challenges competing against their global peers due to the enormous legacy investment by European, Japanese, and American brands in the complex engineering and design needed for producing internal combustion engine-driven cars.

Looking ahead, however, the rising popularity of electric cars has provided China with an opportunity to gain prominence and dominate an important technology sector. Two attributes of EVs favor China. First, EVs tend to be simpler in engineering design than internal combustion engine cars, and thus Chinese manufacturers can catch up easily and compete effectively with their global peers. Second, EVs depend on batteries, an area in which Chinese companies dominate the global market. The Chinese government has incentivized the sale of and investments in EVs, as the new technology provides an important avenue for reducing air pollution across China. The Chinese government has also chosen to make EVs one of the 10 commercial sectors central to its "Made in China 2025" effort to boost advanced industrial technology and Chinese competitiveness.

According to Forbes, in 2017, over 1 million electric cars were sold around the world, a new record. The number of Teslas, Nissan Leafs, and other EVs in circulation worldwide has surpassed 3 million (in 2017), an expansion of 50% from 2016. There were approximately 760,000 EVs on American roads, along with a further 820,000 in Europe, but China's fleet of electric cars is by far the largest, with over 1.2 million. EVs held a 2.2% share of the Chinese automobile market in 2017 (as compared to 1.2% for the United States).

Despite a sluggish global car market and declining overall automobile sales in the Chinese market in 2018 (down 6% for the year compared to the previous year), EVs have continued to increase sales in China. NIO, a new electric car maker that was founded in 2014 and had an initial public offering (IPO) in 2018, is Tesla's counterpart in China. By December 2018, NIO had delivered about 11,000 vehicles and is expected to continue on its growth path, despite strong competition from Tesla, both domestically and abroad.

Seven of the world's top 10 EV battery manufacturers are in China, which enjoys over 50% of the global market share (see Fig. 7.6). Tesla and Panasonic's joint "Gigafactory" in Nevada (capable of producing 20 GWh per year) has been the global benchmark for producers of lithium-ion batteries for EVs. However, Chinese leaders such as Contemporary Amperex Technology (CATL) and Build Your Dreams (BYD) are pushing forward with their own aggressive expansion plans to equal and possibly surpass the Gigafactory's capability.

Foreign battery manufacturers have tried to enter the Chinese market, but have often failed. In 2017, only 6 of the 98 battery companies operating in China were foreign. The Chinese government's Made in China 2025 policy supports the creation of mega capacity (upwards of 40 GWh) for the top three producers of Chinese batteries. Leading Chinese battery manufacturers have also formed strategic ventures with fellow Chinese companies. As an example, CATL formed two joint ventures with automobile company SAIC Motor. The Optimum Nano Innovation Alliance represents another effort to integrate key domestic players across the value chain of EV battery production.

Chinese battery company leaders are beginning to expand globally. CATL, the leading Chinese battery manufacturer, has announced plans to open its first battery plant in Germany in 2022. In a significant reversal of traditional technology transfers, CATL will bring innovative new battery technology to the German (and European) automobile markets.

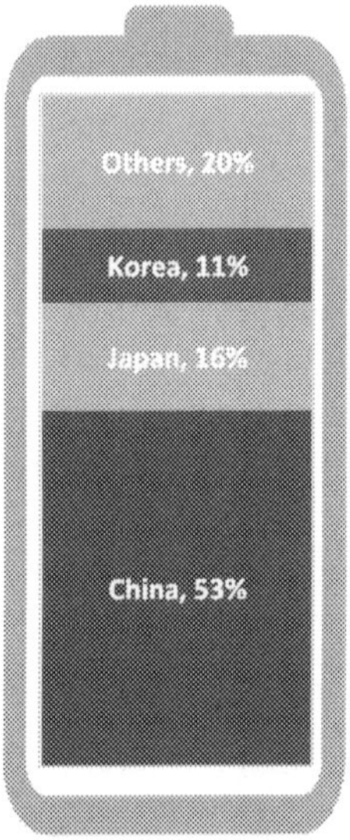

	Company	Global market share, 2017 (%)[a]	Country
1	Contemporary Amperex Technology (CATL)	19	China
2	Panasonic	16	Japan
3	Build Your Dreams (BYD)	12	China
4	OptimumNano	9	China
5	LG Chem	7	Korea
6	Guoxuan High-Tech	5	China
7	Samsung SDI	4	Korea
8	Beijing National Battery Technology	3	China
9	BAK	3	China
10	Funeng Technology[b]	2	China
	Others	20	

[a] *Based on EV lithium-ion battery shipments(GWh)*.
[b] *United States-invested*.

Fig. 7.6 The global EV battery market is dominated by Chinese companies; 7 out of the global top 10 battery manufacturers are Chinese.
Source: China EV 100.

While the United States is the leader in most of the technologies necessary to build an autonomous vehicle, one area in which China leads is vehicle-to-everything (V2X) communication technology. V2X includes vehicle-to-vehicle (V2V), vehicle-to-infrastructure (V2I), vehicle-to-network (V2N), and vehicle-to-pedestrian (V2P) operations.

There are two protocols for V2X: dedicated short-range communication (DSRC), which is based on Wi-Fi technology and cellular-V2X (C-V2X), which is part of the 4G and 5G protocols. DSRC was developed in 2008 and had not made much progress in commercial applications. However, C-V2X offers great compatibility with current cellular infrastructure and a clear evolution path to 5G. C-V2X is supported by companies like Huawei, QUALCOMM, Intel, and mobile carriers around the world.

China leads V2X in two ways. First, China is building V2X compatible cellular base stations much faster than the United States. According to an August 2018 study by consulting firm Deloitte, China has built about 350,000 cell sites since 2015, compared with fewer than 30,000 in the United States.

Second, China more quickly update its urban infrastructure than many other countries. In order to enable communication between traffic lights, traffic signs, and cars, many urban transportation infrastructures need to be updated. The city of Wuxi in Jiangsu Province had updated more than 200 intersections by June 2018 so that automakers can test V2X in real road conditions (Xu, 2018).

Despite its strong position in EVs and the battery market, China is a close second behind the United States in the self-driving automobile industry. Most of the major players in China have R&D teams in both China and the United States. Even though China has an abundant supply of mid-level engineers, it lacks sufficient senior engineers with experience in autonomous driving. China's Made in China 2025 policy has EVs as one of its core pillars—coupled with the large market for cars in China, the policy will drive innovation for Chinese companies in this key sector in the years ahead.

7.4   Moving forward in the innovation path

China has placed innovation at the center of a comprehensive policy of developing its domestic market and shoring up global competitiveness. It has made great strides in global innovation across a wide array of domains and has overtaken the United States in key R&D parameters such as number of researchers, publications, and patents. Its rank on the GII has increased steadily over the last decade, and as of 2019, it is fair to say that China has emerged as a key innovative player in the world.

China's strengths are particularly notable in mobile payments, AI, and EVs. Together, they are bellwethers for China's future and for the global competitiveness of its multinationals. As Chinese firms ratchet up their investments in innovation, they are poised to out-innovate their global peers, leaning on a smart combination of abundant low-cost talent and coordinated government support for global growth.

References

Chen, D., Zheng, S., & Guo, L. (2018). The impact of science and technology policies on rapid economic development in China. In L. Casanova, P. Cornelius, & S. Dutta (Eds.), *Entrepreneurship and the finance of innovation in emerging markets*: Elsevier. https://www.elsevier.com/books/financing-entrepreneurship-and-innovation-in-emerging-markets/casanova/978-0-12-804025-6. [Chapter 3].

China Internet Network Information Center. (2018). https://cnnic.com.cn/.

Global Innovation Index (GII). (2018). https://www.globalinnovationindex.org. [Accessed May 2019].

International Monetary Fund (IMF). (2019). *World Economic Outlook*. April 2019 https://www.imf.org/external/datamapper/NGDPD@WEO/OEMDC/ADVEC/WEOWORLD. (Accessed May 2019).

National Bureau of Statistics of China. (2013). *China Statistical Yearbook 2013*. Beijing: China Statistics Press. Available at http://www.stats.gov.cn/tjsj/njsj/2013/index.htm.

Simon Kucher & Partners. (2019). *How behavioral science can unleash digital payments adoption*. https://www.simon-kucher.com/sites/default/files/2019-01/SimonKucher_Report_Payment%20Adoption_Final.pdf.

Xu, C. (2018). LTE-V2X Wuxi IoT Expo 2017. https://www.youtube.com/watch?v=Fkg-wHr-RTsQ&t=186s Published April 2018. (Accessed June 2019).

Further reading

Allen, G. (2019). Understanding China's AI strategy. In *Center for new American security*. https://www.cnas.org/publications/reports/understanding-chinas-ai-strategy. (Accessed February 2019).

Casanova, L., Cornelius, P., & Dutta, S. (2018). *Entrepreneurship and the finance of innovation in emerging markets*. Elsevier. https://www.elsevier.com/books/financing-entrepreneurship-and-innovation-in-emerging-markets/casanova/978-0-12-804025-6.

Chen, T. (2019). The cross-border payment war of WeChat Pay and Alipay. *Walkthechat*. https://walkthechat.com/the-cross-border-payment-war-of-wechat-pay-and-alipay/. (Accessed February 2019).

Deloitte. (2018). *5G: The chance to lead for a decade*.

Global Innovation Index (GII). (2019). www.globalinnovationindex.org. (Accessed May 2019).

Haour, G., & von Zedtwitz, M. (2016). *Created in China: How China is becoming a global innovator*. London: Bloomsbury Information Ltd.

Holzmann, A. (2018). *China's battery industry is powering up for global competition*. Mercator Institute for China Studies (October 24) https://www.merics.org/cn/node/8371.

Lee, K.-F. (2018). *Ai superpowers: China, Silicon Valley, and the new world order*. Boston: Houghton Mifflin Harcourt.

Liu, S. (2016). *Creating autonomous vehicle systems*. O'Reilly. https://www.oreilly.com/ideas/creating-autonomous-vehicle-systems. (Accessed October 2016).

McCarthy, N. (2018). Electric car sales are surging in China. *Forbes*. https://www.forbes.com/sites/niallmccarthy/2018/06/01/electric-car-sales-are-surging-in-china-infographic/#4a3b7389d1f7. (Accessed June 2018).

National Natural Science Foundation of China. (2019). http://www.nsfc.gov.cn/publish/portal1.

Worldpay. (2018). *Global payments report.* https://www.worldpay.com/global/insight/articles/2018-11/global-payments-report-2018.

Yip, G. (2017). *China's Next Strategic Advantage: From imitation to innovation.* MIT Press.

Xinhua. (2019). China's mobile payment users reach 583m in 2018. *China Daily.* http://www.chinadaily.com.cn/a/201903/03/WS5c7b3ccaa3106c65c34ec6a9.html. (Accessed March 2019).

Zhang, S. (2018). Exclusive: Ant financial shifts focus from finance to tech services: Sources. *Reuters.* https://www.reuters.com/article/us-china-ant-financial-regulation-exclus/exclusive-ant-financial-shifts-focus-from-finance-to-tech-services-sources-idUSKCN1J10WV. (Accessed June 2018).

Zhou, Y., Lazonick, W., & Sun, Y. (2016). *China as an innovation nation.* Oxford, United Kingdom: Oxford University Press.

Chinese multinational companies move beyond price competition

A lot of people, including business leaders, think the future belongs to China. Globalization is not a zero-sum game, but we need to hone our skills to stay in play.

Jon Meacham (Executive Editor and Executive Vice President at Random House)

Acronyms

CAGR	compound annual growth rate
E20	emerging markets 20: Argentina, Brazil, Chile, China, Colombia, Egypt, India, Indonesia, Iran, Malaysia, Mexico, Nigeria, the Philippines, Poland, Republic of Korea, Russia, Saudi Arabia, South Africa, Thailand, and Turkey
G-7	Group of 7: Canada, France, Germany, Italy, Japan, United States, and United Kingdom
GDP	gross domestic product
GFC	Global Financial Crisis
IEA	International Energy Agency
IMF	International Monetary Fund
MNCs	multinational companies

China has traditionally relied on low production costs to produce competitively priced products for global markets. But with a growing domestic market and a robust export engine, Chinese exports have evolved significantly since the 1980s and 1990s. While low-tech products such as textiles has decreased from 20% of Chinese exports in 2000 to around 3% of exports in 2018, high-technology equipment and services have increased significantly; electrical equipment (26%) and machinery including computers (17%) morphed into large components of China's export portfolio. Increased labor and production costs in China spurred this evolution, aided by the realization that technological innovation and brand equity are necessary to compete successfully in global markets (Chattopadhyay & Batra, 2012; Kumar & Steenkamp, 2013; Peng, 2012).

Given that Chinese firms are relatively young, many have continued to rely on price competition while gradually building brand equity, utilizing the low costs of domestic production, integrated value chains, and logistics to their advantage. When they did not enjoy a technological lead or brand recognition, Chinese firms have leaned on their cost advantages relative to developed economy peers to compete on price in foreign markets. However, as they build brand equity and establish technological dominance or parity, Chinese firms have hiked their price points to earn higher profit margins and to invest in future innovation. Lenovo and Huawei, for instance, have become legitimate technology leaders in their respective product categories, even though they initially relied on cost leadership (see below).

The Era of Chinese Multinationals. https://doi.org/10.1016/B978-0-12-816857-8.00008-2

This chapter presents a price and brand comparison of different product and service categories. Analyses in Chapter 1 demonstrated that Chinese companies frequently prioritized revenue growth over gross margins to cater to monetizable consumer segments. Yet, additional comparisons indicate that China's cost leadership strategy is evolving, with significant implications for established leaders and developed economy competitors.

8.1   Chinese companies compete on price

To gain a holistic view of the extent of China's price competition, we compared the prices of similar US and Chinese-made products from companies that hold the highest market share in their respective consumer segments. We focused on the following goods: computers, smartphones, tablets, fitness wearables, and air conditioners. We chose these specific product categories because they are high value-added products, have the highest market share in the world, and are available for sale in the same ecommerce platforms (e.g., Amazon or Walmart).[1] For personal computers (i.e., desktops and laptops), two out of the five largest companies are Chinese, Lenovo and Acer, followed by American brands HP, Dell, and Apple. American firms have long dominated this market, but Chinese companies have made inroads. Figs. 8.1 and 8.2 list the prices of top laptop and desktop brands (see Table 8.1) across different categories, taken from the e-commerce retailer Amazon. The data is differentiated according to a set of performance characteristics based on the intended use: home, work, and gaming. The prices refer to the highest value within the category for each brand. We observed that US brands consistently offer the highest prices across different laptop categories. The higher price reflects the technological sophistication of their products, and most importantly, the high brand equity from which US brands benefit. However, Chinese firms such as Lenovo (see Box 8.1) have grown significantly over the last two decades to assume the highest market share in the global laptop and desktop markets (see Table 8.1). Lenovo's brand equity increased after it acquired IBM's Thinkpad division in 2004. Lenovo continued to avail itself of the Thinkpad brand in subsequent years after the acquisition. However, in 2012, it discontinued Thinkpad to build up Lenovo's own brand. Even as a globally reputable brand with technological sophistication at par or better than its American competitors, Lenovo still pursues a policy of competing on price, as shown by the data in Figs. 8.1 and 8.2.

Meanwhile, American brands remain well poised to leverage brand equity to inflate price without compromising competitiveness. In both "home" and "travel" categories, Apple continues to capture most of the value and profits, thereby securing the highest market capitalization relative to its competitors. In the "work" category, HP is the price leader, followed closely by Apple. In "gaming," HP is likewise at the helm, but is nearly outmatched by Dell.

---

[1] In the selection process, we avoided nation-wide discount sales such as "Black Friday."

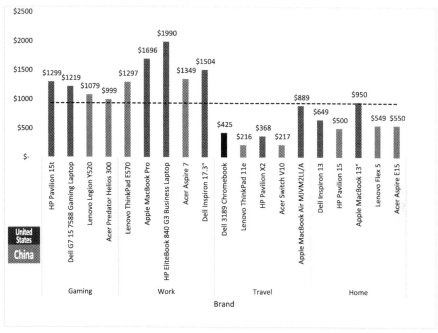

Fig. 8.1 Laptop prices for top Chinese and US brands.
Source: Amazon.com, (Accessed March 2019).

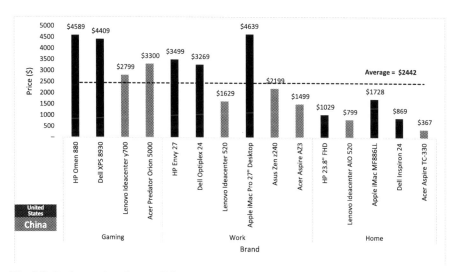

Fig. 8.2 Desktop prices for top Chinese and US brands.
Source: Amazon.com, (Accessed March 2019).

Table 8.1   Largest global personal computer[a] shipments by vendor (% share) as of Q3 2018.

No.	Company	Market share (%)	Headquarters[b]
1	Lenovo	24.0	China
2	HP Inc.	22.8	United States
3	Dell	17.0	United States
4	Apple	7.2	United States
5	Acer Group	7.1	China
6	Others	21.9	–

[a] Personal computers consist of both desktops and laptops.
[b] Data for Hong Kong and Taiwan are included under China.
Source: Forbes, https://www.forbes.com/sites/jeanbaptiste/2018/10/31/lenovo-retakes-1-spot-in-global-pc-market-beating-hp-and-dell/#3f84e77d3f00, (Accessed March 2019).

Box 8.1 Lenovo Group Ltd.—A global leader in computer shipments

Lenovo Group Limited, with its subsidiaries, specializes in the provision of commercial and consumer personal computers, along with mobile Internet devices such as tablets, mobile phones, and others. It offers hardware and software services, and has also diversified into business management/planning, finance, and global supply chains. Lenovo was founded in 1984 and is headquartered in Quarry Bay, Hong Kong. Lenovo propelled itself to become a frontrunner in the PC market in 2004, when it acquired IBM's PC division. This allowed Lenovo, a predominantly Asia-based company, to expand into the United States and other developed markets. The company was able to seamlessly integrate into the US market at both business and cultural levels. In 2009, Lenovo became the first PC vendor to split markets into "emerging" and "mature," as well as develop different strategies for each. Other PC vendors adopted this successful approach soon thereafter. Lenovo further expanded the breadth of its products and services after acquiring IBM's server business and mobile phone manufacturer Motorola in 2014. As of 2019, Lenovo is the number one PC vendor by market share, largely due to its joint venture with Japanese personal computer and laptop vendor Fujitsu. It is also a strong contender in the mobile phones market. It has grown by 5.8% in terms of revenues in 2018. Revenues and profits for 2018 were $45.35 billion and $6.27 billion, respectively. Lenovo is forecast to grow by 12.3% in the 2018–19 fiscal year as the company regains traction in the commercial PC market. Lenovo's market capitalization is $11.089 billion, with the highest market share in the PC market. To date, Lenovo's direct investments have primarily been in the IT sector (72.4%), with a majority of investments concentrated in the Asia/Pacific region (55.2%). However, Lenovo has increased its investments in Europe and in the United States/Canada. The company has also invested in other sectors such as industrials, financials, consumer discretionary, and more.

For smartphones, the market dynamics are different. Fig. 8.3 presents a summary of prices across the world's major smartphone manufacturers (see Table 8.2). Samsung is the price leader, benefitting from a high level of technological sophistication as well as global brand equity. Samsung was the first smartphone manufacturer to launch a foldable screen phone in 2019, and Interbrand ranked the company sixth in its 2018 Best Global Brands. Huawei sells the second highest priced item in the premium segment, followed by Apple. Drawing from its roots in telecommunications, Huawei has also risen rapidly (see Box 8.2) to emerge as the second largest player in the global smartphones market, rivaling Samsung. (It announced a folding screen phone soon

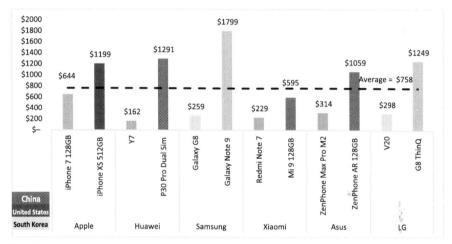

Fig. 8.3 Prices of cheapest and most expensive smartphones by brand for top US, Korean, and Chinese brands—March 2019. Note: the *lighter* color indicates the least expensive item. *Source:* Amazon US, www.amazon.com, (Accessed March 2019).

Table 8.2 Largest global smartphone shipments by vendor (% share) as of Q2 2018.

No.	Company	Market share (%)	Headquarters[a]
1	Samsung	20	Korea
2	Huawei	15	China
3	Apple	11	United States
4	Xiaomi	9	China
5	Oppo	8	China
6	Vivo	7	China
7	LG	3	Korea
8	Lenovo	3	China
9	HMD Global	1	Finland
10	Tecno	1	China
11	Others	22	–

[a] Data for Hong Kong and Taiwan are included under China.
Source: Counterpoint, https://www.counterpointresearch.com/us-market-smartphone-share/, (Accessed March 2019).

Box 8.2 Huawei Technologies Co.—A telecommunications equipment and consumer electronics world leader from China

Huawei Technologies Co. Ltd., an employee-owned company, is a global tele-communications giant specializing in a range of products and services, including telecommunications networks, IT, smart devices, and cloud services. The company was founded in 1987 and is headquartered in Shenzhen, China. Part of Huawei's successes stem from a number of milestones. In 1993, the company developed the most powerful telephone switch in China. Huawei also gained contracts to build a national telecommunications network for the People's Liberation Army. (The company's CEO, Ren Zhengfei, was previously an engineer in the People's Liberation Army.) By 1996, following a change in governmental policies, the state promoted Huawei. The firm's domestic market share increased and, toward the end of 2018, the company became the second largest vendor of smartphones worldwide. It sold 52 million units, with a market share of 14.6% at the time. Outpaced only by Samsung, Huawei even overtook Apple in Q3 of 2018, to become ranked second worldwide in market share. Huawei is expected to ship up to 260 million units in 2019 and to dominate 50% of the Chinese market. The company is also continuously expanding its presence internationally, with acquisitions in Japan and Israel. Huawei experienced a compound annual growth rate (CAGR) of 26% in revenue from 2017, amounting to $105 billion in 2018, and a CAGR of 21% in operating profit from the previous year, on the order of $10.7 billion in 2018. Huawei's total assets stood at $97.1 billion in 2018. As of 2019, Huawei is one of the most global Chinese companies with over 50% of its revenue accrued overseas.

---

after the Korean company.) However, Interbrand ranked Huawei's global brand 68th in the 2018 Best Global Brands, far below that of Samsung and Apple (ranked second). Thus, Huawei's pricing strategy is lower than that of Samsung and Apple for comparable models.

As evident from Table 8.2, Asian firms hold the lion's share of the global smartphone market, with Samsung and Huawei in the first and second ranks, respectively, and Xiaomi and Oppo in the fourth and fifth. As of 2019, Apple is the only American company among the 10 largest globally. Chinese manufacturers Xiaomi, Oppo, and Vivo compete primarily on price, but seek to emulate Samsung and Huawei. Lower production and labor costs, improved efficiency in operations, and a focus on rapid and continuous innovation are the main factors supporting the overall cost leadership of Chinese smart phone firms.

In the fitness wearables market, Chinese firms play an increasingly pronounced role. Xiaomi and Huawei occupied the second and third market share positions in the world in 2018, but both fared significantly less well than Apple, which dominated with 27.4% of fitness wearable goods sold worldwide (see Table 8.3). Similar to the

Table 8.3 Largest global fitness wearables (electronic) shipments by vendor (% share) as of Q4 2018.

No.	Company	Market share (%)	Headquarters[a]
1	Apple	27.4	United States
2	Xiaomi	12.6	China
3	Huawei	9.6	China
4	Fitbit	9.4	United States
5	Samsung	6.8	Korea
6	Others	34.3	–

[a] Data for Hong Kong and Taiwan are included under China.
Source: Statista, https://www.statista.com/statistics/435944/quarterly-wearables-shipments-worldwide-market-share-by-vendor/. (Accessed March 2019).

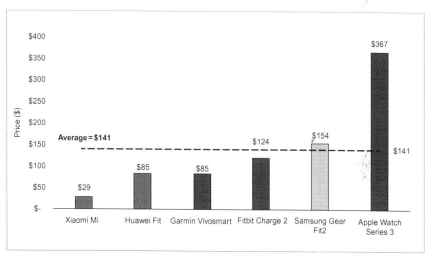

Fig. 8.4 Comparison of fitness wearables' prices between leading brands in emerging countries and in the G-7, 2019.
Source: www.amazon.com, (Accessed February 2019).

laptop and desktop product categories, Xiaomi and Huawei both price their products considerably below the market leader Apple (see Fig. 8.4). It is worth noting that two American firms, Apple and Fitbit, remained poised to capture around 38% of the wearables market value between them.

In sum, Chinese companies are increasingly positioned as protagonists of high-tech consumer product markets—they compete beyond just price. Compared to previous analyses (see Casanova & Miroux, 2018) we observed a steady climb in prices, suggestive of gains in brand equity value. The newer product lines from Chinese companies not only match the quality of products from US companies, but also exhibit similar levels of innovation (e.g., the early launch of foldable smartphone prototypes and 5G phones by Samsung and Huawei).

Examination of white goods, a competitive industry, offers a more complete picture of how Chinese and US companies fare in relation to one another.[2] The prices of white goods—TVs, air conditioners, washing machines, and refrigerators—align with the above identified trend of Chinese firms competing on price, despite having large or dominant market shares in specific product categories. As shown in Table 8.4, Chinese firms hold the top three market shares in the global white goods market. As shown in Fig. 8.5, Midea and Haier sell their air conditioners for far less than the average price offered by LG, but are not very far from their American competitor, Whirlpool. Box 8.3 provides more details on the rise of Haier as one of the global leaders in white goods. Some key elements that led to Haier's ascent are the company's strong focus on innovation, and its active strategy of buying into competitive brands and technologies, such as through the acquisitions of Western leaders like GE Appliances in June 2016.

Chinese companies also compete on price in several other product categories, including service segments such as the airline industry. The lower purchasing power of the average Chinese customer can partially explain the continuation of this trend. To estimate China's average purchasing power, consider the differences in nominal gross domestic product per capita (GDP/capita) across different nations. According to the IMF (2019), China's GDP/capita is $10,150 about a fourth of the average in the European Union (EU) at $36,540 or Japan at $41,020, and just over a seventh of the United States at $64,770. Consequently, Chinese companies are incentivized to design products and services that the domestic market can afford to purchase. Exported around the world, these products and services contributed to gains in the market share of these companies globally.

Table 8.4 Largest white goods sales (% share) by vendor as of 2018.

No.	Company	Market share (%)	Headquarters[a]
1	Midea Group	16.33	China
2	Qingdao Haier	10.63	China
3	Gree Electric Appliances	10.32	China
4	Whirlpool	9.24	United States
5	Electrolux	6.26	Sweden
6	LG	3.93	Korea
7	SEB SA	3.15	France
8	Other	40.13	–

[a] Data for Hong Kong and Taiwan are included under China.
Source: Statista, https://www.statista.com/statistics/461288/major-domestic-appliances-sales-worldwide/; Forbes. https://www.forbes.com/global2000/list/#header:revenue_sortreverse:true_industry:Household%20Appliances, (Accessed March 2019).

[2] We did not include comparative analyses of cars since these Chinese products are not widely sold in the United States.

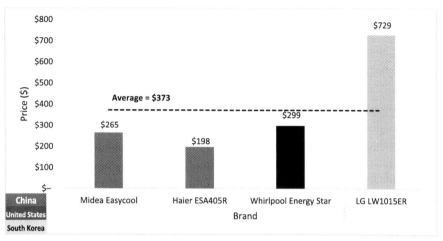

Fig. 8.5 Prices for air conditioners by top US, Chinese, and Korean brands—February 2019. *Source:* Wal-Mart USA, https://www.walmart.com/, (Accessed February 2019).

Box 8.3 Haier Group Corporation—White goods leadership through acquisition

Haier Group Corporation is an industrial conglomerate that specializes in the production and sale of home appliances such as refrigerators, TV sets, washing machines, consumer electronic goods, kitchenware, and numerous other products. Haier was founded in 1984, and is headquartered in Qingdao, China. Under the leadership of its chairman, Zhang Ruiman, Haier became a global super-company. Ruiman's experiments and innovation in management and leadership styles led Haier to grow domestically and internationally from its origins as a refrigerator manufacturer. With the advent of the Internet of Things, Haier transformed from a traditional manufacturing company to one specializing in smart appliances. In 2018, Haier experienced 10% revenue growth from the previous year, with 266.1 billion yuan ($38.7 billion) in revenue. It earned a profit of 33.1 billion yuan ($4.8 billion) in 2018, experiencing a 10% growth from the previous year. Haier has diversified investments, with 55.3% in consumer discretionary, 15.8% in IT, 10.5% in financials, 10.5% in industrials, and 7.8% in health care, materials, and infrastructure combined. A majority of their investments (88.9%) are concentrated in the Asia/Pacific region. Additionally, 5.8% of investments are in Europe, while 1.9% each are in Latin America and the Caribbean, United States and Canada, and Middle East/Africa. Haier's ownership structure is not clearly known. Although it is listed as having partial public ownership, the company claims to be a "collective" (one owned by its employees). Haier also has strong connections with the state. Over the years, Haier has embodied a company culture of "quality," a strategy used to gain consumer confidence in international markets that had low regard for Chinese products. Haier has undergone a number of high-profile acquisitions. As of early 2019, it owns Casarte, GE Appliances, Fisher & Paykel, and many more.

8.2   Comparing input costs, a Chinese advantage

Experts often refer to the Chinese companies' low labor cost as a major advantage, and for this reason we examined how input costs factor into their price competitiveness. An estimated 70% of the costs of a product or service derive from wages, gasoline prices, and electricity. We compared these prices in China with those of other emerging markets (e.g., Brazil, Mexico, India, and South Korea) as well as leading economies (e.g., the United States, Japan, and Germany). While other markets demonstrate comparable attractiveness in terms of labor costs, we looked at the broader variables underlying the appeal of the Chinese market.

Input prices for Chinese companies are well below those of Germany, Japan, the United States, and South Korea (see Fig. 8.6). In China, Mexico, India, and Brazil, the cost of labor is lower and energy prices are competitive. Companies from these regions can hence afford more flexibility in product pricing. Germany, South Korea, the United States, and Japan, with both higher wages and high electricity costs, have the highest prices for goods and services. The total input costs for the United States are about 4.5 times those of China, highlighting an important source of China's competitive advantage.

The total input costs in China, Mexico, and India are comparable. Nevertheless, Mexican and Indian firms have not achieved the same level of global success as

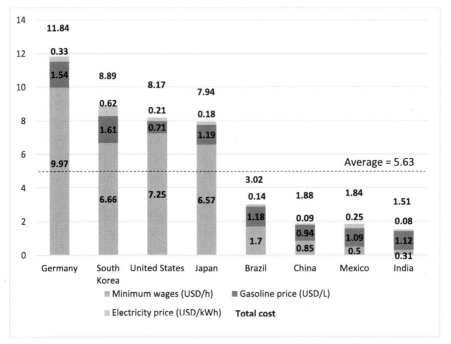

Fig. 8.6 Input costs for China, compared to selected emerging markets and biggest economies (minimum wage, gasoline, and electricity prices).
Source: International Energy (IEA) for gasoline prices, www.wageindicator.org for minimum wages and Statista www.statista.com for electricity prices, (Accessed September 2018).

Chinese firms. Neither Mexico nor India have been able to replicate the rapid growth witnessed in China through the 2010s. Mexican and Indian firms have not been able to enjoy the growth afforded by a large and rapidly growing domestic economy. In addition, Chinese firms have managed to improve production quality; they have excelled in integrating themselves into global supply chains, building effective ecosystems, and investing in R&D and innovation, conditions lacking in other emerging markets including Mexico, Brazil, and India.

While wage rates afford China an advantage, the ratio of revenues and assets per employee is much higher in the United States than in China. Figs. 8.7 and 8.8 plot revenues per employee with return on assets in different industries to consider China's overall industry efficiency compared to other emerging market (E20) and G7 countries in the following areas: (1) technology, media, and telecom, as well as (2) manufacturing (motor vehicles, aerospace, industrial machinery, and engineering). We have included companies in the Fortune Global 500 in 2018.

In Figs. 8.7 and 8.8, companies above and to the right of the line are positioned as the most efficient; this area of the graph indicates higher revenue per employee, with lower assets invested per employee.[3] Chinese companies such as Lenovo,

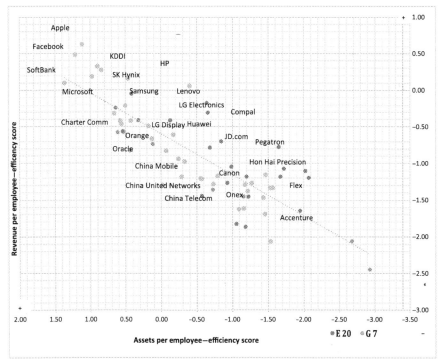

Fig. 8.7 Assets per employee vs revenues per employee in technology, media, and telecom industry in 2018, Fortune Global 500.
Source: Authors based on 2018 Fortune Global 500 data, (Accessed September 2018).

---

[3] The line of best fit represents the average capital expenditure and return on human capital.

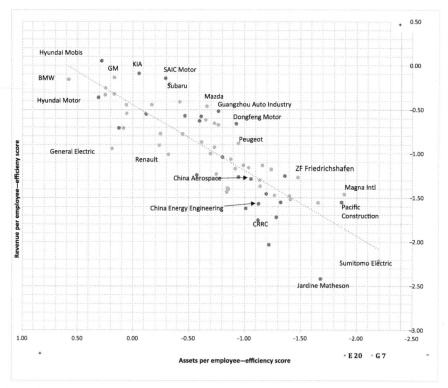

Fig. 8.8 Assets per employee vs revenues per employee in manufacturing (motor vehicles, aerospace, industrial machinery, and engineering) industry in 2018, Fortune Global 500. *Source:* Authors based on 2018 Fortune Global 500 data, (Accessed September 2018).

LG Electronics, Huawei, Pegatron, and Compal are in a stronger position to compete on price compared to traditional multinationals to the left of the line such as Orange, Oracle, and Canon, which do not appear as efficient. Likewise, in the manufacturing industry, Chinese companies like Guangzhou Auto Industry, Dongfeng Motor, and SAIC Motor are well positioned to compete on price, whereas traditional multinationals such as GE, German auto manufacturer BMW, and the French auto manufacturer Renault fall short.

8.3   China's evolving brand recognition

Efficiency and brand leadership are not one and the same. Companies use brand recognition as key leverage to draw further appeal to their products. Powerful brands are linked to quality, reliability, and customer awareness. Examining international brand rankings further draws to the fore China's longstanding cost leadership in contrast to American and European brand differentiation, now dominated by the likes of Amazon, Apple, Google, Microsoft, among others. We focus on China's representation in Brand

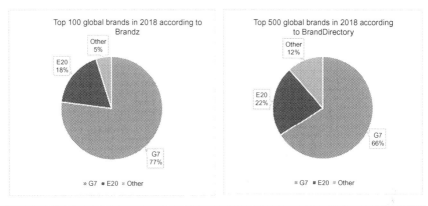

Fig. 8.9 Top 500 (Brandirectory) and top 100 (BrandZ) global brands and their distribution by countries, 2018.
Source: Fortune Global 500, 2018 and Brandirectory's Global Brand 500, 2018 https://brandfinance.com/knowledge-centre/reports/brand-finance-global-500-2019/, and BrandZ, 2018 www.brandZ.com, (Accessed February 2019).

Finance's Global 500 Brandirectory, and in BrandZ. The former ranks companies based on an economic valuation of how much a company can charge for a product or service due to its brand recognition, while the latter ranks the 100 most valuable brands. In the following analyses, we charted the Brandirectory and BrandZ rankings for Chinese companies relative to Group of 7 (G-7) firms.

Both rankings shown above make clear that G-7 economies dominate brand recognition (Fig. 8.9). A full two-thirds of the ranked Brandirectory companies are from G-7 economies, as are 77% from BrandZ. E20 firms fare poorly in comparison but are still more represented in both 2019 rankings relative to previous years. To underscore this data's relevance, we have compared China's presence in the Fortune Global 500 with that of G-7 economies. We found a notable difference in the concentration of Chinese companies, of which China makes up 22.2% of firms in the Fortune Global 500 relative to about 15% in the Brandirectory and BrandZ rankings. Fig. 8.10 demonstrates that US companies make up a much larger ratio of the directories based on brand value.

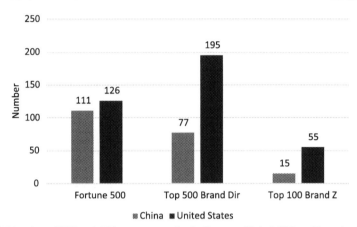

Fig. 8.10 Number of US and Chinese companies in Fortune Global 500 and brand value rankings, 2018.
Source: Fortune Global 500, 2018 and Brandirectory's Global Brand 500, 2019 https://brandfinance.com/knowledge-centre/reports/brand-finance-global-500-2019/, and BrandZ, 2018 www.brandZ.com, (Accessed February 2019).

While the number of Chinese companies in the Fortune Global 500 is converging with the number of US companies, Chinese companies face a long road ahead to catch up on brand equity, recognition, and differentiation. Most Chinese companies are much younger than their American counterparts, suggesting that their smaller strides in brand value are significant. Given that global competition is new for these firms, there are a few remarkable examples of quickly earned success. For example, just 35 years after its creation, Chinese bank ICBC ranked 8th in Brandirectory (see Chapter 5), and China Mobile, with only 20 years of operation, occupied the 15th position in 2019 (see Table 8.5).

Despite the lag, China has made significant inroads in brand equity. For example, in 2009 Chinese brands accounted for about 9% of the firms in the top 500 global brands ranked by Brandirectory; by 2018, this ratio had risen to 15% (Fig. 8.11). Furthermore, Chinese firms account for almost half of the top 25 most valuable global brands in 2019 (11/25), with clear improvement in rankings relative to the previous year. For example, ICBC advanced from 10th to 8th, Huawei from 25th to 12th, Ping An from 29th to 14th, and Toabao made its first ranking appearance (see Table 8.5). These comparisons show that Chinese brands are clearly improving in value and competitiveness relative to other global brands.

Even as American companies maintain dominant positions across the top global brands (see Fig. 8.12), the scenario is changing as several Chinese firms upend the status quo by wresting spots among the top 25 best ranked brands in the world. We can expect more Chinese firms to enter the select group of the world's most valuable brands as their investments in global recognition, new technologies, and innovation start to pay off.

Table 8.5 The top 25 most valuable brands in the world according to Brandirectory (Chinese brands in *bold*).

2019	2018	Name	Country	2019	2018	2019	2018
1	1	Amazon	United States	$187,905M	$150,811M	AAA−	AAA−
2	2	Apple	United States	$153,634M	$146,311M	AAA	AAA+
3	3	Google	United States	$142,755M	$120,911M	AAA	AAA+
4	6	Microsoft	United States	$119,595M	$81,163M	AAA	AAA+
5	4	Samsung	Korea	$91,282M	$92,289M	AAA−	AAA+
6	5	AT&T	United States	$87,005M	$82,422M	AA+	AAA−
7	7	Facebook	United States	$83,202M	$76,526M	AAA−	AAA+
8	**10**	**ICBC**	**China**	**$79,823M**	**$59,189M**	**AAA+**	**AAA+**
9	8	Verizon	United States	$71,154M	$62,826M	AAA	AAA−
10	**11**	**China Construction Bank**	**China**	**$69,742M**	**$56,789M**	**AAA**	**AAA**
11	9	Walmart	United States	$67,867M	$61,480M	AA+	AA+
12	**25**	**Huawei**	**China**	**$62,278M**	**$38,046M**	**AAA−**	**AAA−**
13	13	Mercedes	Germany	$60,355M	$47,936M	AAA−	AA+
14	**29**	**Ping An**	**China**	**$57,626M**	**$32,609M**	**AAA−**	**AAA−**
15	**12**	**China Mobile**	**China**	**$55,670M**	**$53,226M**	**AAA**	**AAA**
16	**26**	**Agricultural Bank of China**	**China**	**$55,040M**	**$37,321M**	**AAA**	**AAA**

Continued

Table 8.5 The top 25 most valuable brands in the world according to Brandirectory (Chinese brands in ***bold***)—cont'd

2019	2018	Name	Country	2019	2018	2019	2018
17	15	Toyota	Japan	$52,291M	$43,701M	AAA	AAA
18	**18**	**State Grid Corporation of China**	**China**	**$51,292M**	**$40,944M**	**AA+**	**AA+**
19	**17**	**Bank of China**	**China**	**$50,990M**	**$41,750M**	**AAA**	**AAA**
20	**47**	**WeChat**	**China**	**$50,707M**	**$22,415M**	**AAA+**	**AAA**
21	**20**	**Tencent (QQ)**	**China**	**$49,701M**	**$40,774M**	**AAA**	**AAA**
22	27	Home Depot	United States	$47,056M	$33,748M	AAA–	AAA–
23		**Taobao**	**China**	**$46,628M**		**AAA–**	
24	21	T (Deutsche Telekom)	Germany	$46,259M	$40,152M	AAA–	AA+
25	30	Walt Disney	United States	$45,750M	$32,590M	AAA	AAA+

Source: https://brandirectory.com/rankings/global-500-2019, (Accessed March 2019).

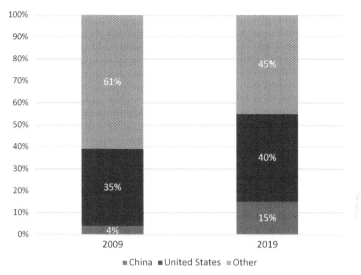

Fig. 8.11 Share of E20, G-7, and rest of the world in top 500 global brands, 2019.
Source: Fortune Global 500, 2018 and Brandirectory's Global Brand 500, 2019 https://brandfinance.com/knowledge-centre/reports/brand-finance-global-500-2019/ (Accessed February 2019).

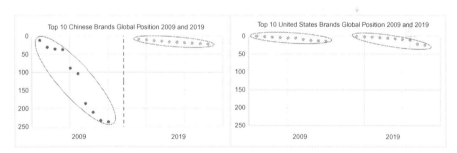

Fig. 8.12 Rank of top 10 brands in China and the United States, 2009–19.
Source: Brandirectory's Global Brand 500, 2019, https://brandfinance.com/knowledge-centre/reports/brand-finance-global 500-2019/, and BrandZ, 2018 www.brandZ.com, (Accessed February 2019).

8.4 When will Chinese brands become household names?

Chinese firms have gained significant leading positions in several sectors globally over a short period of time. The country's rapidly growing domestic market fueled much of this growth, as companies leveraged their lower input costs and fine-tuned production efficiencies. After successfully addressing the needs of domestic Chinese customers (many with low purchasing power), Chinese companies have been able to transfer this experience to compete overseas on price across multiple product categories, amassing leadership positions on a global scale.

As China placed a greater emphasis on globalization, its companies like Lenovo and Huawei led the charge by repositioning their brands for leadership on the international stage. Chinese companies have moved beyond cost leadership as its top priority and are focusing more on innovation and technology to consolidate brand leadership and solidify their market standing.

The gradual but significant turn away from cost leadership has shifted the way Chinese manufacturing operates, as factory managers in China increase wages in order to retain workers. The incoming loss of its cheap labor advantage has led to increased automation across Chinese factories. Accordingly, Chinese companies have pivoted from manufacturing components and assembling systems for Western brands to scale up and develop their own capacity to innovate. Even as they become formidable competitors, Chinese companies are still less efficient than many of their Western counterparts in some key metrics such as revenues per employee (see Chapter 1). Our analysis of the world's most valuable brands indicate, however, that Chinese firms—while not yet on equal footing—have gained ground compared to, for instance, their American peers.

References

Casanova, L., & Miroux, A. (2018). *Emerging market multinationals report 2018.* Emerging Markets Reshaping Globalization. https://www.johnson.cornell.edu/Portals/32/EMI%20 Docu/EMR/EMR2018_V3_FIN-11Jan.pdf. (Accessed June 2019).

Chattopadhyay, A., & Batra, R. (2012). *The new emerging market multinationals: Four strategies for disrupting markets and building brands.* New York: McGraw Hill.

International Monetary Fund (IMF). (2019). *GDP per capita data.* https://www.imf.org/external/datamapper/NGDPDPC@WEO/OEMDC/ADVEC/WEOWORLD. (Accessed May 2019).

Kumar, N., & Steenkamp, J.-B. (2013). *Brand breakout. How emerging market brands will go global.* Basingstoke: Palgrave Macmillan.

Peng, W. (2012). The global strategy of emerging multinationals from China. *Global Strategy Journal, 2,* 97–107. https://doi.org/10.1111/j.2042-5805.2012.01030.x.

Tencent: An innovative tech giant[*] 9

*Technology can bring benefits to the human race; humans should
make good use of technology and refrain from its evil use; and
technology should strive to solve the problems it brings to society*
Pony Ma, Founder and CEO of Tencent at Second Digital China Summit,
April 2019

Acronyms

B2B	business to business
B2C	business to consumer
CAPEX	capital expenditure
Freemium	free and premium
M&A	mergers and acquisitions
MAU	monthly average user
MMOs	massively multiplayer online games
NBA	National Basketball Association
O2O	online to offline
PCCW	Pacific Century Cyberworks Ltd.
QQ	Tencent's first instant messaging service
R&D	Research and development
VAS	value-added services
VC	venture capital
Weixin	Tencent product called WeChat in the global market

Tencent is a powerhouse purveyor of innovative services: from media and entertainment, to online advertisement and mobile payment. The company's success
across a wide range of market frontiers is made all the more visible by its stellar
growth: in 2018, the company's operating profit increased 8% from the previous
year to $14.19 billion, all the while its revenue swelled 32% to $45.46 billion. This
chapter takes stock of Tencent's rise as an emerging multinational in China's rapidly thriving innovation ecosystem. We examine Tencent's interconnected network
of services, and how this "universe" powered the company's growing clout in China
and beyond.

---

[*]This chapter builds on another one published in Casanova, L., Cornelius, P., & Dutta, S. (2018).
Entrepreneurship and the Finance of Innovation in Emerging Markets. Elsevier. https://
www.elsevier.com/books/financing-entrepreneurship-and-innovation-in-emerging-markets/
casanova/978-0-12-804025-6.

The Era of Chinese Multinationals, https://doi.org/10.1016/B978-0-12-816857-8.00009-4

Tencent Holdings, Ltd., is a technology conglomerate and the fifth-most valuable Internet company in the world as of May 2019. Based in Shenzhen, the Chinese investment holding company touts a market capitalization of $474 billion as of March 2019, trailing closely behind US-based Internet giants Google Inc./Alphabet Inc. ($739 billion), Amazon Inc. ($782 billion), Facebook Inc. ($537 billion), and Alibaba Group Holding Ltd. ($508 billion) from China.

9.1 Tencent's early days

Tencent first burst onto the scene as an instant messaging service (QQ) in 1998, but its lack of external funding proved an early barrier. Without charging users, the company failed to secure loans from Chinese banks constrained by restrictive regulations. Regardless of Tencent's projected value, its founders could not find a loan for their fixed capital company and were forced to look elsewhere to meet their needs. Tencent received its first windfall from a conditional equity offer: $2.2 million for a 40% stake, shared equally between Pacific Century Cyberworks Ltd. (PCCW) and IDG Capital. There was one catch: the equity funding was contingent upon Tencent amending its business plan and reaching 4 million registered users.

What followed would mark the beginning of a story of astonishing growth. By April 2000, Tencent received the funding that it needed, as it had reached close to 10 million users. South African company Naspers provided an additional $32 million equity investment in 2001, which afforded Tencent the necessary time and resources to expand QQ's user base and generate additional revenue. In time, it would become evident that Tencent was one of Naspers' most successful venture capital (VC) investments. By March 2019, Naspers 46.5% stake in Tencent was worth $134 billion, significantly more than Naspers itself (Meyer, 2018).

As mobile phones gained popularity in the early 2000s, Tencent found new means to monetize its user base. Tailoring its service to computers and mobile phones, Tencent developed Mobile QQ, a state-owned China Mobile Communications Corp., which charged users a fee of 5 yuan ($0.85) per month, sharing 20% of its revenue with Tencent. This early step into mobile communication laid the groundwork for Tencent to surge to profit by 2001 and for the blockbuster value-added services to come.

However, Tencent had yet to establish its own revenue stream independent of any partner. It thus launched "Q coin," an online currency system, in 2005, which became the de facto standard for all purchases on the Tencent ecosystem. Soon, it unveiled its first website (www.tencent.com) a QQ portal to boost revenues through advertising. Tencent bet on a "freemium" (free and premium) model, whereby a growing revenue base ensured free services for nonpaying users. Virtual goods, which included virtual add-on items (e.g., ringtones, virtual pets, clothing, and jewelry), reflected this strategy. Once Tencent launched the QQ leisure game portal, hosting games developed in-house and elsewhere, laying bare its interconnected service advantage.

In its mission to compete with other social media platforms, Tencent transferred the bulk of its engineers toward mobile development and set the stage for its crowning achievement, Weixin (called WeChat in the global market). Today, WeChat combines WhatsApp's messaging features, Snapchat's quick photo chat,

Facebook's social networking functions, and Instagram's photo-sharing abilities. The company set in motion a universe of verticals from food ordering to ridesharing made possible by tools such as Online-to-Offline (O2O) services. By 2015, the company waded into cloud computing, announcing a staggering investment of $1.57 billion over 5 years, a gambit certain to bear far-reaching implications.

9.1.1   Venture capital investments

As Tencent focused its efforts on forging an ecosystem of linked *services*, it also ensured its success by creating a system of linked *companies*. The company leaned on a series of strategic VC investments beginning in 1999. While it made investments in other parts of the world, most were in China or in its natural market of neighboring countries. Tencent accelerated its investment pace over the years, for instance, investing in more than 163 deals globally in 2018 compared to 143 in 2017 (Deng, 2019). Its investments in 2015–17 totaled more than $30 billion.

We analyzed 211 VC investments Tencent made between 2015 and 2018 and found that 59% of these investments were made in China, 26% in the United States, 3% in South Korea, and 2% each in Hong Kong and India. Of the top 25 VC investments, 21 were in China alone. Over time, the value of China's share increased to approximately 80%, followed by 13% in South Korea, 5% in the United States, and 1% in India. This increased investment in Asian countries resulted in Tencent's extraordinary regional competitive advantage. With a firm grasp on the Asian market, Tencent sought to expand globally by increasing its investments into Europe and North America.

We also found that while a majority of the 211 investments were below $1 billion mark, the company made nine investments over $1 billion.

We also analyzed the industry breakdown of Tencent's VC investments. Almost 35% (91) of Tencent's 211 VC investments were in Internet companies, followed by 26% (68) and 12% (32) in telecom and software, respectively. Gaming companies received 9% (24) of investments, indicative of Tencent's intent to consolidate its leadership position in this industry. While most of Tencent's VC investments were in Internet and mobile service industries, over time, the trend shifted to include investments in the transportation and logistics industry.

All told, Tencent's VC investments were critical to broadening the company's innovation ecosystem and further monetizing its loyal user base. As a result, Tencent was able to expand its leadership position in certain business segments (notably, gaming, which produces the majority of the company's revenue). See Appendix for Tencent's top 25 VC investments from 1999 to 2018.

9.2   Internationalization

Following rampant success in China, Tencent sought to promote its products and services to a more global audience. Tencent invested $2 billion on internationalization, focusing on international patent applications, adapting WeChat for international users, and expanding gaming for a global audience.

From 2008 to 2014, 51% of its investments were in the United States, 40% in China, 5% in South Korea, 2% in India, and 2% in Russia (CBinsights, 2014). Tencent Cloud, a public cloud service provider, has expanded globally to over 23 countries including India, the United States, Germany, South Korea, and numerous others. With global competitors such as Amazon, Microsoft, and Google, Tencent Cloud still has a long way to go.

Tencent is likewise expanding internationally in myriad markets and industries ranging from gaming, education, media, to e-commerce. VIPKID, an online education platform, is supported by Tencent. The company is also continuing to increase its monetization in artificial intelligence (AI). As of 2017, Tencent announced the opening of an AI research facility in Seattle, Washington where research in imaging recognition and voice recognition is underway, to integrate WeChat with voice-controlled assistance. Such expansions worldwide will not only increase the firm's presence in the international market but also challenge global businesses to connect with Tencent in order to reach the Chinese market.

9.2.1   Increasing patent filings

Tencent's international expansion began with filing a series of worldwide patents and utility model applications, first in 2002, and from 2005 to 2007. Tencent quickly ramped up expansion efforts between 2008 and 2010, doubling its filings relative to the previous 2 years. Most of the filings were in information technology and telecommunications, two areas at the heart of research and development (R&D) strategy and infrastructure development. In 2014, Tencent increased its patent filings by 200% over the previous year, the second largest increase in patent filings in the world (World Intellectual Property Organization, 2015). On average, Tencent applies for more than 2000 patent applications yearly, with more than 200 patent applications in the United States, Europe, Japan, and South Korea. In 2018, Tencent filed 1168 patents for AI, surpassing Samsung with 1047 patent filings (Shead, 2018). To continue growth while avoiding patent infringements, in 2018, Tencent announced a patent agreement with Google to develop future technologies in concert (Chen, 2018).

9.2.2   Taking WeChat global

WeChat is Tencent's most public internationalization effort to date. WeChat combines the functionality of free text, voice, and videos messaging, along with functions to post social updates (a la Facebook), call cabs (a la Uber), and share videos (a la Snapchat), as well as other mobile payment and game functions. Tencent has allocated significant resources to make the app compatible with iOS, Android, Blackberry, and Windows phones outside of China. WeChat was most heavily marketed and integrated in India, Malaysia, Indonesia, Thailand, and the Philippines, some of China's natural markets. In 2013, Tencent opened offices in Singapore, the Philippines, Malaysia, and the United States, spending $6.4 million, $6.4 million, $8.8 million, and $5.4 million, respectively, to expand the user base of WeChat in these markets (FDImarkets, 2017).

WeChat also made gains in market share in African and Latin American countries such as South Africa, Brazil, Argentina, and Mexico. As a result, WeChat rapidly amassed around 1.09 billion users as of 2018, up from 50 million in 2011 (Statista, 2018). More recently, however, Tencent has curbed its strategy of expansion through WeChat, and has instead focused on enhancing its ecosystem in mainland China.

9.2.3   Mergers and acquisitions and investment in gaming to expand global footprint

Tencent followed a different approach when internationalizing its gaming sector, first by purchasing major gaming companies, and then supporting VC firms to encourage start-ups. The company has been on a shopping spree for popular games amassing companies that have produced some of the most popular titles since 2008. In 2009, Tencent purchased Riot Games Inc., a prolific and profitable US game developer. By 2012, it bought 48% of US-based Epic Games Inc., the developer of Unreal Engine, 49% of Level Up International Holdings, a Singaporean online game operator (Lu, 2012), and paid for two rounds of investment in Kamcord, a US mobile game-streaming service. A year later, the Chinese giant purchased a 6% stake in Activision Blizzard Inc., World of Warcraft's developer, for an estimated $1.4 billion (Table 9.1).

Meanwhile, Tencent teamed up with Capstone Partners, LLC., a Korean VC firm, to invest in several small South Korean game start-ups. In 2015, Tencent made two substantial investments in San Francisco video game developers. Its stakes in both small start-ups and large companies proved a successful internationalization strategy, as companies like Riot Games opened office in the United States and across the world. These offices afforded Tencent better access to diverse markets all the while strengthening Riot Games' local relationships. Tencent's start-up investments, on the other hand, indicate a commitment to diversification into videogame production. Its most notable transaction in this area was its $8.7 billion acquisition of Finnish company Supercell Oy, the developer of "Clash of Clans." The purchase from SoftBank Group Corp. in June 2016 solidified Tencent's presence in the mobile gaming industry (Osawa & Needleman, 2016).

9.2.3.1   Nubank in Brazil

Continuing with its international expansion, in October 2018 Tencent invested in Nubank, a Brazilian privately held online-only bank that had received approval from Brazil's government to offer loans. Tencent invested $180 million in Nubank, with $90 million invested toward a capital increase and $90 million invested for acquiring partial stakes from Nubank's shareholders (Shieber, 2018). This opportunity is an important one, as Nubank may become a central player in Brazil's financial sector if Brazil decides to move to a cashless economy. Nubank has already issued 5 million credit cards, and Tencent will have the opportunity to strengthen its fintech portfolio, a valuable asset to use against its competitor Alibaba. Tencent's investment in Nubank marks the company's first-ever investment in a stand-alone online bank.

Table 9.1 Tencent's M&A investments by size from 2013 to 2019. *Note:* Only investments higher than $300 million are listed.

Announced date	Transaction type	Target	Country of destination	Size of Tencent's investment ($mm)	Aggregate amount raised ($mm)[a]
June 21, 2016	Merger/acquisition	Supercell Oy	Finland	8600.00	–
November 12, 2017	Merger/acquisition	Uber Technologies, Inc.	United States	8000.00	–
September 11, 2018	Merger/acquisition	Amer Sports Corporation (HLSE:AMEAS)	Finland	6468.80	–
April 10, 2017	Private placement	Flipkart Online Services Pvt. Ltd.	India	3900.00	7110.90
November 3, 2015	Private placement	Meituan Dianping (SEHK:3690)	China	3300.00	4375.00
July 26, 2013	Merger/acquisition	Activision Blizzard, Inc. (NasdaqGS:ATVI)	United States	2338.77	–
January 31, 2019	Private placement	PT Go-Jek Indonesia	Indonesia	2000.00	4050.00
July 3, 2018	Private placement	China Media Capital Inc.	China	1506.06	1506.06
August 25, 2017	Private placement	PT Go-Jek Indonesia	Indonesia	1500.00	2050.00
February 28, 2017	Private placement	GRAIL, Inc.	United States	1211.66	1211.66
October 6, 2017	Private placement	ANI Technologies Private Limited	India	1080.60	2700.84
December 31, 2015	Private placement	Beijing Homelink Real Estate Brokerage Co. Ltd.	China	927.8	927.8
March 25, 2019	Private placement	Ke.Com	China	800	800
September 26, 2018	Merger/acquisition	Bluehole Studio Inc. (nka:Krafton Inc.)	South Korea	730	–
March 8, 2018	Private placement	Wuhan Douyu Network Technology Co., Ltd.	China	631.01	957.01

January 16, 2018	Private placement	ZiroomShenghuo Asset Management	China	621.13	621.13
August 2, 2016	Private placement	Yixin Group Limited (SEHK:2858)	China	550	810
June 15, 2015	Merger/acquisition	iDreamSky Technology Limited	China	545.49	–
April 18, 2018	Private placement	LeshiZhixin Electronic Technology (Tianjin) Co., Ltd.	China	478.18	1482.55
September 15, 2018	Private placement	Shanghai Lantu Information Technology Co., Ltd.	China	450	600
September 16, 2013	Private placement	Sogou Inc. (NYSE:SOGO)	China	448	448
June 12, 2015	Merger/acquisition	Bona Film Group Limited	China	404.92	–
December 20, 2016	Private placement	Bona Film Group Limited	China	359.8	382.29
April 30, 2014	Private placement	Beijing Koudai Technology Co., Ltd.	China	350	362
March 21, 2013	Private Placement	Epic Games, Inc.	United States	330	330

[a] This number reflects the estimated value of the total new money raised through private placement rounds.
Source: Standard & Poor's Capital IQ. (Accessed May 2019).

9.3 Tencent's connected universe and unique business model

What makes Tencent stand out from the crowd is that it is an entire universe of inter-linked businesses rather than a single company. Tencent's gaming business is at the center of this universe, around which the instant messaging platforms (e.g., QQ messenger, WeChat, and Qzone) orbit. The company's other services, the "outer planets" (i.e., its online search, software and apps, e-commerce platforms, web portal, omni-channel/location-based services, mobile payments, entertainment, and social media platforms) cements user loyalty. Altogether, Tencent's comprehensive suite of products provides a platform for brands to engage with customers through multiple touch points, contributing to a "new retail model" sure to inspire other tech companies to follow suit.

In the following section, we delve deeper into Tencent's universe, exploring each element (Fig. 9.1) and how they interconnect.

9.3.1 Gaming

Inclusive of Supercell, Tencent has become the largest gaming company in the world with $11.1 billion in revenue in 2015 (Newzoo, 2016). Tencent owns stakes in the most

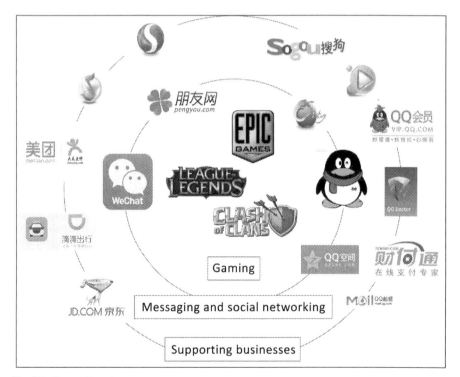

Fig. 9.1 Tencent's universe.
Source: Authors' analysis based on Tencent annual reports.

popular massively multiplayer online games (MMOs) including League of Legends, Crossfire, and Dungeon Fighter Online, which collectively brought in $3.75 billion in 2017 (Takahashi, 2016). In 2018, Tencent's smartphone games saw a 12% increase in revenues from 2017 (a much smaller growth, however, than in the previous year) (Xu, 2019). League of Legends, the only product of Los Angeles-based Riot Games, was one of the most popular online games in the world with over 111 million monthly players with revenues of $1.4 billion, behind Fortnite and Dungeon Fighter online. Riot Games operate 24 offices around the world with 2500 employees.

Tencent avoided many of the risks of pay-to-play games by employing its "freemium" model once again. Tencent was also able to garner significant revenues and increase customer demand by promoting games on WeChat and QQ, enticing gamers and nongamers alike. By designing its own games and strategically investing and acquiring game developers, Tencent was able to reduce competition with other game distributors. The icing on the cake is Tencent's ability to promote its games to the large user base on its own social platforms, generating cash flow and reducing marketing costs simultaneously. And yet, outside of China, most gamers play without knowing that many of the games are actually owned by a Chinese company—Tencent.

9.3.2   Messaging and social networking

As shown above, much of Tencent's success is due to the "network effect" inherent in its social media and instant messaging services. The following platforms fall under its umbrella:

- *QQ messenger* is a chat messenger service with more than 780 million monthly active user accounts in China (Statista, 2018). Its monthly active users, however, are decreasing as popularity shifts in WeChat's favor.
- *WeChat* ("Weixin" in China) is Tencent's crown jewel, with almost 1 billion users worldwide (Statista, 2018).
- *Qzone* is a social network that enables users to write blogs, keep diaries, send photos, listen to music, and watch videos. Launched in 2005, Qzone has reached close to 900 million monthly users, most of whom access the service via smart devices.
- *Pengyou* is an online social network marketed primarily for Chinese students and white-collar workers, designed for corporate outreach as users can become "fans" of companies, which in turn make use of the platform to engage consumers.

9.4   Tencent supporting businesses

Tencent encourages users to stay within its own universe of services by offering a comprehensive suite of products in the form of supporting businesses.

The supporting businesses at Tencent are as follows.

9.4.1   Search engine and email

- *Sogou.com* is integrated into WeChat and is a Chinese search engine that enables users to search text, images, music, and maps.
- *QQ mail* is an email service like Gmail.

9.4.2   Software and apps

- *QQ Doctor* is a free antivirus software.
- *QQ Pinyin* transliterates Chinese using the pinyin method so that users can convert words from pinyin to traditional or simple Chinese.
- *QQ Software Manager* is a tool that allows users to install and uninstall Tencent's software, like Google Play on Android devices or the AppStore in Apple devices.
- *QQ Player* is a multimedia player for video and music files.

9.4.3   Online-to-offline (O2O) services

- *Didi Dache* is a ridesharing app. Tencent invested $15 million in Didi Dache in 2013 to allow users to pay cab fees through WeChat. The following year, $100 million in investments from Tencent and other venture capital firms led to the merger and acquisition (M&A) of the local subsidiary prior to it becoming a global ridesharing app.

9.4.4   Payment platforms

- Tencent has incorporated mobile payment capabilities in WeChat since 2013.
- *Tenpay* supports business-to-business (B2B), business-to-customer (B2C), and customer-to-customer payments since 2005. Tenpay is used in settlements and licenses, and as such, is backing WeChat Pay and all of Tencent's payment systems including QQ wallet.
- *WeChatPay* transfers money between WeChat users (peer-to-peer) and allows users to make payments online and with participating offline retailers within WeChat. As of 2018, WeChatPay captured 40% of the Chinese mobile payment services market in China (Statista, 2018). Alibaba's Alipay is Tencent's biggest mobile payment rival.

Tencent's payment platforms overtake other mobile payment platforms by competitors such as Alibaba and Baidu. It offers services such as payments overseas and web payments from mobile phones.

Tencent also operates its own licensed online banks, along with competitors such as Baidu and Alibaba. Tencent's online bank (WeBank) is the strongest in China, with net profits at 1.448 billion RMB for 2017, which is 1 billion RMB higher than its closest competitor MyBank (Alibaba). WeBank lent twice the amount lent by MyBank in 2017. Tencent continues to enter the fintech sector, in industries such as banking, securities, insurance, and third party payments among others.

9.4.5   Entertainment platforms

- *QQShow* is an avatar-based social platform that adheres to the freemium model to outfit digital avatars with virtual goods.
- *QQMusic* is an online music streaming service. QQMusic joined with market leader China Music Corporation in $2.7 billion merger in 2016. In February 2018, Tencent bought 10% of the Swedish music streaming company Spotify.
- *Tencent Pictures* distributes films and in 2015 launched Tencent Penguin Pictures in Shanghai to begin producing films. As of 2019, Tencent Pictures has financed Men in Black, International and Terminator, and Dark Fate and in 2020 is planning Top Gun: Maverick.

9.5   Unique business model

Recognizing the potential of a connected products ecosystem, Tencent fielded a connection strategy to expand its business building on its current business model (see Fig. 9.2). In 2015, the company launched its "Internet-Plus" strategy. Its key initiatives and objectives are as follows:

- "Enriching products and services available within [Tencent's] platforms. For example, [Tencent] introduced personal micro-loan products and municipal services, such as visa applications, to Mobile QQ and Weixin."
- "Promoting [its] online payment services through enriched payment scenarios, increasing [Monthly Average Users] (MAU) of [their] mobile payment services by over 7 times year-on-year."
- "Growing its mobile utility services, including security, browser and application store, strengthening infrastructural supports to [their] mobile products."
- "Investing in equity stakes in leading companies in related Internet verticals, such as Internet Plus Holdings, to provide best-in-class services to [their] users."(Tencent, 2015).

One of Tencent's major strengths is its diverse array of revenue streams, more so than other major players in social media. While Facebook and Google/Alphabet receive 98% and 86% of their revenues, respectively, from advertising, Tencent only rakes in 17% of its revenue through advertising. Rather, Tencent anchors its efforts in three main revenue categories:

- *Fee-based revenue*: subscriptions and purchase of virtual goods within games and social networks to add items or levels/functionality to their in-game experience.
- *Traffic-based revenue*: online advertising through cost-per-display, cost-per-thousand, cost-per-click, or cost-per-acquisition.
- *Transaction-based-revenue*: small fees accrued for transactions (e.g., WeChat utility payments).

Tencent's revenue as of December 31, 2018 is $45.46 billion, up 32% from the previous year. Online advertising contributed about $8.4 billion alone, sporting 44% growth from 2017. Other sources (including e-commerce) reported up to $11.34 billion, 80% higher revenues than in 2017. Value-added services (VAS) alone have increased from $12.4 billion in 2015 to $25.67 billion in 2018, as visible in Fig. 9.3, but

For mechants	For users	For tencent
• Access to large user base • Unified user log-in enables CRM and targeted advertising • Online payment facilitates transactions	• Always connected • Access to rich mix of content, services and transactions • Control multiple smart devices	• Deepen user stickiness via broadened product offering • Increase traffic conversion through transactions and advertising • Tap into new markets unlocked by mobile Internet

Fig. 9.2 Tencent's "connection" strategy.
Source: Tencent. (2018). Annual report 2018. https://www.tencent.com/en-us/articles/17000441554112592.pdf (Accessed May 2019).

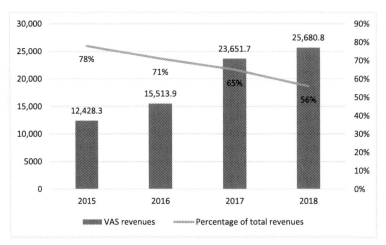

Fig. 9.3 Tencent's VAS revenues (in million US$) from 2015 to 2018. Exchange rate used was as of December 31, 2018, 1 RMB=0.14 US$.
Source: Authors' analysis and Tencent annual reports.

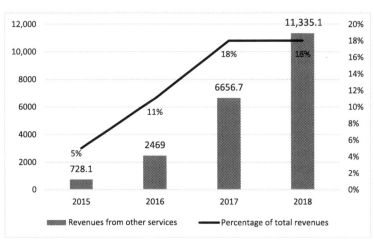

Fig. 9.4 Revenues from Tencent's other services (in million US$), from 2015 to 2018. Exchange rate used was as of December 31, 2018, 1 RMB=0.14 US$.
Source: Authors' analysis and Tencent annual reports.

they represent a decreasing share of Tencent's total revenues, from 78% in 2015 to 56% in 2018 (Tencent, 2018). Fig. 9.4 illustrates the growing importance of other revenues (from cloud and payment services). In 2015, they amounted to only $728 million and accounted for 5% of total revenues. By 2018, they accounted for 18%, a reflection of the ongoing growth of mobile payment and cloud services in China. Indeed, from 2017 to 2018, the number of mobile payment users in China grew by 10.7% to 583 million users (Technode, 2019). In 2018, the value of e-payments reached $41.51 tril-lion, 28 times larger than 5 years earlier (Caixin, 2019).

9.6 Protected environment and collaborative competition

China's policies on disseminating information are among the world's most restrictive. This guarantees homegrown companies such as Tencent, Alibaba, and Baidu a "protective wall" against outside competition. The government censors TV and the news media monitors popular social media platforms like WeChat, and American Internet giants, like Google, Facebook, YouTube, and Twitter, have been blocked in China for years. Tencent bears a strong relationship with the government thanks to its savvy in navigating the regulatory environment, key to its stronghold in China. Critics have condemned Tencent's cozy relationship with the Chinese government, but the latter is expected to take further board seats and ownership stakes in exchange for granting new licenses,.

Three giants dominate the Chinese Internet industry, often collectively referred to as "BAT": Baidu, Alibaba, and Tencent. These three Chinese companies have invested in or acquired hundreds of start-ups in recent years, especially those that produce apps that can connect online users with offline services. This three-way competition has encouraged Tencent to explore different niche areas, through either organic or inorganic means.

In a joint venture bid to challenge Alibaba's dominance, Tencent and Baidu teamed up with conglomerate Wanda Group in 2014. Wanda, a real estate and movie theater chain group, took a 70% stake, while Tencent and Baidu took 15% each in the RMB 5 billion (about $814 million) joint venture (Shu, 2014). The partnership promoted Tencent's online payment platforms, including Tenpay and Weixin Payment. As a result, TenPay and Weixin Payment became the preferred payment method across all of Wanda's businesses, including its movie theaters. Tencent also gained access to Wanda-owned movies, TV shows, and online dramas. Before this joint venture, Alipay had 80% of the market share, but this subsequently decreased to 54%. In 2018, WeChatPay was the most widely used e-payment platform in China, with more than 900 million users, besting Alipay's 500 million users (Jacobs, 2018).

BAT's competition is particularly intense in the O2O space (buying goods offline though apps online). Alibaba and Tencent were principal investors in two O2O companies, Meituan and Dianping, which merged at the end of 2015. While the two companies were quite different, one of their core similarities was a focus on discount coupons. Meituan was an unabashed Groupon clone founded by Wang Xing, while Dianping, referred to as the "Chinese Yelp," was founded before its American counterpart, and often rewarded members discounts if they bought meals at reviewed restaurants with their friends (Cendrowski, 2015). A bevy of competitors encroached upon Dianping and Meituan, including Baidu-backed Nuomi Holdings Inc. As a result, Tencent and Alibaba agreed to join resources to compete against Nuomi.

Similarly, China's biggest taxi-hailing apps, Tencent-backed Didi Dache and Alibaba-backed KuaidiDache, merged after a costly price war, to become Didi Chuxing earlier in 2015. This deal helped the combined entity successfully ward off the threat from Uber Technologies Inc., which eventually sold its stake to the combined entity. In the deal announced in August 2016, Uber agreed to swap its China operations for a 20% stake in Didi Chuxing, valued at $28 billion in its latest fund-raising round. Combined with Uber's China business, valued at around $8 billion, Didi had a valuation of around $36 billion.

Meituan.com	Leading O2O platform for urban and lifestyle services
JD.com	China's largest ecommerce retailer
LY.com	Travel service website
Leju.com	Online real estate trading platform
58.com	China's largest categorized information website
BBS.DXY.CN	China's largest professional medicine website
Cheetah Mobile	Number 1 global mobile tools
Kingsoft.com	China's leading software provider
NAVINFO.com	China's leading digital map content solution provider
Yiche.com	Number 1 website for car consumers
Sogou.com	Third largest search engine
Melllahuo.com	China's largest online fast fashion platform for women
Guahao.com	Professional online medical care service in China

Fig. 9.5 Examples of Tencent's stakes in other verticals.
Source: Author analysis based on Tencent annual reports.

This example of "collaborative competition" is suggestive of how the three Internet giants are not averse to teaming up when they feel it is advantageous to do so, an important factor behind the accelerated growth of these three companies, particularly Tencent. Fig. 9.5 lists examples of verticals that Tencent reached through cooperation, investments and M&A.

9.7 Challenges

Tencent does face some hurdles which it must overcome in order to continue its rapid growth rate. The most notable challenge is expanding WeChat usage to the rest of the world. With 93% of consumers in Chinese tier-one cities already making use of WeChat, the only way to expand it is abroad. To that end, Tencent must customize the app for each market in which it plans to operate. Whenever WeChat releases updates, Tencent must create versions for 14 countries, in more than 10 different languages. Expanding WeChat's user base will therefore require a series of continuous adjustments and improvements.

Tencent faces another challenge in foreign countries: the perception that users' privacy may be at risk because of Tencent's links to the Chinese government. To combat this, WeChat intends to distance both its operations and brand from Tencent. As opposed to Tencent's organizational structure, WeChat independently maintains its own management team, board of directors, and decision-making capabilities. Moreover, Tencent is not involved in WeChat's daily operations, and serves as a holding company. Meanwhile, Tencent is teaming up with Google and other partners to give WeChat a more "local" feel. In January 2014, Tencent began encouraging Google users to link their accounts to WeChat with the incentive to win a $25 Restaurant.com gift card for inviting Google contacts to join WeChat.

One of Tencent's challenges is generating revenue out of its online gaming sector. Chinese gamers play mostly on PC and mobile platforms (largely as a result of a government ban on consoles that lasted up to 2013). The players generally expect that games on these platforms are free. Tencent's freemium revenue model has helped the firm to overcome this challenge.

China's varied levels of Internet infrastructure pose another challenge. While the country has made great strides to expand high-speed Internet capabilities, connection speed, and stability trail the United States and other developed countries. Tencent is collaborating with China's telecom giants, such as China Unicom and China Mobile, to combat nuisances like game lag and dropped connections by introducing high-speed fiber optic lines for second- and third-tier cities. Finally, Tencent has been all but locked out of the US market. While WeChat remains a runaway success in China, it has fared poorly contending with American social media giants like Facebook and Instagram. To date, Tencent's most successful US-based investments bring content back to China, rather than the other way around (such as agreements to stream content from the National Basketball Association (NBA), Warner Bros., and HBO on Tencent's video platform).

9.8   Looking ahead

Tencent, named the most valuable Chinese brand (BrandZ, 2018) and the fifth most valuable brand in the world, is one of the few companies capable of generating its own licensing revenue. While its main competitors Alibaba and Baidu have their own connected ecosystems, the sheer success of Tencent's "one-stop shop" philosophy is difficult to replicate, especially in the gaming industry, a chief accelerator of company growth. Facebook is also trying to provide a more comprehensive customer experience a la Tencent, but we believe that it is unlikely to soon garner the same traction that Tencent already holds.

Tencent will likely retain its lead in the gaming industry. A chief accelerator of company growth, Tencent's gaming assets afford the opportunity for increasing per user revenue as the company continues to expand its game portfolio push in-game purchases.

Because Tencent only receives less than a quarter of its revenue from advertising, this margin gives Tencent significant room to grow. Our forecast indicates this growth will continue as more of Tencent's revenue stems from online payment. Rating agencies have shown great confidence in Tencent's ability to maintain high profitability— Tencent's revenue diversity is key to its ability to generate free cash flow, which also reassures investors.

That being said, Tencent heavily depended on the Chinese market, and it will be critical for Tencent to translate its connection strategy to work in international markets. The company will need to find innovative ways to expand WeChat's reach beyond China and bring its gaming assets to other countries.

Moving forward, Tencent is also looking to provide technology solutions to conventional industries to reduce costs (notably, cloud computing and AI). Tencent plans to roll out these services for logistics, education, energy, and automobile industries, as well as e-commerce and health care.

During personal interviews with company executives in December 2018, the latter described ways that Tencent may spread its influence ever wider to gain more users, even as the B2C market reaches saturation in China. As Tencent celebrated its 20th anniversary in 2018, the company is now solidly positioned as a comprehensive Internet company.

Appendix

Top 25 Tencent VC investments from 1999 to 2018, by size of investment.

Order	Target	Country	Industry	Announced date	Size ($mm)	Buyer/investors
1	Postal Savings Bank of China Co., Ltd. (SEHK:1658)	China	Retail banking	December 8, 2015	7028.53	Ant Financial Services Group; Canada Pension Plan Investment Board; China Life Insurance Company Limited (SEHK:2628); China Telecom Corporation Limited (SEHK:728); DBS Capital Investments Ltd.; International Finance Corporation; J.P. Morgan (China) Venture Capital Investment Company Limited; Temasek Holdings (Private) Limited; **Tencent Holdings Ltd., Investment Arm;** UBS Group AG (SWX:UBSG)
2	Didi Chuxing Technology Co., Ltd.	China	Transportation delivery	May 12, 2016	4800.0	Alibaba Group Holding Limited (NYSE:BABA); Ant Financial Services Group; Apple Inc. (NasdaqGS:AAPL); Bank of Communications Co., Ltd. (SEHK:3328); China Life Investment Holding Company Limited; China Minsheng Investment Group Corp., Ltd.; China Poly Group Corporation; Poly Real Estate Group Co.,Ltd. (SHSE:600048); SoftBank Group Corp. (TSE:9984); **Tencent Holdings Ltd., Investment Arm**

3	China Internet Plus Group	China	Group buying (Internet)	October 13, 2017	4000.0	Canada Pension Plan Investment Board; China Development Bank Capital Corporation Ltd.; Coatue Management, L.L.C.; GIC Pte. Ltd.; IDG Capital Partners; Mubadala Development Company PJSC; Sequoia Capital China; **Tencent Holdings Ltd., Investment Arm**; The Priceline Group Inc. (nka:Booking Holdings Inc. (NasdaqGS:BKNG)); Tiger Global Management LLC; TrustBridge Partners *Buyer Funds*: China-UAE Investment Cooperation Fund
4	Flipkart Online Services Pvt. Ltd.	India	E-commerce	April 10, 2017	3900.0	eBay Inc. (NasdaqGS:EBAY): Microsoft Corporation, Investment Arm; SoftBank Investment Advisers; **Tencent Holdings Limited (SEHK:700)** *Buyer Funds*: SoftBank Vision Fund
5	Meituan Group, Inc. (nka:China Internet Plus Group)	China	Group buying (Internet)	November 3, 2015	3300.0	Baillie Gifford & Co Limited; Canada Pension Plan Investment Board; Capital Today; China Development Bank Capital Corporation Ltd.; China International Capital Corporation Limited (SEHK:3908); DST Global; Sequoia Capital China; Temasek Holdings (Private) Limited; **Tencent Holdings Limited (SEHK:700)**; TrustBridge Partners

Continued

Order	Target	Country	Industry	Announced date	Size ($mm)	Buyer/investors
6	Didi Chuxing Technology Co., Ltd.	China	Transportation delivery	June 17, 2015	3000.0	Alibaba Capital Partners; Capital International, Inc.; China Investment Corporation; Coatue Management, L.L.C.; D. E. Shaw & Co., L.P.; Hillhouse Capital Management, Ltd.; Ping An Ventures; Russian Direct Investment Fund; SoftBank Corp. (nka:SoftBank Group Corp. (TSE:9984); Temasek Holdings (Private) Limited; **Tencent Holdings Ltd., Investment Arm** *Buyer Funds:* Russia-China Investment Fund
7	JD Logistics	China	*E-commerce*	February 13, 2018	2500.0	China Development Bank Capital Corporation Ltd.; China Life Insurance Company Limited (SEHK:2628); China Merchants Technology Holdings Co., Ltd.; China Structural Reform Fund Co., Ltd.; Hillhouse Capital Management, Ltd.; ICBC International Holdings Limited, Investment Arm; Sequoia Capital China; **Tencent Holdings Ltd., Investment Arm**
8	GRAIL, Inc.	United States	Healthcare	February 28, 2017	1211.66	Amazon.com, Inc. (NasdaqGS:AMZN); Arch Venture Partners, L.P; Bristol-Myers Squibb Company (NYSE:BMY); Celgene Corporation (NasdaqGS:CELG); Johnson & Johnson UK Treasury Company Limited; McKesson Ventures; Merck & Co., Inc. (NYSE:MRK); **Tencent Holdings Limited (SEHK:700)**; Varian Medical Systems, Inc. (NYSE:VAR)

	Company	Country	Industry	Date	Amount	Investors
9	PT Go-Jek Indonesia	Indonesia	Logistics	August 25, 2017	1200.0	Alphabet Inc. (NasdaqGS:GOOGL); JD.com, Inc. (NasdaqGS:JD); Temasek Holdings (Private) Limited; **Tencent Holdings Limited (SEHK:700)**
10	NEXTEV LIMITED	China	Automotive	November 8, 2017	1000.0	Baillie Gifford & Co.; China Asset Management Co., Ltd.; China Investment Corporation; CITIC Capital Partners; Lone Pine Capital LLC; Russian Direct Investment Fund; **Tencent Holdings Ltd., Investment Arm** *Buyer Funds*: Russia-China Investment Fund
11	Suzhou Tongcheng Travel E-Commerce Co., Ltd.	China	E-commerce	July 3, 2015	967.59	Beijing Wanda Culture Industry Group Co. Ltd.; CITIC Capital Partners; **Tencent Holdings Ltd., Investment Arm** *Buyer Funds*: Tencent Collaboration Fund
12	Beijing Homelink Real Estate Brokerage Co., Ltd.	China	Real estate brokerage	December 31, 2015	927.8	Baidu, Inc. (NasdaqGS:BIDU); Huasheng Capital; **Tencent Holdings Limited (SEHK:700)**
13	Guazi.com Inc.	China	Internet	March 1, 2018	818.0	Capital Today; DST Global; FountainVest Partners; GIC Pte. Ltd.; H Capital; ICBC International Holdings Limited; IDG Capital Partners; Sequoia Capital China; Shougang Fund; Taihe Capital; **Tencent Holdings Ltd., Investment Arm**; Yunfeng Capital
14	Beijing XiaojuKeji Co., Ltd.	China	Transportation delivery	December 9, 2014	700.0	DST Global; Temasek Holdings (Private) Limited; **Tencent Holdings Ltd., Investment Arm**

Continued

Order	Target	Country	Industry	Announced date	Size ($mm)	Buyer/investors
15	Lyft, Inc.	United States	Transportation delivery	March 11, 2015	680.0	Alibaba Capital Partners; Didi Chuxing Technology Co., Ltd.; Fontinalis Partners, LLC; Icahn Enterprises L.P. (NasdaqGS:IEP); Rakuten, Inc. (TSE:4755); **Tencent Holdings Ltd., Investment Arm**
16	Guangzhou Douyu Network Technology Co., Ltd.	China	Game streaming	March 8, 2018	631.01	**Tencent Holdings Limited (SEHK:700)**
17	Shanghai Lazhasi Information Technology Co., Ltd.	China	Internet	August 27, 2015	630.0	Beijing Hualian Mall (Singapore) Commercial Management Pte. Ltd.; China Media Capital; CITIC Private Equity Funds Management Co., Ltd.; Gopher Asset Management Co., Ltd.; Horizon GreenTech Ventures; JD.com, Inc. (NasdaqGS:JD); Sequoia Capital China; Slender West Lake Investment Limited; **Tencent Holdings Ltd., Investment Arm**
18	ZiroomShenghuo Asset Management	China	Internet	January 16, 2018	621.13	General Atlantic LLC; Haixia Capital Management Co., Ltd.; Huasheng Capital; New Hope Group Co., Ltd.; Sequoia Capital China; Source Code Capital; Strait Capital Corp.; Sunac China Holdings Limited (SEHK:1918); **Tencent Holdings Limited (SEHK:700)**; Warburg Pincus LLC

19	Beijing Mobike Technology Co., Ltd	China	Transportation	June 15, 2017	600.0	Bocom International Holdings Company Limited. Investment Arm: Farallon Capital Management, L.L.C.; Hillhouse Capital Management, Ltd.; ICBC International Holdings Limited, Investment Arm; Sequoia Capital China; **Tencent Holdings Ltd., Investment Arm**; TPG Capital, L.P.
20	Yixin Group Limited (SEHK:2858)	China	Investment holding	May 11, 2017	579.4	Bitauto Holdings Limited (NYSE:BITA); China Orient Asset Management Co., Ltd.; **Tencent Holdings Limited (SEHK:700)**
21	Yixin Group Limited (SEHK:2858)	China	Investment holding	August 2, 2016	550.0	Baidu, Inc. (NasdaqGS:BIDU); Bitauto Holdings Limited (NYSE:BITA); JD.com, Inc. (NasdaqGS:JD); **Tencent Holdings Limited (SEHK:700)**
22	NavInfo Co., Ltd. (SZSE:002405)	China	Internet	May 13, 2016	520.55	China Securities Co., Ltd. Investment Arm; Huatai Asset Management Co., Ltd.; Linzhi Jinhua Investment Management Co., Ltd.; LonghuaQifu Investment Co., Ltd.; Nanjing HuataiRuilian Equity Investment Fund Management Partnership Enterprise; Shenzhen Anpeng Capital Innovation Co., Ltd.; **Tencent Holdings Ltd., Investment Arm**: Tianan Property Insurance Co., Ltd. *Buyer Funds*: Beijing Xindongneng Investment Fund (Limited Partnership); Nanjing HuataiRuilian M&A Fund No. 1 (Limited Partnership); Tencent Collaboration Fund

Continued

Order	Target	Country	Industry	Announced date	Size ($mm)	Buyer/investors
23	NEXTEV LIMITED	China	Automotive	August 31, 2015	500.0	Hillhouse Capital Management, Ltd.; JD. com, Inc. (NasdaqGS:JD); Joy Capital; Sequoia Capital China; **Tencent Holdings Ltd., Investment Arm**
24	Shanda Games Limited	China	Gaming	February 7, 2018	478.83	**Tencent Holdings Ltd., Investment Arm**
25	Beijing Weiying Times Technology Co., Ltd.	China	Internet	April 26, 2016	461.87	Dalian Zeus Entertainment Co., Ltd. (SZSE:002354); Everbright Financial Holding Asset Management Co.,Ltd.; Heyi Capital Management (Beijing) Co., Ltd.; iDreamSky Technology Limited; **Tencent Holdings Ltd., Investment Arm** *Buyer Funds*: Shenzhen TianshenZhonghui Investment Center (Limited Partnership)

Source: Authors from various industry reports and analyses.

References

BrandZ. (2018). *Top 100 most valuable global brands.* https://www.brandZ.com.

Caixin. (2019). *Chart of the Day: China's Mobile Payment Transaction Volume Hits $41.51 Trillion in 2018.* Caixin. https://www.caixinglobal.com/2019-03-22/chart-of-the-day-chinas-mobile-payment-transaction-volume-hits-4151-trillion-in-2018-101395789.html. (Accessed January 2019).

CBinsights. (2014). Tencent's accelerated pace of private company investments. *CBinsights.* https://www.cbinsights.com/blog/tencent-private-investment/. (Accessed September 2016).

Cendrowski, S. (2015). This $15 billion deal shows how tough times are for Chinese VC. *Forbes.* http://fortune.com/2015/10/08/china-tencent-alibaba-vc-deal/. (Accessed May 2018).

Chen, L. (2018). Google, Tencent agree to share patents in global tech alliance. *Bloomberg.* https://www.bloomberg.com/news/articles/2018-01-19/google-tencent-agree-to-share-patents-in-global-tech-alliance. (Accessed May 2018).

Deng, I. (2019). Tencent defends investment spree as core strategy amid venture 'capital winter' concerns. *South China Morning Post.* Feb. 20, 2019. https://www.scmp.com/tech/big-tech/article/2186939/tencent-defends-investment-spree-core-strategy-amid-venture-capital.

FDImarkets. (2017). https://app-fdimarkets-com.proxy.library.cornell.edu/library/index.cfm?-fuseaction=company_profiles.profile&selected_tab=2&company_id=57721&x_col=project_year&x_val=2013&x_name=Year:%202013:%20Total. (Accessed January 2017).

Jacobs, H. (2018). One photo shows that China is already in a cashless future. *Business Insider.* https://businessinsider.com/alipay-wechat-pay-china-mobile-payments-street-vendors-musicians-2018-5. (Accessed May 2019).

Lu, G. (2012). Tencent advances in game with new acquisitions and rising revenue. *Technode.* http://technode.com/2012/08/16/tencent-advances-in-game-with-new-acquisition-and-rising-revenue/. (Accessed January 2018).

Meyer, D. (2018). This media firm bet $32 million on Tencent in 2001. Now it's selling a sliver of its investment for $10.6 Billion. *Fortune.* http://fortune.com/2018/03/22/naspers-tencent-cashing-in/. (Accessed March 2019).

Newzoo. (2016). Supercell acquisition: Tencent set to take 13% of this year's $99.6Bn global games market. *Newzoo.* https://newzoo.com/insights/articles/supercell-acquisition-tencent-set-to-take-13-percent-of-the-games-market/. (Accessed January 2019).

Osawa, J., & Needleman, S. (2016). Tencent seals deal to buy 'clash of clans' developer supercell for $8.6 billion. *Wall Street Journal.* http://www.wsj.com/articles/tencent-agrees-to-acquire-clash-of-clans-maker-supercell-1466493612. (Accessed July 2016).

Shead, S. (2018). Baidu leads AI patent applications in China with 2,368 filings. *Forbes.* https://www.forbes.com/sites/samshead/2018/12/04/baidu-leads-ai-patent-applications-in-china-with-2368-filings/#13932ef628ae. (Accessed May 2019).

Shieber, J. (2018). Nubank is now worth $4 billion after Tencent's $180 million investment. *TechCrunch.* https://techcrunch.com/2018/10/08/tencent-cash-values-nubank-at-4-billion/?guccounter=1&guce_referrer_us=aHR0cHM6Ly93d3cuZ29vZ2xlLmNvbvbS8&guce_referrer_cs=DyGEjojFOFx_30J84zz7og. (Accessed June 2019).

Shu, C. (2014). Tencent, Baidu and Wanda form $814M joint venture to take on Alibaba. *TechCrunch.* https://techcrunch.com/2014/08/28/tencent-baidu-and-wanda-form-814m-joint-venture-to-take-on-alibaba/. (Accessed May 2018).

Statista. (2018). *Number of monthly active WeChat users from 4th quarter 2011 to 4th quarter 2018 (in millions).* https://www.statista.com/statistics/255778/number-of-active-wechat-messenger-accounts/. (Accessed May 2018).

Takahashi, D. (2016). League of legends, Clash of Clans, and CrossFire drive digital games to $61.3 B in 2015. *Venturebeat*. http://venturebeat.com/2016/01/26/league-of-legends-clash-of-clans-and-crossfire-drive-digital-games-to-61-3b-in-2015/. (Accessed September 2016).

Technode. (2019). *Briefing: China's mobile payment users reached 583 million last year.* https://technode.com/2019/03/04/briefing-chinas-mobile-payment-users-reached-583-million-last-year/. (Accessed May 2019).

Tencent. (2015). *Annual report 2015.* http://www.tencent.com/en-us/content/ir/rp/2015/attachments/201502.pdf. (Accessed August 2016).

Tencent. (2018). *Annual report 2018.* https://www.tencent.com/en-us/articles/17000441554112592.pdf. (Accessed May 2019).

World Intellectual Property Organization. (2015). *Telecoms firms lead WIPO international patent filings.* http://www.wipo.int/pressroom/en/articles/2015/article_0004.html. (Accessed September 2016).

Xu, T. (2019). Tencent records overall growth in 2018 as gaming revenues stagnate. *Technode*. https://technode.com/2019/03/21/tencent-records-overall-growth-in-2018-as-gaming-revenues-stagnate/. (Accessed May 2019).

Further reading

Bloomberg. (2016). *China said to explore taking stakes in some news websites.* http://www.bloomberg.com/news/articles/2016-05-03/china-said-to-explore-taking-stakes-in-some-news-websites-apps. (Accessed January 2016).

Casanova, L., Cornelius, P., & Dutta, S. (2018). *Entrepreneurship and the finance of innovation in emerging markets.* Elsevier. https://www.elsevier.com/books/financing-entrepreneurship-and-innovation-in-emerging-markets/casanova/978-0-12-804025-6.

Forbes. (2017). *Is WeChat pay taking over Alipay?.* https://www.forbes.com/sites/quora/2017/06/20/is-wechat-pay-taking-over-alipay/#74d0120f3a0b. (Accessed May 2018).

Li, Y. (2015). Kingmakers of China's internet: Baidu, Alibaba and Tencent. *Wall Street Journal*. https://www.wsj.com/articles/kingmakers-of-chinas-Internet-baidu-alibaba-and-tencent-1445451143. (Accessed May 2018).

Millward Brown, WPP. (2018). *BrandZ™ top 100 most valuable global brands ranking and report.* http://brandz.com/admin/uploads/files/BZ_Global_2018_DL.pdf. (Accessed May 2018).

Statista. (2015). *WeChat usage by city tier in China as of October 2015.* https://www.statista.com/statistics/746065/china-wechat-penetration-by-city-tier/. (Accessed May 2018).

Statista. (2017). *Usage of mobile payment services in China as of February 2017.* https://www.statista.com/statistics/746108/china-mobile-payment-service-usage/. (Accessed May 2018).

The growth of HNA—Navigating an uncertain world

...we have to assume our social responsibilities in human welfare. The corporate mission to make profits will sometimes conflict with public interests. Our corporate culture is to try and integrate these two interests. We will not damage public benefit for our own business interests.

**Chen Feng, founder of HNA 2014,
Bloomberg Markets Magazine**

Acronyms

CAAC	Civil Aviation Administration of China
CSR	corporate social responsibility
eMNCs	emerging market multinational companies
EPZ	export processing zone
GFC	Global Financial Crisis
M&As	mergers and acquisitions
MNCs	multinational companies
SEZ	special economic zone
SOE	state-owned enterprise

In little more than 20 years, Hainan Airlines (HNAs) morphed into a large international and diversified conglomerate, HNA Group. From a small provincial airline founded in 1993 in Haikou, the capital of China's Hainan province, HNA rose to global prominence with its forceful campaign of international expansion, culminating in a foreign firm-buying spree from 2014 to 2016, often making international headlines. By 2015, HNA entered the Fortune Global 500, a monumental achievement considering its modest origins (Table 10.1).

HNA is emblematic of the new Chinese global acquirers, ascending spectacularly on the heels of the Global Financial Crisis (GFC), but humbled by the tide's turn since 2017. Shackled by a significant amount of debt, the firm faced financial difficulties and a tightening of government regulations for overseas mergers and acquisitions (M&As) (see Chapter 2). Thereafter, HNA entered a selling-off period to recoup its losses; in 2018, it did not feature in the Fortune Global 500 list. This chapter traces HNA Group's beginnings as a provincial commercial airline competing with state-owned airlines. It tracks its meteoric rise into a large global conglomerate with activities spanning a wide array of industries. We explore the company's structure and business practices and consider the myriad challenges it faces. As we shall see, HNA's experience is an instructive reminder that fast-growing Chinese multinational companies (MNCs) are not immune to sudden reversals of fortune.

The Era of Chinese Multinationals. https://doi.org/10.1016/B978-0-12-816857-8.00010-0

Table 10.1 Fortune Global 500 ranking—Financial data for HNA Group.

HNA group (Fortune Global 500 list data)	December 31, 2014 (million US$)	December 31, 2015 (million US$)	December 31, 2016 (million US$)
Revenues	25,646	29,562	53,035
Profits	206.9	235	278.9
Assets	79,898	95,339	173,095
Fortune Global 500 Rank	464	353	170

Note: In the Fortune Global 500 list, data are for each company's fiscal year, ending on or before March of the publication year, i.e., data for the 2015 Fortune Global 500 list are for the fiscal year that ended on or before March 2015. The 2018 list did not include HNA.
Source: www.fortune.com, accessed April 2019. Data from the 2015, 2016, and 2017 lists of Fortune Global 500.

According to Capital IQ, as of December 2017, HNA Group's total revenues were $86 billion. In December 2018 they amounted to $89 billion, an increase of 4%. However, with the company facing $62.9 billion in total debt, HNA's debt/equity ratio was 170%.

10.1   Key phases of HNA'S growth

HNA's growth is characterized by four developmental phases:

- The first phase (1993–2003): The development of its flagship airline.
- The second phase (2003–08): A period of intense diversification within China.
- The third phase (2008–16): A swift-moving foray into international expansion.
- The fourth phase (since 2017): The sell-off.

10.1.1   1993–2003: Developing a Flagship airline

HNA owes its formation to the confluence of several Chinese central government initiatives in the late 1980s. In 1985, the Chinese government restructured the Civil Aviation Administration of China (CAAC), which afforded local governments more freedom to manage and regulate their own airline operations, the objective of which was to encourage the development of regional airlines to support local growth. In 1988, Hainan—an island in the South China Sea off the coast of Guangdong Province—became independent from Guandong and was designated a special economic zone (SEZ), a status that rewarded exemptions to foreign investors and duty-free status for production inputs.

The liberalization that followed provided an opportunity for the newly endowed province to form its own airline and enhance its transportation infrastructure to take full advantage of its new export processing zone (EPZ) status. To establish the airline, the provincial government recruited two members of the CAAC: Chen Feng and Wang Jian, who together formed the core team that founded HNAs in 1993. Unlike other

Chinese airlines, HNA was not established as a state-owned enterprise (SOE) but as a public-private enterprise with close ties to high-level government officials.

HNAs first set its sights on building a world-class airline. In the largely state-controlled environment of Chinese aviation, its main competitors were the "Big Three": Air China, China Eastern Airlines, and China Southern Airlines, all of which were state-owned, based out of different regions of China, and benefitted from the central government's allocation of both routes and planes. To standout, HNAs strategy focused on safety, service, and branding, which led the airline to buy large Boeing airplanes for its fleet. To avoid a head-on collision with its competitors, HNAs focused on filling market gaps rather than plunging into crowded routes between China and the United States or Western European capitals. The airline found a market in smaller provincial airports in China, and destinations in neighboring Thailand, Malaysia, or Korea. It also became the first Chinese airline to offer nonstop service to Central Europe with a direct flight to Budapest, Hungary.

While the state-controlled Chinese airline industry was difficult to break into, HNAs' expansion efforts enjoyed an early boost. First, American Aviation, a company owned by investor George Soros and a subsidiary of the hedge fund Quantum Fund, bought a 25% stake in the company ($25 million worth of shares) in 1995. HNAs next turned to the Shanghai Stock Exchange, selling $71 million B shares in 1997 and $205 million A shares in 1999. The airline restructured in 1997, and in 2000 the HNA Group was established.

In the 3 years that followed, the company focused on acquiring regional airlines, taking over China Xinhua Airlines (which operated mainly from Tinjua and Beijing), Chang'an Airlines (which provided flights from Xi'an), and Shanxi Airlines (based in *Taiyuan*). In the wake of these acquisitions, HNA became the fourth largest airline in China. Despite this success, several external crises in the late 1990s and early 2000s tested the mettle of the fledgling airline: the 1997 Asian financial crisis sparked a regional decline in air travel demand, while the September 11, 2001 terrorist attacks in the United States provoked a worldwide dip, followed not long after by the 2003 SARS epidemic in Asia, which also kept planes grounded.

Even as the three big state-owned airlines could count on government support to cope with these difficulties, HNA was made to survive on its own. The company implemented a strategy based on upstream and downstream diversification, branching into complementary industries in local hotels and Haikou's Meilan Airport by the turn of the millennium.

10.1.2 2003–08: Domestic diversification

To differentiate itself from its competitors, HNA put a strong emphasis on the quality of its airlines service and diversified into related industries with less state control. HNA capitalized on the booming Hainan tourism industry, acquiring more regional airlines, airports, and local hotels while expanding into tour companies, corporate air travel, and car rental, as well as plane leasing and shipping. As a result of this expansion, HNA Group incorporated HNA Hotel, HNA Tourism, and HNA Capital to its overall corporate structure.

When markets began to turn volatile in 2007, HNA consolidated its assets to optimize performance and reduce losses, strategically closing some businesses. Its logistics business (especially shipping) faced the most restructuring (Kirby, McFarlan, & Eby, 2016). Out of this consolidation, HNA found itself fairly liquid during the 2008 GFC, while cheaply priced assets were making their way to the market. This turn of events presented a golden opportunity for China, whose market weathered the storm with much greater ease than other countries.

10.1.3   2008–16: International expansion

In effect, the GFC triggered HNA's drive for internationalization, and marked a turning point for emerging market multinational companies (eMNCs) as a whole. Much less affected by the crisis than their rivals, many Chinese firms were well poised to acquire assets from financially troubled peers (see Chapter 2). HNA's ambitions to become a world-class company coincided with this fortuitous opportunity.

(a) Expanding HNA's core business through airline acquisition

As demand for international travel expanded in China, it was only natural for HNA to explore providing international flights. However, the Chinese central government only permitted one Chinese carrier to fly each international route, and unlike the three state-owned airlines, HNA did not enjoy privileged treatment from the government regarding international route allocation. International airline acquisition became a shortcut to access such routes. In 2012, HNA bought a 48% stake in Aigle Azur, a French airline with the potential to award HNA access to a lucrative Beijing-Paris route without requiring Chinese government approval. With ownership of Aigle Azur, HNA could earn route approval in France instead of China. (The route finally opened in fall 2018.) This partnership marked the first instance a Chinese company investing in a European airline.

HNA also saw major potential to expand the airline industry into other emerging markets. In 2012, HNA teamed up with the China-Africa Development Fund to set up an aviation company in Ghana, Africa World Airlines, rendering HNAs the first Chinese carrier in Africa (Wharton University of Pennsylvania, 2013). By 2015, HNA became the largest shareholder of the third largest airline in Brazil, Azul Brazilian Airlines, acquiring a 24% stake in the company.

(b) Upstream and downstream diversification

One of the key factors in HNA's expansion was its global pursuit of vertical diversification into a wide array of upstream and downstream industries. Upstream, HNA acquired companies to assist in both aircraft maintenance and pilot training. In 2010 and 2011, it bought two Turkish companies: myTECHNIC, an aircraft maintenance company, and ACT Cargo Airlines (later known as myCargo). From Australia, HNA acquired a leading share in an aviation college and Allco, an aircraft leasing business. HNA followed with an additional acquisition of an aircraft-leasing firm in 2015, the Irish firm Avolon, which later became the largest aircraft-leasing firm in the world after the acquisition of US-based CIT Group's leasing activities in April 2017. By 2011, HNA purchased SEACO, General Electric's container-leasing subsidiary, the fifth largest cargo company in the world, as a result of which HNA Group became a world leader in container leasing when later SEACO acquired Cronos Ltd, a Bermuda-based container leasing group. In 2013, HNA completed the acquisition of GE's subsidiary TIP, the largest trailer-leasing company in Europe. Rounding out its upstream acquisitions, HNA bought two Swiss companies: in 2015, it fully acquired Swissport, the world's largest ground and cargo handling services provider, and in 2016 Gategroup, the second largest airline caterer in the world.

Fueled likewise by the desire to provide consumer services, HNA substantially diversified downstream into hotels. In 2013, it acquired a 20% share in the Spanish HN Hotel Group, the third largest hotel chain in Europe. The conglomerate later became its largest shareholder, after increasing its share to 29%. In 2015, HNA also bought a 10% stake in the French tourism services and residence company, Pierre et Vacances. From 2015 to 2016, the company entered the United States with a 15% interest in Red Lion Hotels, bought for more than $20 billion. A number of acquisitions were worth several billion dollars (see Table 10.2). One of HNA's most publicized deals was its acquisition of a 25% share in Park Hotels & Resorts Inc., which owns Hilton hotels,

Table 10.2 Selected cross-border M&As by HNA, 2015–first quarter 2017.

Date of acquisition	Company	Country of origin	Industry	Price ($ bn)
June 2015	Red Lion Hotels (15%)	United States	Hotels	20.9
July 2015	Swissport	Switzerland	Cargo and aircraft ground handler	2.8
September 2015	Real estate in London	United Kingdom	Real estate	–
September 2015	Avolon Holdings	Ireland	Aircraft leaser	2.6
November 2015	Azul (23.7%)	Brazil	Airline (Brazil)	0.45
July 2016	Gategroup	Switzerland	Airline caterer	1.5
July 2016	SR Technics	Switzerland	Aircraft repair and maintenance	–
October 2016	CIT Group	United States	Aircraft leasing	10.0
October 2016	US Golf Courses	United States	Real estate	0.14
October 2016	Hilton Gorp (25%)	United States	Hotels	6.5
October 2016	Pactera	United States	IT consulting, solution and outsourcing services	6.75
December 2016	Ingram Micro	United States	IT products and services	6.0
December 2016	Carlson Hotels Group	United States	Hotels	–
March 2017	Real Estate on Park Avenue (NY)	United States	Real estate	2.2
February and May 2017	Deutsche Bank	Germany (10%)	Banking	–

Source: Authors, based on data from S&P Capital IQ HNA Group website, and press reports.

for $6.5 billion. As part of its buying spree, HNA also invested in high-end properties Europe, acquiring the iconic 30 South Colonnade Street Building in London, as well as other properties in New York and Hong Kong.

Meanwhile, HNA pursued horizontal diversification, too. In December 2016, it closed a $6 billion deal for Ingram Micro, a US-based IT company specializing in global technology and supply chain services, and one of the world's largest IT distributors. At the time, HNA CEO Adam Xiandong Tan declared that the addition would transform HNA's logistics arm into a supply chain operator with one-stop services while improving efficiencies (Financier Worldwide, 2016). The acquisition would also reward the company with a stronger foothold in high-growth emerging markets through Ingram's large international presence. That same year, HNA also acquired Pactera from the US global investment and asset management firm Blackstone. The Beijing-based company provides IT consulting, solutions, and outsourcing services to a range of multinational firms and is itself the owner of US and Swiss IT firms Innoveo Solutions AG as well as Blue Fountain Media. In 2017, HNA went one step further into horizontal diversification by buying stakes in Deutsche Bank, progressively raising its stakes to become the bank's largest shareholder.

HNA's most intense period of overseas buying activity occurred in 2015–16. In 2016, the peak of HNA's expansion abroad, the company's overseas deals accounted for an estimated 13% of total Chinese overseas M&As. However, the firm needed to take time to digest the acquisitions and adapt to its widespread structure and multicultural environment. HNA's far-ranging deal making resulted in a heavy debt burden. Between 2015 and 2017, HNA borrowed a total of $45.7 billion, mainly through highly leveraged loans. This freewheeling style wasn't entirely new to the company, as it had relied on high leverage financing from its inception. However, this time around, the spree was different in its intensity and international reach. Over time, the stakes grew as HNA targeted much higher-priced assets.

By 2017, HNA Group had become a diversified international conglomerate (see Figs. 10.1 and 10.2), with 45 foreign companies in 18 countries and territories. It had created about 400,000 jobs, 290,000 of them overseas (HNA Group, 2017), and had tripled its assets in three years—to about 230 $ billions by end 2017 according to the company website.

Flushed with the success of its remarkable trajectory, the company set ambitious goals for its future. By 2020, HNA executives hoped to transform into a global industrial

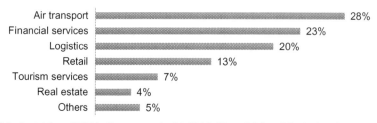

Fig. 10.1 Activities of HNA Group, as of mid-2016. *Note:* "Others" includes airport services, hotels and restaurants, and other industries.
Source: Company information as reported in Nikkei Asian Review (February 11, 2017).

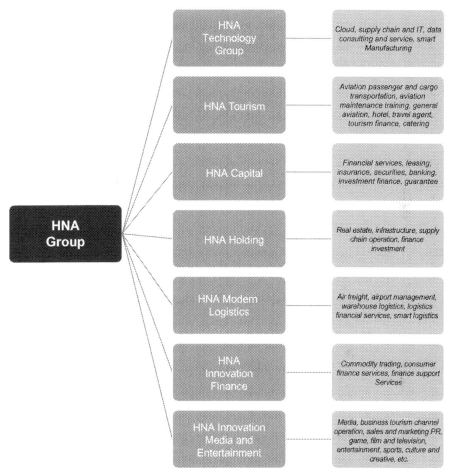

Fig. 10.2 HNA Group, as of March 2017. *Note:* Activities of each entity marked in *italics.* *Source:* Authors based on information from company report "HNA Sharing Dreams," March 2017.

and financial group that would feature among the top 100 of the Fortune Global 500, and in the top 50 by 2030 (Mellor & Wang, 2014). The company expected to achieve this transformation largely through international expansion, with 40% of the group's assets projected to be foreign by 2020 (Wharton University of Pennsylvania, 2013).

10.2 HNA group corporate culture

Much of the rapid growth that HNA experienced can be attributed to the company's strong and pervasive corporate culture, in addition to its willingness to buck industry norms, and its ability to quickly and decisively respond to changing markets. Over the years, management—especially its original founders and Chairman Chen Feng—promoted a culture combining Buddhist teachings and traditional Chinese values, encompassing respect for moral principles and for the common good.

The company worked on instilling its corporate culture and values—that is, "common ideal, common belief, common pursuit, and common philosophy" (HNA Connect, 2017)—through training and development programs. HNA introduced the idea of striving toward a common goal and altruism within a corporate context to its staff throughout all levels of the organization. In several company reports, HNA has emphasized "sharing dreams" and "sharing the happy tomorrow" as values it wanted the company as a whole to project (HNA Group, 2017). In the eyes of HNA's founders and management, the company's success was in part due to employees maintaining cohesiveness, dedication, and loyalty. As the firm developed a corporate culture based on the latter, it also made an effort to retain top talent and preserve an acquired company's management team during transitions. When the company expanded internationally, maintaining such a corporate culture throughout the firm's ever-widening reach became increasingly challenging, as the company needed to make strategic decisions about which parts of company culture would best translate across societal lines.

Through it all, corporate social responsibility (CSR)—a concept more familiar in global business than in traditional Chinese values—played an important part in HNA corporate culture. HNA launched a series of public welfare projects in sectors such as medical assistance, education, poverty alleviation, and culture conservation. Projects included cultural heritage preservation and rehabilitation projects in Nepal after the 2015 earthquake, and a Syrian refugee assistance program. In 2017, the group released its eighth Social Responsibility Report, which, in its English version, paid particular attention to the United Nations Sustainable Development Goals. HNA Group was recognized through various CSR awards, and the company became a four-time winner of the "China Charity Prize," the highest philanthropic recognition given by the Chinese Ministry of Civil Affairs. HNA also participated in charity health projects, earning a UN South–South Corporate Social Responsibility Award for "Brightness Action," its blindness prevention work in Malawi, Zimbabwe, Mozambique, and China.

10.3 Troubled times and strategy shift (late 2017–present)

In the wake of its buying spree, HNA faced mounting challenges. As the company acquired asset after asset, it became difficult to effectively integrate them with HNA Group at such a breakneck pace. Furthermore, this wave of acquisitions entailed significant financial risk, all the more pressing as global growth—including Chinese growth—slowed and the attitude of the Chinese authorities toward overseas acquisitions began to shift.

HNA paid a high premium price for many of its acquisitions (Table 10.2). In addition, it often sought assets with considerable revenues, even if these companies were not profitable or were already loaded with debt. Some observers contend that

HNA's ambitious goal to rise among the Fortune Global 500 was a significant factor at play. (In 2015, HNA entered the ranking of 464 out of 500, and jumped to 170 by 2017.) More importantly, such acquired assets could be used as collateral to back further purchases—a familiar strategy—but one that can prove risky if the borrowing environment changes, or if the value of the acquired assets drops. The buying spree, coupled with assets losses, plunged HNA into debt. By 2017, the company had accumulated debt totaling $94 billion. According to an annual company report, as detailed in Bloomberg, the overall debt rose by 21% in 2017, with short-term borrowing climbing by 25% to about $30 billion (Campbell & Ho, 2018). Total debt amounted to about 20 times HNA's earnings before interest and taxes, a ratio worse than most global nonfinancial companies of comparable size, according to Bloomberg data (Campbell & Ho, 2018). Borrowing costs surged to about $5 billion for the full year, an increase of more than 50% over the year prior, triggering a serious liquidity crisis.

Meanwhile, the Chinese government began scrutinizing the debt levels of the country's most acquisitive companies. The government's decision to rein in capital outflows, in particular overseas M&As, meant a sudden and significant change of gear. In this new environment, some lenders began to restrict credit access to high-flying borrowers that had driven the M&A surge (see Chapters 2 and 4). As one of the largest conglomerates, HNA was one of the hardest hit. Doubts emerged as to HNA's capacity to shoulder its high financial burden, in spite of the company's reassurances to its creditors.

HNA's complex financing and ownership structure exacerbated suspicions, as discerning individual shareholders proved difficult at first glance (Barboza, 2017; Financial Times, 2017). While it had resorted to the stock market and stock issuance to raise funds, HNA also maintained a close relationship with the Chinese government, occasionally securing financing from state-owned banks, including the China Development Bank, the China Construction Bank, and the Export and Import Bank of China (Barboza, 2017). HNA denied rumors of ties with the Chinese Communist party. Some details about HNA's ownership structure were finally revealed mid-2017, following a transfer of shares from one of HNA's main shareholders, Guan Jun, to the Hainan Province Cihang Foundation, a charity with a branch registered in China and another in New York. After the transfer, these two branches held 52% ownership of HNA, while the company's two chairmen, Chen Fang and Wang Jian, each held almost 15%, and the other chairmen and HNAs Holding Company split the remaining shares (Walt, 2017). Following Chairman Wang Jian's death in France after an accident in August 2018, the charity's share of the firm rose to 67% (Reuters, 2018b). Despite these revelations, questions over HNA's shareholding structure, and the company's ultimate ownership, would continue to dog the company.

Such suspicions were doubly detrimental for HNA. They led to increased scrutiny in recipient countries, and most importantly, rendered it more difficult to obtain financing from abroad, just as Chinese banking scrutiny and credit tightening made loans from Western banks more important. Global giants including HSBC Holdings Plc. and Bank of America Corp. reportedly began steering clear of the group

(Chan, 2017; David, Browning, & Chan, 2017). By late 2017, reports surfaced of the company's difficulties meeting its financial obligations. HNA reversed course and sold off assets, raising more than $40 billion from 2017 to 2018 (Hornby & Ju, 2019). The firm first aimed to dispose of hotels, properties, and insurance companies to recoup some losses while preserving its core assets. Some of HNA's disinvestments (see Table 10.3) are as follows:

- Offloading real estate properties in Shanghai, Hong Kong, Australia, the United Kingdom and the United States One of its most significant property sales was that of 245 Park Ave. in New York City, originally purchased in 2017 (Ho, 2018).
- Divesting its entire stakes in Hilton's listed entities: Hilton Worldwide Holdings, Hilton Grand Vacation, and Park and Hotel Resort for a total of $8.5 billion in 2018.
- Progressively reducing its shares in Deutsche Bank to 6.3% (as of February 2019), after previously being its largest shareholder (Schuetze & Ruwitch, 2018). Bloomberg reports in early 2019 indicated that HNA planned to eventually dispose of its entire stake.
- Selling Hong Kong International Construction Investment Management Group to Blackstone, the US global investment and asset management firm.

By early 2019, HNA was also trying to sell Pactera and Ingram Micro, both acquired in 2016. In less than 2 years, the HNA empire had shrank dramatically.

Finally, in an effort to streamline the organization and refocus its strategy around its core aviation business, HNA adjusted its structure. As of early 2019, HNA Capital and HNA Technology no longer operated as separate entities under the HNA Group umbrella but as business units of the Group.

Most of HNA's asset sales through mid-2018 produced profits (Steinberg & Xie, 2018). However, with mounting pressure from debt repayments, it proved increasingly difficult for the company to guarantee optimal deals out of asset sales. Even as the pace of divestiture moved fast, debt remained high: for instance, HNA had $2.5 billion due in bond repayment and loan reimbursement by the end of 2019.

10.4 Future prospects

As of 2019, HNA's future remains uncertain. The group expected the pressure to ease by mid-2018 and declared, that year, that its long-term goal to become a world-class enterprise was unshaken (Miller, 2018). As financial strain increased over time, however, HNA Group had no choice but to start selling some of its core aviation business. In March 2019, HNA sold Gategroup, the promising airline caterer it has acquired in 2017. The company also planned to sell Swissport. In April 2019, HNA relinquished its hold on the budget airline Hong Kong Express, a bright spot in its portfolio given the rising demand in Asia for short, cheap flights. (Cathay Pacific Airways bought the airline). Likewise, in April 2019, HNA Holdings Group Ltd. (later known as CWT International Ltd.) halted trading as it failed to service a $179 million loan; CWT assets were seized in turn. Even Hainan Airlines, the jewel in HNA's crown, suffered: a court in Shandong, China, froze part of the airline's shares in March 2019 as a result of a contract dispute with a local aircraft leasing firm.

Table 10.3 Shedding off assets—Most important HNA divestments. 2018–April 2019.

Date	Asset	Outcome	Industry/ sector	Price, US$
January 2018	Property in Australia (Sydney)	Sold	Real estate	$150 million
February–March 2018	Property in Hong Kong (Kai Tak land)	Sold	Real estate	$2.8 billion
March–April 2018	Park and Hotel Resorts; Hilton Worldwide Holding and Hilton grand Vacation	Divested its stake	Hotels	$8.5 billion
April 2018	Deutsche Bank	Reduced its stake	Banking	~$375 million (est.)
May 2018	Property in the UK (London)	Sold	Real estate	$440 million
May 2018	Property in the US (San Francisco)	Sold	Real estate	$330 million
June 2018	NH Hotels	Divested its stake	Hotels	$729 million
July 2018	Warehouses in Singapore	Sold		$535 million
July 2018	Hotel Company Radisson Holdings	Sold	Hotels	$2 billion
August 2018	Azul	Divested its stake	Airline	
August 2018	Avolon	Divested its stake	Aircraft leaser	$2.2 billion
November 2018	Property in New-York (Park Avenue)	Sold	Real estate	$150 million
January 2019	Property in New-York	Sold	Real estate	$422 million
February 2019	Deutsche Bank	Further reduced its stake	Banking	$410 million
March 2019	Hong Kong International Construction Investment Management	Divested its stake	Construction, property investment and management	$894 million
April 2019	Gategroup	Sold	Airline caterer	–
April 2019	Hong Kong Express	Sold	Airline	$628 million

Source: Authors based on Bloomberg, Reuters and other financial press reports.

The diversification and acquisition-based growth strategy that HNA relied upon to transform itself into a key player in the Asian airline industry was in the end at the root of its problem once scaled to the global level. Diversification upstream and downstream helped HNA to face competition from within—that is, the three dominant Chinese state-owned airlines. However, when expanding overseas, some of its acquisitions (in banking, IT industries, or high-end real estate) did not seem to fit into an "integrated value chain" rationale, at least not while the pace of the buying spree proved too swift for proper integration. HNA Chairman Chen Feng acknowledged this lack of synergy, noting in 2018: "Our business has become so big that we need to improve efficiency…" (Reuters, 2018a).

This glut of acquisitions left HNA financially vulnerable to changes in the business environment, whether a slowdown in economic growth or a shift in the government's attitude toward outbound M&As. In particular, the increased government scrutiny on prolific but highly indebted buyers such as HNA further precipitated the company's difficulties. While it was not the first time that HNA shed acquisitions, the sheer scale of HNA's latter troubles had no precedent in the company's history.

Some observers contend that Chinese authorities will keep HNA from going bankrupt, partly due to the debt owed to China's state-owned banks. Indeed, in 2018 HNA reportedly received a line of credit from two Chinese state-owned banks: China Citic Bank Corp and Bank of China Ltd. (Trivedi & Steinberg, 2018). The Chinese government further agreed to suspend public trading of some HNA units' shares, in an effort to stabilize the group. As of 2019, China Development Bank, the airline's largest creditor, supervises HNA's asset sales. The company may, at the end, return to its roots: its core aviation business.

HNA's experience may be a source of inspiration for fast-growing Chinese multinationals. Like all multinationals, Chinese firms can fall victim to overly quick expansion or excessive debt. Some of the characteristics that proved successful in the local Chinese business environment may not be adequate in a global context. For instance, to compete effectively in China requires speed and agility, but cross-border M&As require a different kind of agility, and the learning curve can be steep. Successfully integrating new acquisitions has long been a challenge, whatever be the profile, history, size, or nationality of the acquirer. In its rapid-fire sequence of cross-border acquisitions, HNA did not have the time it needed to learn from and digest its acquisitions. In addition, growth at a breakneck speed risks engendering a false sense of security. Whereas initial success may depend on a combination of factors—including factors specific to a domestic market such as a huge unserved demand and a favorable policy environment—sustained success often demands additional qualities and evolving strategies. A complex ownership structure and lack of transparency can also be disadvantageous for firms when venturing abroad, since suspicions regarding ultimate owners can be reason enough to block access to foreign markets and financial resources. HNA suffered from such suspicions, and its efforts to resolve them were, for some observers, too little and too late.

References

Barboza, D. (2017). A Chinese Giant is on a global buying spree. Who's behind it? *New York Times*. https://www.nytimes.com/2017/05/09/business/hna-group-hainan-airlines-china-deals.html.

Campbell, M., & Ho, P. (2018). The $94 billion mystery: What will be left of HNA's empire? *Bloomberg Businessweek*. https://www.bloomberg.com/news/articles/2018-05-03/the-94-billion-mystery-what-will-be-left-of-hna-s-empire.

Chan, V. (2017). HSBC steps up scrutiny of Chinese conglomerate HNA. *Bloomberg*. https://www.bloomberg.com/news/articles/2017-12-08/hsbc-is-said-to-step-up-scrutiny-of-china-s-indebted-hna-group.

David, R., Browning, J., & Chan, V. (2017). Bank of America halts deals with HNA amid debt concerns. *Bloomberg*. https://www.bloomberg.com/news/articles/2017-07-19/bank-of-america-said-to-halt-deals-with-hna-amid-debt-concerns.

Financial Times. (2017). *Who owns HNA, China's most aggressive dealmaker?*. https://www.ft.com/content/8acfe40e-410b-11e7-9d56-25f963e998b2.

Financier Worldwide Magazine. (2016). *HNA agrees to acquire ingram micro for $6bn*. https://www.financierworldwide.com/hna-agrees-to-acquire-ingram-micro-for-6bn.

HNA Connect. (2017). *Introducing the spirit of HNA—The four commons*. http://connect.hnagroup.com.hk/index.php?issue_id=57.

HNA Group. (2017). *Sharing dreams, company*. www.hnagroup.com/en-us. (Accessed April 2019).

Ho, P. (2018). HNA's $16 billion garage sale faces a setback. *Bloomberg Deals*. https://www.bloomberg.com/news/articles/2018-03-27/collapse-of-hna-s-swiss-ipo-sets-back-16-billion-garage-sale.

Hornby, L., & Ju, S. F. (2019). HNA debt drag forces deviation from flight plan. *Financial Times*. https://www.ft.com/content/df0c99a0-507b-11e9-b401-8d9ef1626294.

Kirby, W. C., McFarlan, F. W., & Eby, J. W. (2016). *HNA group: Global excellence with Chinese characteristics*. Harvard Business School Case 316-013.

Mellor, W., & Wang, J. (2014). *Chinese tycoon rides resort's rise to empire in the sky*. Bloomberg Markets Magazine. https://www.bloomberg.com/news/articles/2014-04-10/chinese-tycoon-rides-resort-s-rise-to-empire-in-the-sky.

Miller, M. (2018). *Exclusive: China's HNA group, squeezed on cash, looks to turn corner*. Reuters. https://www.reuters.com/article/us-china-hna-exclusive/exclusive-chinas-hna-group-squeezed-on-cash-looks-to-turn-corner-idUSKBN1F70MF>.

Reuters. (2018a). *China's HNA group, squeezed on cash, looks to turn corner* [January]. https://www.reuters.com/article/us-china-hna-exclusive/exclusive-chinas-hna-group-squeezed-on-cash-looks-to-turn-corner-idUSKBN1F70MF.

Reuters. (2018b). *China's HNA group announces management reshuffle* [August]. https://www.reuters.com/article/us-hna-management/chinas-hna-group-announces-management-reshuffle-idUSKBN1KN0AG.

Schuetze, A., & Ruwitch, J. (2018). China's HNA pares back big stake in Deutsche bank. *Reuters*. https://www.reuters.com/article/us-hna-group-deutsche-bank/chinas-hna-pares-back-big-stake-in-deutsche-bank-idUSKCN1G00A9>.

Steinberg, J., & Xie, S. Y. (2018). HNA, under pressure from Beijing, to sell its overseas empire. *Wall Street Journal*. http://classroom.wsj.com/articles/chinas-hna-to-exit-deutsche-bank-stake-under-pressure-from-beijing-1536307095?mod=searchresults&page=13&pos=4.

Trivedi, A., & Steinberg, J. (2018). Chinese conglomerate HNA gets a lifeline. *Wall Street Journal*. https://www.wsj.com/articles/chinese-conglomerate-hna-gets-a-lifeline-1520045305.

Walt, V. (2017). Mammoth Chinese conglomerate HNA group reveals new details about its ownership. *Fortune*. http://fortune.com/2017/07/24/hna-group-china-new-ownership-structure/.

Wharton University of Pennsylvania. Knowledge@Wharton. (2013). *HNA Chairman Chen Feng's growth strategy: Go global in the downturn*. http://knowledge.wharton.upenn.edu/article/hna-chairman-chen-fengs-growth-strategy-go-global-in-the-downturn/. (Accessed April 2019).

Further reading

Fortune Global 500. (n.d.). http://fortune.com/global500/hna-group/.

Hainan Airline. (2016). *Social responsibility report 2015*. https://www.hainanairlines.com/go/2017.6-6/DOCS/Responsibilities_and_Prospects/HNA_CSR-Report_2016_EN.pdf.

HNA. *Who we are*. http://www.hnagroup.com/en-us/who-we-are/introduction/. (Accessed April 2019).

Ho, J. (2017). *Questions mount over HNA's financial engineering*. Nikkei Asian Review. https://asia.nikkei.com/Business/Company-in-focus/Questions-mount-over-HNA-s-financial-engineering2.

Kihara, T. (2019). *China's HNA speeds up asset sales in 'return to roots'*. Nikkei Asian Review. https://asia.nikkei.com/Business/Companies/China-s-HNA-speeds-up-asset-sales-in-return-to-roots.

Miller, M. (2017). *China's HNA to apply M&A brakes after $50b deal splurge*. Deal Street Asia. https://www.dealstreetasia.com/stories/chinas-hna-tap-ma-brake-50-bln-deal-splurge-74245/>.

Mulholland, S. (2017). *China's HNA reverses buying binge with $4 billion selling spree*. Bloomberg Markets. https://www.bloomberg.com/news/articles/2018-02-08/hna-group-is-said-to-put-4-billion-of-u-s-properties-on-market>.

Sito, P. (2017). Can a US$48 billion global shopping spree take this Chinese company into the fortune 100? *South China Morning Post*. http://www.scmp.com/business/companies/article/2095133/hnas-global-shopping-spree-may-put-it-fortunes-100-list.

Vardi, N. (2017). China Deal machine HNA group sues wealthy Chinese fugitive Guo Wengui. *Forbes*. https://www.forbes.com/sites/nathanvardi/2017/06/16/china-deal-machine-hna-group-sues-wealthy-chinese-fugitive-guo-wengui/#472b7d7d296c.

Conclusion: Chinese firms disrupt the competitive landscape

Acronyms

BRI	Belt and Road Initiative
FDI	foreign direct investment
GDP	gross domestic product
GFC	global financial crisis
OFDI	outward foreign direct investment
R&D	Research and Development
SOE	state-owned enterprise

Chinese firms' increased global presence illustrates China's swift and radical transformation. These firms have grown rapidly and gained scale by leveraging the growing Chinese economy and its huge domestic market, potentially twice the size of both the United States and Europe combined. In the decade following the 2008 Global Financial Crisis (GFC) alone, Chinese firms have substantially increased their global footprint. Hardly visible among the largest firms in the world in 2005, there are now nearly as many Chinese firms in the Fortune Global 500 list as the US firms (111 Chinese firms compared to 126 US firms in 2018). Since the beginning of the 21st century, economic power is shifting toward China, bringing increasing political influence as well.

Chinese firms have invested overseas to obtain natural resources, for intangibles like technology, and to build their brands. In 2015, China became a net foreign direct investment (FDI) capital exporter for the first time and has featured as the second or third largest global investor since then.

Chinese firms' increasing role as major global acquirers has attracted global attention, especially from political and public opinion leaders in developed markets. Their acquisitions have increased since the GFC and peaked in 2016–17—Chinese firms were the second most prolific acquirers in the world in 2016, trailing only the United States. Many of those deals were of a size that would have been unimaginable even a decade ago. For example, Chinese firms bought Syngenta, the Swiss chemical giant, the Italian tire maker Pirelli, and part of the Swedish firm Volvo, demonstrating their increased sophistication and scale. For a country that was low income and mostly rural through much of the 20th century, acquiring flagship firms from advanced economies has been no small achievement.

Undeniably, Chinese firms still lag behind their peers in developed economies and other emerging markets in terms of profits, market capitalization, and global presence.

But this is changing, as is the image of the Chinese firm generally. In their ventures abroad, beyond investing in their natural markets in Asia or other emerging and developing regions, Chinese firms have increasingly expanded into developed markets, as well as in a variety of sectors. The outbound expansion of Chinese firms is no indeed longer confined to traditional industries such as energy, raw materials, and heavy industries but increasingly includes service-based and consumer-related industries. All of these changes point to a significant shift in the rationale and overall strategies behind Chinese overseas investment.

Chinese firms' global ascension has disrupted the global competitive landscape fundamentally. Traditionally, Chinese firms would compete on the basis of lower prices. While this is still the case in many sectors, Chinese companies have begun climbing up the brand recognition ladder and an increasing number of Chinese firms such as Huawei and ICBC (Industrial and Commercial Bank of China) now feature among the top global brands. In part, this change reflects the increasing consumer power of emerging economies, in which a growing middle class offers ample opportunities for growth. In such markets, firms from China are well positioned as they have a long history of experience with local customer demands and regional risks. But the increased brand recognition of Chinese companies has not been limited to emerging markets. Two noteworthy examples include Huawei's advertising efforts in France and the United Arab Emirates: a building-size billboard visible from the banks of the River Seine in Paris in March 2019, or the glitzy Huawei shop in the largest mall in Dubai, the envy of its high-end mobile competitors. Similarly, Haier secured advertising spots on Swiss TV to target Swiss consumers, suggesting that the firm is working hard at building its brand recognition.

Beyond brand building, Chinese firms have invested in their innovation capabilities. This increased innovation, when combined with their historical advantage of price competitiveness, has made Chinese firms serious challengers. Though they are in some respects still dependent on foreign technology, those gaps are narrowing. Chinese firms' success has mirrored China's evolution into an innovation leader, as illustrated in international innovation rankings such as the Global Innovation Index where, in 2018, China (17th in the world) ranked close to Japan (13th), France (16th), and Canada (18th). China is now the world's second-largest spender on Research and development (R&D) activities after the United States. It is one of the few countries able to send humans into the space and is the recognized world leader in 5G. It has also achieved some prominent "firsts": sending robots to the dark side of the moon, exchanging information between Earth and space, and transporting high-voltage electricity across long distances.

Such advancement in quality and innovation is increasingly visible in the products and services Chinese firms offer—including in the digital economy where global technological leaders from China are producing world-leading technologies. Alibaba (Alipay) and Tencent (WeChat Pay) are examples of Chinese innovation leaders in mobile payments that can compete and out-innovate their best competitors from developed markets, thereby raising the bar for global competition.

Chinese firms' global expansion cannot be viewed as merely the consolidation of China's economic might. China's evolving government policies on outward foreign direct investment (OFDI), for instance, also played a crucial role in increasing Chinese firms' overseas investment. As China's policies changed from restriction to liberalization, and then to active guidance and encouragement, Chinese companies have benefited from state support and direction, including through the promotion of national champions. This proximity between the state and business sectors, illustrated by (but not limited to) state-owned enterprises (SOEs), has been essential to the development of Chinese enterprises. Even as it substantially liberalized OFDI, the Chinese government still monitors it, taking action to rein in outward investment, especially in periods of massive outflows, and encouraging investments that enhance Chinese competitiveness.

"The land that failed to fail" as a New York Times article in November 2018 put it, China has avoided the economic crises that have devastated other countries in Latin America or other parts of Asia. China has been able to keep the renminbi's exchange rate relatively stable since 2008. This stability, combined with a strong relationship between business and the state, has been one of the key success factors of Chinese firms.

Chinese firms have built on the immense scale of their domestic market, access to significant financial resources, an increasingly educated human resource pool, and rising competences in technological innovation to become formidable competitors for established incumbents from developed markets. Many sectors across multiple geographies have begun to feel this disruptive shock.

As of 2018, China's economy was the same size as the US economy in 2004, while growing at a faster pace than the United States (6.6% for China in 2018 as compared to 3.8% for the United States that year). China has gone international while still at a nominal GDP/capita of $9000 while most Western companies did not venture abroad until their home economy reached a higher GDP/capita. While the rest of the emerging world has bet its development on attracting investments, China has staked its future on nurturing its own national champions in key sectors, encouraging them to go abroad. Applying a strategy of learning by doing, and embracing risk as necessary for growth, Chinese firms have leveraged their international experience to strengthen activities at home.

Some of the favorable conditions that contributed to China's rapid growth and its firms' remarkable ascent have changed however. Protectionism in particular has become a reality, with an overt trade war between the two largest economies in the world. The effects will likely echo through the rest of the global economy, harming Chinese firms' prospects along the way. Negotiations between the United States and China to resolve this conflict have been in an on and off mode while historically high tariffs were imposed, with no conclusion by mid-2019. Regardless of the outcome of the negotiations, it is clear that the rule-based global trading system that developed in the second half of the 20th century is fraying.

Beyond trade, technology is the key issue at stake and the trade war is morphing into a war for technology dominance. Tariff hikes, export restrictions, increased control on inward investment, including restrictions on business acquisitions by foreigners, all deeply affect technology-related sectors. The case of telecoms is particularly illustrative, with the US adopting a number of measures on national security grounds that de facto targets Chinese firms such as Huawei, preventing it from accessing the

US market or acquiring technology equipment from the US firms. The United States is encouraging other countries to adopt similar restrictions. Even if other nations do not go as far as the United States, some are adopting a much more cautious approach to investment by Chinese firms. These developments reveal a significant paradigm shift, transitioning away from a world in which China could rely on an open global environment as a source for growth and a basis for global expansion.

Despite these elements of uncertainty, the underlying motivations for Chinese outward investment remain. On the one hand, access to natural resources, markets, know-how, and technology as well as brand building will continue to be key drivers of outward investment for Chinese companies. On the other, the Chinese government is likely to keep encouraging outbound investment in line with its overall strategy for the transformation of China into a high value-added and innovation-driven economy. In this context, it seems likely that Chinese OFDI will continue its upward trend, albeit at a slower pace. One can also expect that Chinese OFDI will shift geographically, with more investment in Belt and Road Initiative (BRI) countries and other countries in Latin America and Africa. Among advanced economies, Europe may continue to be a top priority for Chinese investment due to its less confrontational environment.

Given recent policy developments, some Chinese firms may choose to temporarily slow their international expansion and refocus on growth in the domestic market. One can also anticipate renewed efforts by the Chinese government to develop capabilities at home to lessen the country's dependence on foreign players in key technologies. Yet, there is no going back. The global expansion of Chinese firms is but one aspect of China's broader return—as the powerful nation it once was—on the global scene.

Time will tell if we are entering a phase of China-led globalization. The reactions of Western shareholder-driven companies to competition from these newcomers will likely determine how this new phase unfolds and Western incumbents will need to better understand their Chinese peers both to collaborate and compete with them. The new world that is emerging requires a rethinking of many of the dogmas taught in business schools, endorsed by many economists and business leaders and echoed by the press in developed markets. Beyond free and open markets, privatization, and deregulation, there is a need for more inclusive medium- and long-term planning, coordination of different stakeholders, and sacrificing short-term profits for long-term growth and the overall welfare of the country. These new discussions are starting both in China and in the West. This book seeks to inform these critical conversations.

Index

Note: Page numbers followed by *f* indicate figures, *t* indicate tables, and *b* indicate boxes.

Printed in the United States
By Bookmasters